THE MODERN LIBRARY

of the World's Best Books

THE

HINDU

TRADITION

The publisher will be pleased to send, upon request,

an illustrated folder listing each volume in

THE MODERN LIBRARY

THE
HINDU
TRADITION

EDITED BY

AINSLIE T. EMBREE

Readings in Oriental Thought
General Editor: WILLIAM THEODORE DE BARY

THE MODERN LIBRARY · NEW YORK

Hindu literature

FIRST MODERN LIBRARY EDITION, *February, 1966*

© *Copyright, 1966, by* RANDOM HOUSE, INC.

Library of Congress Catalogue Number: 66–13011

*Acknowledgments for material used in this volume appear on the
following page.*

THE MODERN LIBRARY
is published by
RANDOM HOUSE, INC.

BENNETT CERF   DONALD S. KLOPFER

MANUFACTURED IN THE UNITED STATES OF AMERICA

ACKNOWLEDGMENTS

The editor wishes to thank the following for permission to reprint material included in this volume:

George Allen & Unwin Ltd and The Macmillan Company—*The Hindu View of Life* by S. Radhakrishnan.

Sri Aurobindo Ashram—*The Life Divine* by Aurobindo Ghose.

Bharatiya Vidya Bhavan—*History and Culture of the Indian People,* Vol. III (*The Classical Age*), ed. by R. C. Majumdar.

The Bodley Head Ltd and T. Werner Laurie—*The Satakas or Wise Sayings* by Bhartrihari, trans. by J. M. Kennedy.

The Christian Literature Society—*The Poems of Tukārām,* trans. by J. N. Fraser and K. B. Marathe.

The Clarendon Press, Oxford—*The Sikh Religion,* Vol. I, by M. A. MacAuliffe, *Tiruvācagam* by Manikkavāchakar, trans. by G. U. Pope, *Bhagavad Gītā,* trans. by K. T. Telang in *Sacred Books of the East,* Vol. VIII, *The Vedānta Sūtra* with commentary of Rāmānuja, trans. by George Thibaut, in *Sacred Books of the East,* Vol. XLVIII.

Columbia University Press—*Introduction to Oriental Civilizations: Sources of the Indian Tradition,* ed. by W. T. de Bary, Stephen Hay, Royal Weiler, and Andrew Yarrow (1958).

Narayan Desai—*The Gita According to Gandhi* by M. K. Desai.

Ganesan & Co. (Madras) Private Ltd.—*Writings and Speeches of Bal Gangadhar Tilak.*

Kutub Popular Private Limited—*Gītā Govinda* by Jayadeva, trans. by George Keyt.

Macmillan & Co. Ltd.—*Nationalism* by Rabīndranāth Tagore, *The Autobiography of Maharishi Devendranath Tagore,* trans. by Satyendranāth Tagore and Indira Devi.

(vi) *Acknowledgments*

The Macmillan Company—*Songs of Kabīr* by Rabīndranāth Tagore. Copyright 1915 by The Macmillan Company, Renewed 1942 by Rathindrinath Tagore.

Lutterworth Press—*A Sixteenth Century Indian Mystic* by W. G. Orr.

Oxford University Press—*The Thirteen Principal Upanishads* by R. E. Hume.

Philosophical Library—*The Mahābhārata*, trans. by P. C. Roy, ed. by S. C. Nott.

Royal Asiatic Society—*Harsacarita* by Bāna, trans. by E. B. Cowell & F. W. Thomas.

Shanti Sadan—*Rāmāyana* by Valmiki, trans. by Hari Prasad Shastri, Vol. I.

M. S. Srinivas—*Artha Śāstra* by Kautilya, trans. by R. Shamasastry.

The Theosophical Publishing House—*Avatāras* by Annie Besant.

Vedanta Society—*The Gospel of Rāmakrishna*, trans. by "M."

YMCA Publishing House—*Hymns from the Rigveda* by A. A. Macdonnell, and *Hymns of the Tamil Śaivite Saints* by F. Kingsbury and G. E. Phillips.

PREFACE

This book is an exploration of the meaning of the Hindu tradition, one of the greatest and most enduring of mankind's many attempts to create an order of existence that would make life both tolerable and meaningful. The physical setting is the land known to the western world since ancient times as India, a word borrowed by the Greeks from the Persians who, because of the difficulty they had with the initial *s*, called the great Sindhu River (the modern Indus) the "Hindu." It was this word that came to be applied by foreigners to the religion and culture of the people who lived in the land watered by the two rivers, the Indus and the Ganges, although the people themselves did not use the term. They had, in fact, no words to describe their religion as distinct from that of others, except those that implied that the way of life known to them and to their fathers was the way of truth. They had, however, a variety of names for their homeland: one, Jambudvīpa, indicated it was the land of the rose-apple tree; another, Bhāratavarsha, indicated it was the land of the sons of a mighty king. But by whatever name they called it, they regarded their land, as one of the scriptures put it, as "the best of the divisions of the world," where gods were glad to be born as mortals, for nowhere else were men so certain of finding "the way to the pleasures of Paradise, or the greater blessings of final liberation" (see page 216).

The method adopted here for the exploration of the
Hindu tradition is to give selections from religious, literary,
and philosophic works that express the ideas and values,
the unquestioned assumptions and the persistent doubts,
that have characterized Indian life for the past three thousand years. This method means that certain important aspects of culture have been excluded—any consideration of
art and architecture, for example, or any sustained examination of the non-Hindu religions of India—but it also means
that much has been included. A fundamental feature of the
Hindu tradition is that there is no dividing line between
sacred and secular, no area of belief or custom that is
alien to religious influence. For this reason there are many
selections dealing with the ordering of social life and the
management of political relationships, as well as a few that
express the Hindu attitude to human love and passion.
There are, regrettably, few that touch upon the Hindu
scientific contribution. The reason is simply that the texts
are too technical or too obscure to yield a meaning com-
prehensible in ordinary literary terms. It is also true that
most of the selections come from what is often referred to
as "the high tradition," the literary and learned stratum
of society, as distinct from the Hinduism of the common
man, who may know nothing of the great works of classical
antiquity. But there are numerous examples of the hymns
and devotional songs that provide religious sustenance to
all classes, and, furthermore, while the Indian villager may
not be familiar with the actual Sanskrit texts, their values
permeate his thinking and their stories are part of his
everyday life.

The arrangement of the material is chronological, not
topical. This arises from the conviction that the richness
and complexity of the Hindu tradition can be seen only
as an attempt is made to suggest its growth and its development over the centuries. Because of the lack of a clear
historical framework, this cannot be done with any assurance of success, but at least it is possible to gain some sense

of the vitality of a tradition that has frequently, and erroneously, been described as static.

No claim is made that this book represents "what Hindus believe today." Since one purpose is to make clear the extraordinary diversity of Hindu belief, such a claim would be useless. Yet though the emphasis is on the past, the Hindu tradition is today living and vibrant—more so, perhaps, than it has been for two hundred years—and its roots are assuredly in the values and ideals of the great religious and literary works.

In editing a book of this kind, one's debts are so many and so obvious as scarcely to need acknowledgment. The greatest debt, however, is to William Theodore de Bary and his co-workers, particularly Royal Weiler and Stephen Hay, who produced *Sources of Indian Tradition* (Columbia University Press). Not only have many translations been taken from that work, but it has been used as a guide for both fact and interpretation. I am responsible, however, for all the statements made in the introductions and headings to the selections.

Ainslie T. Embree

Columbia University

EXPLANATORY NOTE

With each selection will be found the name of the work from which it is taken, and also the source of the translation. This is expressed as briefly as possible, but the full data can be found by consulting the list of sources at the end of the book.

The transliteration of Indian words follows, in general, that adopted in *Sources of Indian Tradition*, but since the translations are the work of many scholars, there is almost inevitably some variation. Long vowels have been indicated by a macron (ā, ī, ū). The long *ā* is pronounced as *a* in *father*, while the short *a* is pronounced as the *u* in *but*. In some of the selections the long vowels are marked with a slightly different symbol (å). The *sh* sound is, in a few places, indicated with *ś*.

CONTENTS

~~~~~~~~~

PREFACE   vii

EXPLANATORY NOTE   x

Part One

THE ROOTS OF THE TRADITION

*(The Age of the Vedas and the
Upanishads, c. 1500-550 B.C.)*

INTRODUCTION

CHAPTER I   The Ordering of the Universe   9

The Ancient Gods—*Varuna—Usha, the Dawn—
Indra—Agni—Soma.* The Origin of the Universe—
*Time as Creator—Sacrifice as Creator—The One as
Creator.* The Meaning of Sacrifice. Death.

CHAPTER II   The Social Order   32

The Duty of Charity. War. Charms and Spells for a
Good Life—*Against Jaundice—Against Serpents—
To Compel a Woman's Love—For Success in Trading.* In Praise of the Cow. The Place of the Brāhman. The Crowning of a King—*King of Kings—The*

Chosen One—The Enduring Ruler. Earth as Mother-land.

CHAPTER III   The Crown of the Vedic Age: The
Upanishads   48

The New Meaning of Sacrifice. Brahman: The Search
for the Ground of the Universe. Ātman: The Real
Self. The Identity of Brahman and Ātman. Karma
and Transmigration. Emancipation from Karma.

Part Two

THE GROWTH OF THE TRADITION

(550 B.C.–300 A.D.)

INTRODUCTION

CHAPTER IV   The Exposition of Life's Duties   74

The Class Structure—*The Statement of the Ideal—
Mutual Dependence of the Classes*. The Four Stages
of Life—*The Student—The Householder and Family
Life—The Hermit—The Homeless Wanderer*. The
Recognition of Life's Limitations. The Possibility of
Growth and Change. Life as Sacrament. A Widow's
Act of Devotion.

CHAPTER V   The Maintenance of the Social Fabric   101

Kingship as a Remedy for an Evil Society. The Danger of Anarchy. War and Peace. Ashoka's Vision of
True Conquest.

CHAPTER VI   The Search for Salvation   117

Man's True Nature—*The Way of Salvation: Duty—
The Way of Salvation: Knowledge—The Way of
Salvation: Devotion*. Incarnation: The Response to

Human Need. Adoration of Shiva. The Great Heresies of the Tradition—*Buddha's First Sermon*—*The Jain Vision of Life.*

CHAPTER VII   The Universe of the Great Epics   136

The Mahābhārata: The Founding of the Royal Line. The Rāmāyana: The Defence of Dharma.

Part Three

THE FLOWERING OF THE TRADITION

(300-1200 A.D.)

INTRODUCTION

CHAPTER VIII   The Literary Reflection   157

The Pleasure of Love—*The Pain of Love*—*The Perils of Love.* A Wife's Devotion. Divine and Human Love. The Celebration of a Prince's Birth. The Science of Pleasure. Caution and Commonsense.

CHAPTER IX   The Philosophic Statement
                of the Tradition   180

The Basis of Logical Thinking: Nyāya—*The Atomic Nature of Reality: Vaisheshika*—*Proof of the Sacred Texts: Mīmāmsā*—*The Dualism of Matter and Spirit: Sānkhya*—*The Way of Discipline: Yoga*—*Non-Dualism: The Vedānta of Shankara*—*Qualified Non-Dualism: The Vedānta of Rāmānuja.*

CHAPTER X   Sacred History   208

A Story of Origins: The Churning of the Ocean. The Price of Devotion: The Triumph of Prahlāda. The Lineage of Kings. Sacred Geography. The Nature of History.

Part Four

THE TRADITION AND
THE PEOPLE'S FAITH

INTRODUCTION

CHAPTER XI In Praise of Shiva   232

A Description of Shiva. Appar—*Consecration to Shiva—Triumph Through Shiva.* Sambandar—*Shiva's Glory—The Lord is Everything.* Mānikkavāchakar— *A Song to Awaken Shiva.* Sundaramūrthi—*Shiva's Dwelling Places.* Rāmaprasād—*Shiva's Consort, Kali.* Lallā—*The Indwelling Lord.*

CHAPTER XII In Praise of Vishnu as Krishna and
Rāma   246

Purandaradāsa—*Stomach Austerity.* Jnānadeva—*A Prayer for Grace.* Tukārām—*The Burden of the Past.* Mīrābāī—*Krishna's Bride.* Sūrdās. Chaitanya. Tulasīdās.

CHAPTER XIII The Meeting of Hindu and Muslim
Devotion   261

Kabīr. Nānak—*Morning Prayer.* Dādū.

Part Five

THE TRADITION AND
THE MODERN WORLD

INTRODUCTION

CHAPTER XIV Acceptance and Reform   278

Rāmmohan Roy: Rationalist Prophet—*Original*

Hinduism—A Defence of Hinduism. Debendranāth Tagore: Mysticism and Reform. Keshub Chunder Sen: Christ and India. M. G. Rānade: The Need for Social Reform.

CHAPTER XV Rejection and Revival   299

Dayānanda Saraswatī: Aggressive Reformer—*God and the Veda—Against Christianity—Against Islam*. B. G. Tilak: The Call to Action. Srī Rāmakrishna: Sainthood and the Modern World. Vivekānanda: Hindu Prophet to the Western World. Mrs. Annie Besant: Theosophy's Interpretation of Hinduism.

CHAPTER XVI Four Twentieth Century Statements 325

Rabīndranāth Tagore: A Vision of India—*Nationalism*. Sri Aurobindo: A Vision of Spiritual Evolution. Mahātma Gāndhi: A Vision of the Good Life. Sarvepalli Rādhakrishnan: A Vision of Hinduism.

SOURCES OF ENGLISH TRANSLATIONS AND SELECTIONS 349

PART ONE

THE ROOTS OF
THE TRADITION

~~~~~~~~~

(THE AGE OF THE VEDAS AND THE

UPANISHADS, C. 1500-550 B.C.)

INTRODUCTION

The Hindu tradition is rooted in the Vedic Age, the period of Indian history that extends from about 1500 B.C. to 600 B.C. Although this long expanse of time was marked by great religious and social changes, and conditions differed widely throughout the subcontinent, the Age had a unity and style that sets it apart. Chronologically, it was defined on the one side by the disappearance of the ancient Harappa culture and the coming of the Aryan peoples; on the other, by the establishment in the sixth century of important kingdoms in North India. From that time to the present, organized political life has existed in the area. Culturally, the designation "Vedic" indicates the dominant cultural and religious influence of India—the creation of a body of literature, the *Vedas*, which has served to undergird every aspect of the civilization.

The Vedic Age was a time of fusion of different cultures and traditions, concerning the exact origins of which we know little, but whose existence is apparent in the richness and complexities—as well as the contradictions—of the Hindu way of life. One source that almost certainly contributed to this cultural amalgam was the great civilization that centered on the Indus Valley cities of Harappa and Mohenjodaro. The physical remains of this extraordinary culture were only discovered in this century; its existence till then had not even been guessed at. It endured for nearly a thousand years, covering much of northwest India with an elaborately organized commercial and administrative system. Many aspects of later Hinduism—the god Shiva, for example—appear to have had prototypes in the Indus Valley civilization. Another source of the cultural heritage was the widely scattered peoples who spoke Dravidian languages, the modern representatives of which are Tamil and Telugu. It is possible that these peoples were closely related, either ethnically or in terms of cultural influence, with the Indus Valley civilization. Probably such features of popular Hinduism as zoomorphic deities, the use of animals to symbolize the supernatural, were Dravidian in origin, as may have been such important concepts of Indian thought as the belief in transmigration. The third great source of cultural ideas and practices was the peoples who migrated into northwest India in the first half of the second millennium B.C. These were the people known as Aryans, although the word indicates linguistic affinities, rather than a race. Their religious and social concepts, as well as their language, were similar to those of the peoples who migrated westward to Europe.

While not all the chief features of the Hindu tradition can be traced to the Aryans, nevertheless it was they who imposed a distinctive order and character upon the Vedic Age. The evidence of this influence—and the great unifying feature of the period—is a vast body of literature, one of the most magnificent achievements of the human spirit in any place or time. Collectively referred to as the *Veda*, it is these writings that provided the roots for the later growth of the Hindu tradition.

The *Veda* is not a book in the ordinary sense, nor even a collection of books, like the Bible. It is, rather, the name given to the extremely diverse materials composed over a period of a thousand years by a priestly class. As such, it exhibits changes and developments within the general structure of the society but it has a unity imposed by a common and continuing concern with the religious ritual.

This vast corpus of scripture can be classified under four headings that indicate both content, and, very roughly, the chronological development of the materials. First of all are the *Samhitās*, collections of hymns used in the ritual. There are four of these collections, the *Rig Veda, Yajur Veda, Sāma Veda,* and *Atharva Veda.* The *Rig Veda,* the oldest and the most important of these, consists of about one thousand hymns of varying length, some of which may have been written before the Aryans had entered India, while others were written hundreds of years afterwards. Many of the hymns were created by the priests for specific needs of the ritual services that were the heart of Vedic religion, but even those that are from the most ancient strata of the tradition are products of careful literary craftsmanship. They are not, then, the spiritual outpourings of the heart of primitive man at the dawn of history, as has sometimes been suggested; they are the achievement of a highly developed religious system. The *Yajur Veda* and *Sāma Veda* are essentially technical texts and formulae used in the ritual, and are based in large part on the *Rig Veda.* The *Atharva Veda* is different from the other three, consisting largely of spells and incantations. While it is the latest of the *Samhitās* to have received its definitive form, it contains material that is very ancient, and, since it is less concerned with the ritual and more with the problems of ordinary life, provides many insights into the thinking of the people.

The second class of Vedic literature, the *Brāhmanas* are interpretations in prose of the meaning of the ritual acts of the older *Samhitās.* The interpretations frequently take the form of fanciful allegories, with great dependence on supposed etymological derivations of important words, but they provide an indication of the way in which an attempt was made to bring the past into relationship with changing patterns of thought and social life. Within the tradition itself, they fulfilled the valuable function of maintaining the continuity of essential belief and practice, for even

though the *Brāhmaņas* represented different schools and
sects, they all acknowledged the authority of the older
texts. A third category of the *Veda, the Āranyakas*, or
"Forest Books," treated the details of the rituals of the
former collections as symbols of hidden truths. The *Upanishads, the fourth category*, are outgrowths of the *Āranyaka*
literature, but they display a great freedom of speculation
in the discussion of the symbolic meanings of the old ritual. In subsequent Indian thought, the *Upanishads* have a
dominant place and quite outshadow the more ancient
texts.

This Vedic literature—*Samhitā, Brāhmana, Āranyaka,*
and *Upanishad*—was handed down orally, a fact which
probably explains such characteristic features as repetition
and the use of set modes of expression. Even after the in-
vention of writing the *Veda* was transmitted orally, probably reflecting the enormous emphasis in the tradition on
the sanctity of the spoken word. This emphasis meant that
great care was taken to see that the text was correctly
memorized, and for this reason there is great uniformity in
the texts throughout the ages.

Taken together, the four categories of Vedic literature
comprise what is accepted by all Hindus as authorita-
tive scripture; indeed, one of the few definitions comprehensive enough to include all Hindus is that they
are the people who accept the *Veda* as normative for religious faith and practice. There are, as we shall see, other
classes of scripture, but the *Veda* is unique. It is *shruti,*
"what is heard," or revealed; another great class of scripture is called *smriti,* "what is remembered," or tradition.
For the orthodox, the *Veda* is eternal, and not the product
of human minds. Yet it is not like the Bible or the Koran;
it is the record of the truth as it was "discovered" by the
great rishis, or saints, of ancient time rather than a revelation from God. What is enjoined within the system is not
belief in the teachings so much as an attempt to redupli-
cate the spiritual experiences of these saints; the argument
is that they have found truth, and that this can be verified

through a repetition of their disciplines. Two important points should be noted. One is that, despite the assertion of the absolute truth of the *Veda*, different interpretations could exist within the framework of orthodoxy because of the variety of ideas within the literature itself. The other is that while the scripture of Hinduism is the *Veda*, the religion of the people of Vedic times was not Hinduism. That is, while Hinduism indubitably has its roots in the Vedic literature, the term "Hinduism" cannot be appropriately applied to the religion of the period. Many scholars prefer the word "Brahmanism" for the ancient religious tradition.

Since few artifacts have survived that can with certainty be identified with the Vedic Age, our knowledge of the social organization and life of the people is based wholly on religious and literary texts, with consequent limitations imposed by their field of concern. They give, nonetheless, a reasonably clear picture of the general outlines of the society. In the earliest period, society is wholly agricultural and pastoral, with an emphasis on stockbreeding. Clans, not kingdoms, were the basic political unit; a tribal chief's main function was to be a leader in time of war. By the end of the Vedic period the Aryans had extended their control from their original homeland in the Panjab to the Gangetic Plain in the region of the modern Benares. The tribal system was replaced by numerous small kingdoms with permanent capitals, and the king became an hereditary ruler through succession from his father, although not necessarily through primogeniture.

The religion of the Vedic people is the subject of an enormous literature; more than almost any other aspect of the life of ancient India, it has attracted great attention since it first became known to the west in the late eighteenth century. This interest was aroused partly by the great antiquity of the surviving religious texts, which gives them a very special place in the history of religion. There are few religious concepts and practices that are not touched upon in some way in the Vedic literature. Beyond this, they are the fundamental sources for the understanding of future developments in both Indian history and religion. As such they have been recognized in modern times as the great glory of the Indian tradition. But above all, the records of the Vedic Age are interesting in themselves as expressions of the aspirations and achievements of the human spirit.

CHAPTER I

THE ORDERING OF
THE UNIVERSE

~~~~~~~~

While it is impossible to reduce the Vedic literature to a systematic statement, certain general characteristics stand out. The agricultural life of the people combined with the special features of the Indian climate—the brilliance of sunshine, the clarity of atmosphere, the easy beneficence quickly altering to harsh malevolence—made the people sensitive to the natural world. Much of the imagery of the poetry and religion can be understood as the response of the imagination to a Nature that seemed living and animate. Related to this response is another characteristic of the literature of the Vedic Age: the sense of a cosmic order or law pervading the universe. This cosmic law was not made by the gods, although they are the guardians of it. It is reflected not only in the physical regularity of the night and day and of the seasons but also in the moral order that binds men to each other and to the gods. The word (rita) used for this cosmic law becomes a synonym for truth, thus opening up possibilities for the development of wide-ranging philosophical and theological speculations as to the nature of the universe.

The concepts of a living nature and a cosmic law find frequent expression in Vedic mythology. The hymns of the Rig Veda are addressed to many gods, most of whom are closely related to the forces of nature, either as controlling the natural phenomena or as identified with their essential nature. But the gods are not personifications of natural forces in the sense that they emerge as clearly defined anthropomorphic beings; with few exceptions, their characters remain vague and shadowy. The same qualities, for example, are assigned to different deities, and are given epithets indicating supremacy. Nor is there any fixed hierarchical structure among the gods, even though some are regarded as being of greater importance than others. The lack of clear distinction between the gods probably made possible a belief in multiplicity as representing some more fundamental principle of unity.

The Vedic cosmology pictures the universe divided into three parts—earth, atmosphere and heaven—and this triad provides an organizing principle for classifying the gods. Among those whose functions are related to heaven are Varuna, one of the greatest of all Vedic deities, Usha, the goddess of dawn, and Surya, the sun. Indra is the most important of all the atmospheric gods, while Soma and Agni are the chief gods among those classified as having a special relationship to earth. Fuller information on these deities is given in the introductory notes to the hymns. There are in addition many divine or semi-divine beings who do not fit into the three-fold classification, such as family deities, forest spirits, demons, wives of the gods, and abstractions derived from human qualities, such as Faith or Anger.

Questions concerning the creation of the universe and the origin of gods and men are related to the cosmic law in a general way, but the Vedic literature presents a number of myths, which are not all consistent with each other, to explain divine and human existence. Thus at times the universe is represented as having been created by the gods, after the analogy of the work of a carpenter, but at other times it is suggested that the whole of creation, including the gods, is the product of a process of natural generation. The gods, quite as much as men, are "this side of creation." *Sometimes the emphasis is on parentage in the human sense; sometimes a complex and subtle reference is made to the evolution of being from non-being. In all these speculations one sees a willingness to move to new positions, even though this means contradicting themes already entrenched within the tradition.*

The concepts and practices of the sacrificial ritual, which was at the heart of Vedic religion, were also linked to the fundamental understanding of the existence of a cosmic law. *The central physical feature of the religion was not a temple or an image, but an altar on which the sacred fire was lighted and around which the ritual took place.* The sacrifices were mainly things that man himself enjoyed, such as food or the intoxicating soma, a kind of drink whose nature is not now known. These offerings came to be surrounded with rites of extraordinary complexity, the correct performance of which was dependent upon the specialized knowledge of the priests. *The belief grew up that the sacrifice was necessary for the maintenance of the cosmic order, and that "without regular sacrifices all cosmic processes would cease, and chaos would come again."* [1] From this the conclusion was drawn that what was important was not the gods to whom sacrifice was made, nor the materials of the sacrifice, but the sacrificer, who knew the secret formulae that held the cosmos together. *The word that was used for the sacrificer was* brāhman, *which only by extension of its early meaning came to be used for a whole class of people. Originally* brāhman *seems to have meant the spoken words of the ritual, but eventually it stood for the power behind the ritual, the principle that lies at the ground of all being, and hence the end of man's spiritual quest.* [2]

It might be supposed that the attempt to relate man's

---

[1] A. L. Basham, *The Wonder That Was India* (New York: Grove Press, 1959), p. 239.
[2] A distinction should be made between *brahman*, the highest principle of the universe; *Brāhman*, a member of the highest social order; and *Brahmā*, one of the great gods.

existence to the cosmic order would have led to considerable interest in the significance of death, but in fact speculation concerning death occupies only a minor place in the
early texts. The ancient Indian peoples desired death for
their enemies and long life on earth for themselves; when
a man died, his soul rose with the smoke of the burning
body to heaven. In the earliest texts there is no certain indication of any belief in transmigration, that most pervasive of later Indian beliefs. Within the Vedic concepts,
however, there was possibility for the elaboration of this
belief, particularly in the emphasis on an undeviating cosmic law.

In the following selections, these varied aspects of the
ordering of the universe—the nature of the gods, the creation of the universe, the function of sacrifice, man's fate at
death—are set forth in the words of the saints and seers of
the Vedic Age.

THE ANCIENT GODS

Varuna

Varuna, the greatest of the celestial gods, as the guardian of
the cosmic order (*rita*), was responsible for the maintenance
of both the physical and moral order. He caused the sun to
rise and set; the stars shone at his command; he bestowed the
rains that gave life to the earth. The moral laws of the universe were no less fixed and immutable than those that gov-
erned the natural world, and Varuna administered these with
the same unswerving regularity. For this reason, prayers for
forgiveness for wrongs done to others were addressed to Varuna,
since wrongdoing disturbed the order of the universe. Varuna
eventually faded out of the Indian religious consciousness, but
the emphasis on man's participation in an ordered cosmos became an enduring part of the Hindu tradition. The first two
selections given below are from the *Rig Veda*, while the third
is from the *Atharva Veda*, a later compilation of the hymns of

the Vedic people. It is remarkable for the clear assertion of the omnipresence and omniscience of Varuna.

Prayer for forgiveness

Wise, verily, are creatures through his greatness who stayed
    even spacious heaven and earth asunder;
Who urged the high and mighty sky to motion, the Star
    of old, and spread the earth before him.
With mine own heart I commune on the question how
    Varuna and I may be united
What gift of mine will he accept unangered? When may I
    calmly look and find him gracious?
Fain to know this my sin I question others: I seek the
    wise, O Varuna, and ask them.
This one same answer even the sages gave me, Surely this
    Varuna is angry with thee.
What, Varuna, hath been my chief transgression, that
    thou wouldst slay the friend who sings thy praises?
Tell me, Unconquerable Lord, and quickly sinless will I
    approach thee with mine homage.
Free us from sins committed by our fathers, from those
    wherein we have ourselves offended.
O King, loose, like a thief who feeds the cattle, as from
    the cord a calf, set free Vasishtha.
Not our own will betrayed us, but seduction, thoughtless-
    ness, Varuna! wine, dice, or anger.
The old is near to lead astray the younger: even sleep re-
    moveth not all evil-doing.
Slavelike may I do service to the Bounteous, serve, free
    from sin, the God inclined to anger.
This gentle Lord gives wisdom to the simple: the wiser
    God leads on the wise to riches.
O Lord, O Varuna, may this laudation come close to thee
    and lie within thy spirit.
May it be well with us in rest and labour. Preserve us ever-
    more, ye Gods, with blessings.

(from *Rig Veda*, VII:86, in R. T. H. Griffith, *The Hymns of the Rig Veda*, II, p. 82)

His Lordship

Unto the sovereign lord sing a sublime and solemn prayer (*brahman*), one dear unto glorious Varuna, who has spread out the earth, as the butcher does the hide, by way of a carpet for the sun.

Varuna has extended the air above the trees; he has put strength in horses, milk in cows, will-power in hearts, fire in waters, the sun in the heaven, and soma upon the mountain.

Varuna poured out the leather-bag, opening downward, upon the heaven and the earth and the mid-region. Thereby does the lord of the whole creation moisten thoroughly the expanse of earth, as rain does the corn.

He moistens the broad earth and the heaven. When Varuna would have it milked [i.e., would shower rain] then, indeed, do the mountains clothe themselves with clouds and the heroes, showing off their might, loosen those clothes [i.e., disperse the clouds].

This great magic-work (māyā) of renowned spiritual Varuna will I proclaim loudly; of Varuna, who, standing in the mid-region, has measured the earth with the sun as with a measuring rod.

No one, indeed, dare impugn this great magic-work of the wisest god, namely, that the many glistening streams, pouring forth, do not fill up one ocean with water.

release from sin

If we, O Varuna, have offended against a friend, befriended through Aryaman or through Mitra [i.e., gods of hospitality and friendship], or if we have offended against an all-time comrade or a brother or an inmate—whether belonging to us, O Varuna, or a stranger—do you remove that offense from us.

If we have deceived, like gamblers in a game of dice, and whether we really know it or not, all that do you unbind from us, like loosened fetters, O god. Thus may we be dear unto you, O Varuna.

(from *Rig Veda* V:85, in *Sources of Indian Tradition*, pp. 11-12)

As guardian, the Lord of worlds
Sees all things as if near at hand.
In secret what 'tis thought to do
That to the gods is all displayed.

Whoever moves or stands, who glides in secret,
Who seeks a hiding-place, or hastens from it,
What thing two men may plan in secret council,
A third, King Varuna, perceives it also.

sees all that is in secret

And all this earth King Varuna possesses,
His the remotest ends of yon broad heaven;
And both the seas in Varuna lie hidden,
But yet the smallest water-drop contains him.

omnipresent

Although I climbed the furthest heaven, fleeing,
I should not there escape the monarch's power;
From heaven his spies descending hasten hither,
With all their thousand eyes the world surveying.

Whate'er exists between the earth and heaven,
Or both beyond, to Varuna lies open.
The winkings of each mortal eye he numbers,
He wields the universe, as dice a player.

(from *Atharva Veda*, IV:16, in A. Kaegi, *The Rig Veda*, p. 65)

Usha, the Dawn

In the many hymns to the goddess Usha, or Dawn, the descriptions of the beauty of the early morning show the sensitivity of the ancient Indian peoples to the natural world. They are more than nature poems, however, for as elsewhere in the Vedic literature, there is a strong sense of the close relation of the phenomenal world to the deepest concerns of human life. Dawn comes, like a maiden dressed in light, dispelling darkness and driving away evil spirits, making possible a life of ordered regularity. In another poem, the thought that Dawn, the symbol of youthful loveliness, was also ancient, being constantly reborn, suggested to a poet the contrast between the "wasting away of the life of mortals" while the human race itself remained (*Rig Veda* I:92). Perhaps at this very early stage can be seen the characteristic tendency of Indian literature to see nature as a frame for human emotions. The natural world is not understood as something apart from man, but as a reflection of his moods and passions.

This light has come, of all the lights the fairest:
The brilliant brightness has been born effulgent.
Urged onward for god Savitar's uprising,
Night now has yielded up her place to morning.
Bringing a radiant calf she comes resplendent:
To her the Black One has given up her mansions.
Akin, immortal, following each the other,
Morning and Night fare on, exchanging colours.
The sisters' pathway is the same, unending:
Taught by the gods alternately they tread it.
Fair-shaped, of form diverse, yet single-minded,
Morning and Night clash not, nor do they tarry.
Bright leader of glad sounds she shines effulgent:
Widely she has unclosed for us her portals.
Pervading all the world she shows us riches:
Dawn has awakened every living creature.
Men lying on the ground she wakes to action:
Some rise to seek enjoyment of great riches,
Some, seeing little, to behold the distant:
Dawn has awakened every living creature.
One for dominion, and for fame another;
Another is aroused for winning greatness;
Another seeks the goal of varied nurture:
Dawn has awakened every living creature.
Daughter of Heaven, she has appeared before us,
A maiden shining in resplendent raiment.
Thou sovereign lady of all earthly treasure,
Auspicious Dawn, shine here to-day upon us. . . .
Gone are those mortals who in former ages

Beheld the flushing of the early morning;
We living men now look upon her shining:
Those will be born who shall hereafter see her.
Dispelling foes, observer of world order,
Born in due season, giver of enjoyment,
Wafting oblations, bringing wealth and fortune,
Shine brightly here to-day, O Dawn, upon us. . . .
In the sky's framework she has gleamed with brightness;
The goddess has cast off the robe of darkness.
Rousing the world from sleep, with ruddy horses,
Dawn in her well-yoked chariot is arriving.
She brings upon it many bounteous blessings;
Brightly she shines and spreads her brilliant lustre.
Last of innumerable morns departed,
First of bright morns to come, has Dawn arisen.
Arise! The vital breath again has reached us:
Darkness has gone away and light is coming.
She leaves a pathway for the sun to travel:
We have arrived where men prolong existence.

(from *Rig Veda* I:113, in A. A. Macdonnell, *Hymns from the Rigveda*, p. 38)

Indra

While Varuna was perhaps the most honored of the Vedic deities, it was Indra who was regarded as the particular god of the Aryan peoples. Since his name, unlike that of most of the other gods, does not indicate any connection with a natural phenomenon, it is conceivable that Indra may have been an actual historic figure, a leader of the Aryans who was deified after the defeat of the indigenous people of India by the invaders. In any case, he was clearly the God of Battles, to whom men, "rushing to deadly combat, will cry aloud for protection" (*Rig Veda* IV:24). Indra is also a personification of the thunderstorm, and his weapon is a bolt of lightning. Offerings of the intoxicating *soma* drink are also closely associated with his character, and he is frequently portrayed as a drunken brawler.

A vast number of myths and legends have gathered around

this complex figure. The story of his slaying of the demon Vritra is the most important of these, for while its meaning for the Vedic peoples is not altogether clear, the many references to it in the hymns establishes its fundamental character. Vritra, in the form of a serpent or dragon, has shut up the waters and the sun, but after a fierce battle Indra slays him, releasing the life-giving forces. Among the many interpretations that have been made of this myth is the suggestion that it represents the renewal of the year, either through the ending of the winter or the coming of the monsoons. Another possibility is that it represents the actual conflict between the Aryan peoples and those of the Indus Valley civilization. In a wider sense, Vritra may stand for chaos, upon which Indra imposes form and order.

Indra's heroic deeds, indeed, will I proclaim, the first ones which the wielder of the thunderbolt accomplished. He killed the dragon, released the waters, and split open the sides of the mountains.

He killed the dragon lying spread out on the mountain; for him Tvashtar fashioned the roaring thunderbolt. Like bellowing cows, the waters, gliding, have gone down straightway to the ocean.

Showing off his virile power he chose soma; from the three bowls he drank of the extracted soma. The bounteous god took up the missile, the vajra; he killed the firstborn among the dragons.

When you, O Indra, killed the first-born among the dragons and further overpowered the wily tricks (māyā) of the tricksters, bringing forth, at that very moment, the sun, the heaven, and the dawn—since then, indeed, have you not come across another enemy.

Indra killed Vritra, the greater enemy, the shoulderless one, with his mighty and fatal weapon, the thunderbolt. Like branches of a tree lopped off with an axe, the dragon lies prostrate upon the earth.

For, like an incapable fighter, in an intoxicated state, he [Vritra] had challenged the great hero [Indra], the mighty overwhelmer, the drinker of soma to the dregs. He did not surmount the onslaught of his fatal weapon. Indra's enemy, broken-nosed, was completely crushed.

Footless and handless he gave battle to Indra. He [Indra] struck him with the vajra upon the back. The castrated bull, seeking to become a compeer of the virile bull, Vritra lay shattered in many places.

Over him, who lay in that manner like a shattered bull flowed the waters for the sake of man. At the feet of the very waters, which Vritra had once enclosed with his might, the dragon [now] lay [prostrate]

Vritra's mother had her vital energy ebbing out; Indra had hurled his fatal weapon at her. The mother lay above, the son below; Dānu, his mother lay down like a cow with her calf.

In the midst of the water-streams, which never stood still nor had any resting place, the body lay. The waters flow in all directions over Vritra's secret place; Indra's enemy lay sunk in long darkness.

With the demon as their lord and with the dragon as their warder, the waters remained imprisoned. . . . Having killed Vritra, [Indra] threw open the cleft of waters which had been closed.

You became the hair of a horse's tail, O Indra, when he [Vritra] struck at your sharp-pointed vajra—the one god though you were. You won the cows, O brave one, you won soma; you released the seven rivers, so that they should flow.

Neither did lightning nor thunder, nor mist nor hailstorm, which he [Vritra] had spread out, prove efficacious when Indra and the dragon fought. And the bounteous god remained victorious for all time to come.

Whom did you see, O Indra, as the avenger of the dragon, that fear entered into your heart, after you had killed the dragon, and frightened, you crossed nine and ninety rivers and the aerial regions like the falcon?

Indra, who wields the thunderbolt in his hand, is the lord of what moves and what remains rested, of what is peaceful and what is horned. He alone rules over the tribes as their king; he encloses them as does a rim the spokes.

(from *Rig Veda*, I:32, in *Sources of Indian Tradition*, pp. 13-15)

Agni

The god Agni has a special place in the Vedic attempt to create a model of an ordered cosmos. Although addressed as a person, the description given of him is that of the sacrificial fire; many-tongued, he is the mouth by which the gods eat the sacrifices made to them. While in this form he is an earth god, he is also the link with other realms, since he appears in the atmosphere as lightning and in the heavens as the sun. The epithet given to him, "Offspring of the Waters," indicated his relationship with the primeval waters. On earth, his hidden home was wood, out of which he could reveal himself as flame, particularly as the flame of the altar. He is both bearer of the offerings of men to the gods, and the one who brings the gods down to the altar. One may see in these characteristics of Agni the blurring of distinctions and function, and the attribution of essentially contradictory qualities, which in later developments was carried to the logical conclusion of denying the validity of any ultimate differentiation between the gods and, finally, for the quest for a statement of the unity of all being.

I extol Agni, the household priest, the divine minister of the sacrifice, the chief priest, the bestower of blessings.

May that Agni, who is to be extoled by ancient and modern seers, conduct the gods here.

Through Agni may one gain day by day wealth and welfare which is glorious and replete with heroic sons.

O Agni, the sacrifice and ritual which you encompass on every side, that indeed goes to the gods.

May Agni, the chief priest, who possesses the insight of a sage, who is truthful, widely renowned, and divine, come here with the gods.

O Agni, O Messenger, whatever prosperity you bring to

the pious is indeed in accordance with your true function.

O Agni, illuminator of darkness, day by day we approach you with holy thought bringing homage to you,
    Presiding at ritual functions, the brightly shining custodian of the cosmic order (rita), thriving in your own realm.

O Agni, be easy of access to us as a father to his son. Join us for our wellbeing.

(from *Rig Veda*, I:1, in *Sources of Indian Tradition*, pp. 9-10)

Soma

Like Agni, Soma has few anthropomorphic characteristics, and is usually described either in terms of the effect the beverage known as *soma* had on those who drank it or of its power over the gods, especially Indra. Just what *soma* was cannot be decided with certainty, but it was apparently a drink made from a plant, and produced hallucinations of the kind made familiar by modern experiments with a variety of drugs and herbs. It was the essential ingredient of the Vedic rituals, and while it was preeminently the offering made to Indra, it was used in the sacrifices made to all the gods. It conferred on men some of the qualities of gods, including immortality. It had, moreover, the power to cause the sun to rise and set, as well as the ability to confer the blessings of riches and long life. One sees here, then, the tendency already noted of assigning the same functions to different gods—in this case, Soma is given powers normally ascribed to Indra and Varuna. The verses that follow here are from a hymn addressed to Soma. They express very vividly the effects *soma* was supposed to have.

We have drunk Soma and become immortal; we have attained the light the Gods discovered.

Effects of soma

Now what may foeman's malice do to harm us? What, O Immortal, mortal man's deception?

Absorbed into the heart, be sweet, O Indu, as a kind father to his son, O Soma,

As a wise Friend to friend: do thou, wide ruler, O Soma,
   lengthen out our days for living.

These glorious drops that give me freedom have I drunk.
   Closely they knit my joints as straps secure a car.

Let them protect my foot from slipping on the way: yea,
   let the drops I drink preserve me from disease.

Make me shine bright like fire produced by friction: give
   us a clearer sight and make us better.

For in carouse I think of thee, O Soma: Shall I, as a rich
   man, attain to comfort?

May we enjoy with an enlivened spirit the juice thou givest
   like ancestral riches.

O Soma, King, prolong thou our existence as Surya makes
   the shining days grow longer.

King Soma, favour us and make us prosper: we are thy
   devotees; of this be mindful.

Spirit and power are fresh in us, O Indu: give us not up
   unto our foeman's pleasure.

For thou hast settled in each joint, O Soma, aim of men's
   eyes and guardian of our bodies.

When we offend against thine holy statutes, as a kind
   Friend, God, best of all, be gracious.

May I be with the Friend whose heart is tender, who, Lord
   of Bays! when quaffed will never harm me—

This Soma now deposited within me. For this, I pray for
   longer life to Indra.

Our maladies have lost their strength and vanished: they
   feared, and passed away into the darkness.

Soma hath risen in us, exceeding mighty, and we are come
   where men prolong existence.

Fathers, that Indu which our hearts have drunken, Immortal in himself, hath entered mortals.

So let us serve this Soma with oblation, and rest securely in
   his grace and favour.

Associate with the Fathers thou, O Soma, hast spread thyself abroad through earth and heaven.

So with oblation let us serve thee, Indu, and so let us become the lords of riches,

Give us your blessing, O ye Gods, preservers. Never may
   sleep or idle talk control us.
But evermore may we, as friends of Soma, speak to the
   assembly with brave sons around us.
On all sides, Soma, thou art our life-giver: aim of all eyes,
   light-finder, come within us.
Indu, of one accord with thy protections both from behind and from before preserve us.

(from *Rig Veda*, VIII:48, in Griffith, *The Hymns of the Rig
Veda*, II, pp. 198-99)

THE ORIGIN OF THE UNIVERSE

Indra and Varuna are frequently referred to as the creators of
the universe, but from very early times an attempt was made
to go beyond the concept of the world having been created
after the model of a carpenter constructing a building. The
origin of the visible and invisible universe was sought in some
primary principle, rather than in the action of a deity. One of
the most interesting examples of this is seen in the *Atharva
Veda* in a hymn to Kāla, or Time. Kāla is an intellectual abstraction, not a god, and is more correctly thought of as the
source of the universe, rather than as creator. Another abstract
deity, Prajāpati, "Lord of Offspring," seems to be a designation
for the same principle. A hymn to Kāla is given in the first
selection below.

   A very different kind of speculation concerning the origin
of the universe is given in one of the most famous hymns of
the *Rig Veda*, the *Purusha Sukta*, or Hymn of Man. Here the
emphasis is on the creation of animate life and society, rather
than on the physical world. A Primal Man, whose origin is
unexplained in the text, is sacrificed by the gods, and all of
life, including the orders of society, comes into existence. This
concept had an important place in the development of the
sacrificial ritual, for, through analogical reasoning, each ritual
performance was seen as a repetition of the primeval sacrifice.

Each succeeding ritual act was understood to sustain the universe, just as did the first great sacrifice.

Another very fascinating speculation concerning creation is given in the great Creation Hymn of the *Rig Veda*. After a complex statement of the origin of the world, the poet concludes by saying that only the First Principle knows how the earth was created; and then suddenly adds, "or perhaps he knows it not." This phrase is often quoted as evidence of the skeptical mind of the ancient poet, but more probably it indicates the willingness within the Indian tradition to push inquiry to an extreme in the search for some ultimate principle that can be accepted as final and unchanging.

Time as Creator

kala

Time carries [us] forward, a steed, with seven rays, a thousand eyes, undecaying, full of fecundity. On him intelligent sages mount; his wheels are all the worlds. This Time moves on seven wheels; he has seven naves; immortality is his axle. He is at present all these worlds. Time hastens onward, the first god. A full jar is contained in Time. We behold him existing in many forms. He is all these worlds in the future. They call him Time in the highest heaven. It is he who drew forth the worlds, and encompassed them. Being the father, he became their son. There is no other power superior to him. Time generated the sky and these earths. Set in motion by Time, the past and the future subsist. Time created the earth; by Time the sun burns; through Time all beings [exist]; through Time the eye sees. Mind, breath, name, are embraced in Time. All these creatures rejoice when Time arrives. In Time rigorous abstraction, in Time the highest, in Time divine knowledge, is comprehended. Time is lord of all things, he who was the father of Prajāpati. That [universe] has been set in motion by him, produced by him, and is supported on him.

(from *Atharva Veda* XIX:531-38, in Muir, *Original Sanskrit Texts*, V, p. 408)

Sacrifice as Creator

Thousand-headed Purusha, thousand-eyed, thousand-footed—he having pervaded the earth on all sides, still extends ten fingers beyond it.

Purusha alone is all this—whatever has been and whatever is going to be. Further, he is the lord of immortality and also of what grows for food.

Such is his greatness; greater, indeed, than this is Purusha. All creatures constitute but one quarter of him, his three quarters are the immortal in heaven. . . . Being born, he projected himself behind the earth as also before it.

When the gods performed the sacrifice with Purusha as the oblation, then the spring was its clarified butter, the summer the sacrificial fuel, and the autumn the oblation.

The sacrificial victim, namely, Purusha, born at the very beginning, they sprinkled with sacred water upon the sacrificial grass. With him as oblation the gods performed the sacrifice, and also the Sādhyas [a class of semidivine beings] and the rishis [ancient seers].

From that wholly offered sacrificial oblation were born the verses and the sacred chants; from it were born the meters; the sacrificial formula was born from it.

From it horses were born and also those animals who have double rows of teeth; cows were born from it, from it were born goats and sheep.

When they divided Purusha, in how many different portions did they arrange him? What became of his mouth, what of his two arms? What were his two thighs and his two feet called?

His mouth became the brāhman; his two arms were made into the rājanya; his two thighs the vaishyas; from his two feet the shūdra was born.

The moon was born from the mind, from the eye the sun was born; from the mouth Indra and Agni, from the breath the wind was born.

From the navel was the atmosphere created, from the head the heaven issued forth; from the two feet was born the earth and the quarters (the cardinal directions) from the ear. Thus did they fashion the worlds.

Seven were the enclosing sticks in this sacrifice, thrice seven were the fire-sticks made, when the gods, performing the sacrifice, bound down Purusha, the sacrificial victim.

With this sacrificial oblation did the gods offer the sacrifice. These were the first norms (*dharma*) of sacrifice. These greatnesses reached to the sky wherein live the ancient Sādhyas and gods.

(from *Rig Veda* X:90, in *Sources of Indian Tradition*, pp. 16-17)

The One as Creator

Then was not non-existent nor existent: there was no realm of air, no sky beyond it.

What covered in, and where? and what gave shelter? Was water there, unfathomed depth of water?

Death was not then, nor was there aught immortal: no sign was there, the day's and night's divider.

That One Thing, breathless, breathed by its own nature: apart from it was nothing whatsoever.

Darkness there was: at first concealed in darkness this All was undifferentiated chaos.

All that existed then was void and formless: by the great power of Warmth was born that One.

Thereafter rose Desire in the beginning, Desire, the primal seed and germ of Spirit.

Sages who searched with their heart's thought discovered the existent's kinship in the non-existent.

Transversely was their severing line extended: what was above it then, and what below it?

There were begetters, there were mighty forces, free action here and energy up yonder.

Who verily knows and who can here declare it, whence it
   was born and whence comes this creation?
The Gods are later than this world's creation. Who knows
   then whence it first came into being?
He, the first origin of this creation, whether he formed it
   all or did not form it,
Whose eye controls this world in highest heaven, he verily
   knows it, or perhaps he knows not.

(from *Rig Veda* X:129, in Griffith, *The Hymns of the Rig
Veda*, II, pp. 575-76)

THE MEANING OF SACRIFICE

While the centrality of the sacrificial rituals in early Indian
religion is clear, the nature and meaning of the actual performances is often obscure. This is due partly to developments that
took place throughout the centuries in the religious tradition
and partly to the complexity of the concepts involved. In the
earliest period the sacrifice seems to have been performed in
order to win the favor of a god by making a gift for which he
would return riches and a long life. Thus in one hymn offerings
are made to Indra who is told, in a rather peremptory fashion,
to accept them and "then fix thy mind upon bestowing treasure." (*Rig Veda* I:54). Related to this was the thought of
the sacrifice as a thank-offering, a gift made for favors received.

   An important development took place when the conclusion
was reached that if a sacrifice were properly performed the gods
could not withhold the boon requested. In other words, the
sacrifice was understood to be able to provide the results desired, and the will of the gods became almost irrelevant. The
power of sacrifice in bringing about the creation of the world
has already been noted in the Hymn of Man, and the sacrificial
ritual thus assumed enormous importance within the whole
cultural tradition. One result of this belief in the potency of
the ritual was an exaltation of the role of the performer. Since
the ritual was of such great consequence, it had to be correctly

performed; the misuse of a word or phrase might lead to disaster. The sacrificer was thus regarded as controlling a power that could bring blessing or destruction. The priest therefore became a key figure in the whole drama of the cosmic order. This development undoubtedly explains in part at least the unique function of the Brāhman in Indian culture, for he was a man who controlled the secrets of the universe. A further result of this attitude towards sacrifice and the role of the sacrificer was that the gods became less important than the performer and the ritual act.

The following selections are taken from a *Brāhmana*, one of a class of Vedic literature that deals, in great detail, with the ritual performances. They illustrate the way in which the significance of the sacrifice was heightened by seeing analogies and correspondences between the materials of the sacrifice and other materials. Especial significance was seen in word similarities, and the kind of etymological reasoning shown here occupies an important place in Indian literature. The second selection indicates the extent of the claims made by the Brāhman priests.

After that (the priest) pronounces the offering-prayer to Tanūnapāt. Tanūnapāt, doubtless, is the summer; for the summer burns the bodies (tanūn tapati) of these creatures. The gods, at that time, appropriated the summer, and deprived their rivals of the summer; and now this one also appropriates the summer, and deprives his rivals of the summer: this is the reason why he pronounces the offering-prayer to Tanūnapāt.

He then pronounces the offering-prayer to the Iḍs. The Iḍs (praises), doubtless, are the rains; they are the rains, inasmuch as the vile, crawling (vermin) which shrink during the summer and winter, then (in the rainy season) move about in quest of food, as it were, praising (īḍ) the rains: therefore the Iḍs are the rains. The gods, at that time, appropriated the rains, and deprived their rivals of the rains; and now this one also appropriates the rains, and deprives his rivals of the rains: this is the reason why he pronounces the offering-prayer to the Iḍs.

He then pronounces the offering-prayer to the barhis (covering of sacrificial grass on the altar). The barhis, doubtless, is the autumn; the barhis is the autumn, inasmuch as these plants which shrink during the summer and winter grow by the rains, and in autumn lie spread open after the fashion of barhis: for this reason the barhis is the autumn. The gods, at that time, appropriated the autumn, and deprived their rivals of the autumn; and now this one also appropriates the autumn, and deprives his rivals of the autumn; this is why he pronounces the prayer to the barhis.

(from *Śatapatha Brāhmana*, I:5:3:10-27, in *Sacred Books of the East*, XII, p. 147)

DEATH

When the Vedic people thought of the future life they generally pictured a place where those who had satisfied the gods —both through the performance of sacrifices and the living of a life in accordance with the moral order—enjoyed pleasures which were an extension of those of life on earth, differing in quantity but not in kind. On a more sophisticated level, death was also equated with that state of non-existence (*asat*) of which the hymns speak so frequently. To live, was to be ruled by cosmic law, that ordering of existence that applied to both men and gods; to die, was to pass into the order of non-existence, a realm in some way outside the cosmic law. This sense that death was identified with non-existence is reflected in the reiterated desire to live "a hundred autumns," and, quite probably, in the attempt through ritual and sacrifice to set a limit to Death's claims.

Go hence, O Death, pursue thy special pathway apart from that which Gods are wont to travel.

To thee I say it who hast eyes and hearest: Touch not our
offspring, injure not our heroes.

Divided from the dead are these, the living: now be our
calling on the Gods successful.

We have gone forth for dancing and for laughter, to further times prolonging our existence.

Here I erect this rampart for the living; let none of these,
none other, reach this limit.

May they survive a hundred lengthened autumns, and may
they bury Death beneath this mountain.

As the days follow days in close succession, as with the
seasons duly come the seasons,

As each successor fails not his foregoer, so form the lives of
these, O great Ordainer.

Live your full lives and find old age delightful, all of you
striving one behind the other.

May Tvashtar, maker of fair things, be gracious and
lengthen out the days of your existence.

Let these unwidowed dames with noble husbands adorn
themselves with fragrant balm and unguent.

Decked with fair jewels, tearless, free from sorrow, first let
the dames go up to where he lieth.

Rise, come unto the world of life, O woman: come, he is
lifeless by whose side thou liest.

Wifehood with this thy husband was thy portion, who
took thy hand and wooed thee as a lover.

From his dead hand I take the bow he carried, that it may
be our power and might and glory.

There art thou, there; and here with noble heroes may we
o'ercome all hosts that fight against us.

Betake thee to the lap of Earth the Mother, of Earth far-
spreading, very kind and gracious.

Young Dame, wool-soft unto the guerdon-giver, may she
preserve thee from Destruction's bosom.

Heave thyself, Earth, nor press thee downward heavily:
afford him easy access, gently tending him.

Cover him, as a mother wraps her skirt about her child, O
Earth.

Now let the heaving earth be free from motion: yea, let a
    thousand clods remain above him.
Be they to him a home distilling fatness, here let them
    ever be his place of refuge.
I stay the earth from thee, while over thee I place this
    piece of earth. May I be free from injury.
Here let the Fathers keep this pillar firm for thee, and
    there let Death make thee an abiding-place.

(from *Rig Veda* X:18, in Griffith, *The Hymns of the Rig
Veda*, II, pp. 406-07)

CHAPTER II

THE SOCIAL ORDER

〰〰〰〰〰

For an understanding of the development of the Hindu tradition some knowledge is necessary of the social life of the people in the great creative periods, for very frequently the religious and philosophical ideas appear in a quite new light when they are seen reflected through the patterns of the lives of the people in their ordinary concerns. And while it is probably true that it is difficult to consider religious ideas apart from social structure in any society, in Indian culture it is manifestly impossible. Not only was every stage of life from birth to death marked by formal sacramental acts, but there was scarcely an action or custom, however trivial or commonplace, that did not have a sanction beyond mere utility. This means that while Indian culture is probably more "religious" than almost any other, at the same time religious rites and practices often have a very casual performance, sometimes suggesting to outsiders a lack of genuine piety. The explanation is, of course, a different understanding of the nature of the secular and sacred. It may be noted in passing that the religious consciousness that surrounds commonplace acts is an important element in transmitting the heritage, since the style and tone of the high culture can penetrate in this way

to cultural levels that may be quite unfamiliar with the
philosophical presuppositions underlying them.

The selections included in this chapter are intended to
suggest how some aspects of ancient Indian experience
have had a particularly influential role in the growth of the
Hindu tradition. Many of the passages are from the
Atharva Veda, which is largely a collection of incantations
and charms that have an intimate relationship to the everyday lives of the people. A distinction is sometimes made
between the levels of religious and cultural experience displayed in the Rig Veda and the Atharva Veda, with the
suggestion that the Atharva Veda preserves the record of a
more primitive religious understanding, with an emphasis
on magic. This distinction probably should not be stressed
too much, however, for both in the great sacrificial rituals
of the Rig Veda and in the rather crude charms and spells
of the Atharva Veda a comparable spirit can be recognized. There is in both an almost unbounded faith in the
power of the priestly class to control the processes of life,
and, linked to this, a feeling that while the universe may
contain many elements hostile to man, nevertheless,
means of control are available. This point is worth stress-
ing in connection with the Indian social order, for there
seems to be little evidence, at least in the early literature,
of any acquiescence on the part of man to natural forces or
any sense of fatalism, those two attitudes popularly attrib-
uted to Indian society.

THE DUTY OF CHARITY

The stress in the Vedic hymns on the offering of gifts to the
gods as an essential feature of religious experience was generalized to include the concept of the duty of liberality to all who
were in need. The motivation for charity is not, therefore, an

appeal to compassion based on an understanding of human suffering or of common brotherhood, but rather a recognition of the right of the recipient of a gift to share in the good fortune of the donor. The duty of almsgiving, which is a prominent feature of all Indian religions, is clearly foreshadowed in the following hymn from the *Rig Veda*.

The Gods have not ordained hunger to be our death: even to the well-fed man comes death in varied shape.
The riches of the liberal never waste away, while he who will not give finds none to comfort him.
The man with food in store who, when the needy comes in miserable case begging for bread to eat,
Hardens his heart against him—even when of old he did him service—finds not one to comfort him.
Bounteous is he who gives unto the beggar who feebly comes to him in want of food.
Success attends him in the shout of battle. He makes a friend of him in future troubles.
No friend is he who to his friend and comrade, who comes imploring food, will offer nothing.
Let him depart—no home is that to rest in—, and rather seek a stranger to support him.
Let the rich satisfy the poor implorer, and bend his eye upon a longer pathway.
Riches come now to one, now to another, and like the wheels of chariots are ever moving.

(from *Rig Veda*, X:117, in Griffith, *The Hymns of the Rig Veda*, II, p. 561, revised)

WAR

In recent years the place of non-violence in the Indian tradition has received much emphasis, but it is worth remembering that throughout India's history military prowess has been exalted and the waging of war has been regarded as an essential feature of political life. The early Aryans gloried in the ability of their horses and chariots to strike terror into the hearts of their enemies, the people of the land, and their favorite god, Indra, was a great military hero. The selection given here was probably a kind of incantation which, when recited before battle, gave special potency to the weapons of the warriors.

The warrior's look is like a thunderous rain-cloud's, when, armed with mail, he seeks the lap of battle.
Be thou victorious with unwounded body: so let the thickness of thy mail protect thee.
With Bow let us win kine, with Bow the battle, with Bow be victors in our hot encounters.
The Bow brings grief and sorrow to the foeman: armed with the Bow may we subdue all regions.
Close to his ear, as fain to speak, She presses, holding her well-loved Friend in her embraces.
Strained on the Bow, She whispers like a woman—this Bowstring that preserves us in the combat.
These, meeting like a woman and her lover, bear, mother-like their child upon their bosom.
May the two Bow-ends, starting swift asunder, scatter, in unison, the foes who hate us.
With many a son, father of many daughters, He clangs and clashes as he goes to battle.
Slung on the back, pouring his brood, the Quiver vanquishes all opposing bands and armies.
Upstanding in the Car the skilful Charioteer guides his strong Horses on whithersoe'er he will.
See and admire the strength of those controlling Reins which from behind declare the will of him who drives.
Horses whose hoofs rain dust are neighing loudly, yoked to the Chariots, showing forth their vigour.
With their forefeet descending on the foemen, they, never flinching, trample and destroy them. . . .
He lays his blows upon their backs, he deals his blows upon their thighs.

Thou, Whip, who urgest horses, drive sagacious horses in
the fray.

It compasses the arm with serpent windings, fending away
the friction of the bowstring:

So may the Brace, well-skilled in all its duties, guard man-
fully the man from every quarter.

Now to the Shaft with venom smeared, tipped with deer-
horn, with iron mouth.

Celestial, of the Rain God's seed, be this great adoration
paid.

Loosed from the Bowstring fly away, thou Arrow, sharpened by our prayer.

Go to the foemen, strike them home, and let not one be
left alive.

(from *Rig Veda*, VI:75, in Griffith, *The Hymns of the Rig
Veda*, I, pp. 645-47)

CHARMS AND SPELLS
FOR A GOOD LIFE

Valuable sources of information regarding the everyday life of
the ancient Indian peoples are contained in the numerous incantations and spells of the *Atharva Veda*. They feared the
demons and evil spirits who haunted the forests, but, even
more, they feared the sorcerers who had the power to control
the forces of evil. Scarcely differentiated from the malign spiritual forces were the natural sources of death and injury—dis-
eases, wild beasts, serpents. In their world, as in the Psalmist's,
pestilence walked in darkness, and destruction wasted at noon-
day. This did not mean, however, that they felt helpless before
the dark powers; on the contrary, through their armory of spells
and magic formulae they were confident of their ability to
meet and master the external world. And in addition to charms
for protecting life, they had a wide variety of spells to bring

about the birth of sons, to gain success in trading, and to compel the love of men and women.

Examples of these ancient spells are given here. Presumably they were accompanied by symbolic actions which, in consort with the spoken word and the proper materials, brought about the desired ends. This process of "sympathetic magic" is found in many cultures, but it appears to have been elaborated to an unusual degree within the Indian tradition and, through being related to the high religious and philosophical tradition, to have played a unique part in the development of society.

Against Jaundice

Unto the sun let them both go up—your heartburn and your yellowness; with the color of the red bull do we envelop you.

With red colors do we envelop you for the sake of long life; so that this person may be free from harm and may become non-yellow.

Those cows that have Rohinī [the Red One] as presiding divinity, as also cows which are red—their every form and every power—with them do we envelop you.

Into the parrots do we put your yellowness and into the yellow-green birds. Similarly into the turmeric [or yellow wagtail?] do we deposit your yellowness.

(from *Atharva Veda*, I:22, in *Sources of Indian Tradition*, p. 20)

Against Serpents

Let not the serpent, O gods, slay us with our children and with our men. The closed jaw shall not snap open, the open one shall not close. Homage to the divine folk [i.e., the serpents, by way of exorcistic euphemism].

Homage be to the black serpent, homage to the one with stripes across its body, homage to the brown constrictor [?], homage to the divine folk.

I smite your teeth with tooth, I smite your two jaws
with jaw; I smite your tongue with tongue; I smite your
mouth, O Serpent, with mouth.

(from *Atharva Veda*, VI:56, in *Sources of Indian Tradition*,
p. 20)

To Compel a Woman's Love

As the wind shakes this Tuft of Grass hither and thither
  on the ground,
So do I stir and shake thy mind, that thou mayst be in love
  with me, my darling, never to depart.
Ye, Asvins, lead together, ye unite and bring the loving
  pair.
Now have the fortunes of you twain, now have your vows
  and spirits met.
When eagles, calling out aloud, are screaming in the joy of
  health,
Then to my calling let her come, as to the arrow's neck the
  shaft.
Let what is inward turn outside, let what is outward be
  within:
Seize and possess, O Plant, the mind of maidens rich in
  every charm.
Seeking a husband she hath come! and I came longing for
  a wife:
Even as a loudly-neighing steed my fate and fortune have I
  met.

(from *Atharva Veda*, II:30, in Griffith, I, pp. 70-71)

For Success in Trading

I stir and animate the merchant Indra: may he approach
  and be our guide and leader.

Chasing ill-will, wild beast, and highway robber, may he
    who hath the power give me riches.
The many paths which Gods are wont to travel, the paths
    which go between the earth and heaven,
May they rejoice with me in milk and fatness that I may
    make rich profit by my purchase.
With fuel, Agni! and with butter, longing, mine offering I
    present for strength and conquest;
With prayer, so far as I have strength, adoring—this holy
    hymn to gain a hundred treasures.
Pardon this stubbornness of ours, O Agni, the distant
    pathway which our feet have trodden.
Propitious unto us be sale and barter, may interchange of
    merchandise enrich me.
Accept, ye twain, accordant, this libation! Prosperous be
    our ventures and incomings.
The wealth wherewith I carry on my traffic, seeking, ye
    Gods! wealth with the wealth I offer,
May this grow more for me, not less: O Agni, through
    sacrifice chase those who hinder profit!

(from *Atharva Veda*, III:15, in Griffith, I, pp. 116-17)

IN PRAISE OF THE COW

Although the unique place accorded to the cow is one of the
best-known features of the Hindu tradition, it is difficult to define the nature of the relationship of the cow to the religious
structure. This is probably partly to be explained by the fact
that no very close analogy exists elsewhere, and therefore one
cannot draw upon other cultural examples to illumine the situation, but it is also to be explained in terms of changing
values within the tradition itself. To say that the cow is regarded as sacred is probably correct, but in a tradition notable
for the proliferation of deities and for the willingness of people
to create plastic representations, it is remarkable that there is

no "cow goddess" nor is the cow—as distinct from the bull—
found in the form of an idol in temples. Furthermore, the prohibition on cow-killing and the eating of beef, which characterizes Hinduism from the early centuries of the Christian era,
was apparently unknown in Vedic times.

From very early times, however, the cow was revered as the
possessor of great power. It is frequently suggested this is the
natural reaction of an agricultural people to an animal valuable
for plowing, transportation, fertilizer, and food, but this nat-
uralistic interpretation would scarcely seem to account for the
quite extraordinary sanctity that is associated with the cow.
Probably one must look for the explanation in some very primitive acceptance of the cow as a totem, and then, at a later
stage, in the tendency for Indian thinkers to see special significance in finding identities between the cosmic order and the
familiar objects of the everyday world. The cow and her manifold useful properties provided a peculiarly satisfying object for
identification. The following verses in praise of the cow are
taken from a long hymn where, through a process of mystical
identifications, the cow becomes the whole visible universe.

Worship to thee, springing to life, and worship to thee
   when born!
Worship, O Cow, to thy tail-hair, and to thy hooves, and
   to thy form!
Hitherward we invite with prayer the Cow who pours a
   thousand streams,
By whom the heaven, by whom the earth, by whom these
   waters are preserved. . . .
Forth from thy mouth the songs came, from thy neck's
   nape sprang strength, O Cow.
Sacrifice from thy flanks was born, and rays of sunlight
   from thy teats.
From thy fore-quarters and thy thighs motion was generated, Cow!
Food from thine entrails was produced, and from thy belly
   came the plants. . . .
They call the Cow immortal life, pay homage to the Cow
   as Death.

She hath become this universe, Fathers, and Rishis, hath become the Gods, and men, and Spirits.

The man who hath this knowledge may receive the Cow with welcoming.

So for the giver willingly doth perfect sacrifice pour milk. . . .

The Cow is Heaven, the Cow is Earth, the Cow is Vishnu, Lord of Life.

The heavenly beings have drunk the out-pourings of the Cow.

When these heavenly beings have drunk the out-pourings of the Cow,

They in the Bright One's dwelling-place pay adoration to her milk.

For Soma some have milked her: some worship the fatness she hath poured.

They who have given a cow to him who hath this knowledge have gone up to the third region of the sky.

He who hath given a Cow unto the Brāhmans winneth all the worlds.

For Right is firmly set in her, devotion, and religious zeal.

Both Gods and mortal men depend for life and being on the Cow.

She hath become this universe: all that the Sun surveys is she.

(from *Atharva Veda* X:10, in Griffith, II, pp. 45-56, revised)

THE PLACE OF THE BRĀHMAN

The nature of the class divisions of Indian society will be noted in more detail in Chapter IV, but reference must be made here to the unique role of the Brāhman. While the class structure is immensely complicated, and varies in character from region to region, everywhere the highest role is assigned to the priestly class, the Brāhmans. That the four classes—the priests (*Brāhman*), warrior (*kshatriya*), peasant (*vaishya*), and serf (*shūdra*) —were regarded as the basic form of the special order is shown in the Hymn of Man in the *Rig Veda*, which is quoted in Chapter I. In social terms, the highest and lowest classes were probably the most important, since the Brāhmans controlled the religious institutions and the shūdras composed the bulk of the composition.

The selection given here indicates the extent of the claims made by the priests, and while the literature from which this type of statement comes was written by Brāhmans who would presumably forward their own class interests, it represents the ideal generally accepted by all classes in the society. Over against the assertion of rights made by the Brāhmans for themselves must be set the role they assigned the shūdras. The general implication is that the lower orders have obligations which can be understood as rights only in a secondary way.

A number of possibilities ought to be kept in mind in reading passages from the ancient texts dealing with class structure. On the one hand, they may be statements of hard social fact, a description of the ways things were, and not the definition of an ideal society. On the other hand, the passages may be examples of rather fanatical pretensions by priests, who while anxious to define the boundaries of the classes, were never actually able to carry out their prescriptions. This would seem, for example, to be the only explanation possible for such statements as "a shūdra is the servant of another, to be slain at will." Such a policy would have led to social anarchy, whereas the emphasis was always on social order.

. . . . Those who spit, or throw filth upon a Brāhman, sit eating hair in the midst of a stream of blood. So long as this Brāhman's cow is cut up and cooked, she destroys the glory of the kingdom; no vigorous hero is born there. It is cruel to slaughter her; her ill-flavoured flesh is thrown away. When her milk is drunk, that is esteemed a sin among the Forefathers. Whenever a king, fancying himself mighty, seeks to devour a Brāhman, that kingdom is broken up, in which a Brāhman is oppressed. Becoming eight-footed, four-eyed, four-eared, four-jawed, two-faced, two-tongued, she (the cow) shatters the kingdom of the oppressor of Brāhmans. (Ruin) overflows that kingdom, as water swamps a leaky boat: calamity smites that country in which a priest is wronged. Even trees, O Nārada, repel, and refuse their shade to, the man who claims a right to the property of a Brāhman. This (property), as king Varuna hath said, has been turned into a poison by the gods. No one who has eaten a Brāhman's cow continues to watch (*i.e.* to rule) over a country. . . .

The gods have declared that the cloth wherewith a dead man's feet are bound shall be thy pall, thou oppressor of priests. The tears which flow from a persecuted man as he laments,—such is the portion of water which the gods have assigned to thee, thou oppressor of priests. The gods have allotted to thee that portion of water wherewith men wash the dead, and moisten beards. The rain of Mitra and Varuna does not descend on the oppressor of priests. For him the battle has never a successful issue; nor does he bring his friend into subjection.

(from *Atharva Veda*, V:19, in Muir, I, pp. 286-87)

THE CROWNING OF A KING

In the early Indian tradition there is nothing that quite corresponds to western political thinking, but this does not mean that questions concerning the nature of human government were not asked. It only means that different questions were asked, and they were answered in a different way. As will be seen (in Chapter V), statecraft understood as the techniques of political control, became the subject matter of an important branch of literature. In the early period, interest centered on the relation of the king to the ritual practices of the religion and his place in the divine order.

Although there are some passages that suggest the king was elected by the people, normally this could have only meant some measure of control by the tribal or village elders. From quite early times—certainly by 600 B.C.—the king was regarded as surrounded by a special sanctity. Two things probably contributed to this. One was the king's participation in the great sacrifices, most notably the horse sacrifice; the other was his membership in a class that was itself divinely ordained. The selections given here, the first of which is taken from a description of the coronation rites and the second of which is from hymns probably sung at the ceremony, emphasize both the king's power and his duty to rule according to the sacred laws of society.

King of Kings

This is the Lord of Indra, this the Lord of Heaven, the Lord of Earth,
The Lord of all existing things: the one and only Lord be thou.
The Sea is regent of the floods, Agni is ruler of the land,
The Moon is regent of the stars: the one and only Lord be thou.
Thou art the King of Earthly Kings, the crown and summit of mankind:
Thou art the partner of the Gods: the one and only Lord be thou.

The Chosen One

Here art thou: I have chosen thee. Stand steadfast and immovable.
Let all the clans desire thee: let not thy kingdom fall away.
Be even here: fall not away: be like a mountain unremoved.
Stand steadfast here like Indra's self, and hold the kingship in thy grasp.
This man hath Indra stablished, made secure by constant sacrifice.

Soma, and Brahmanaspati here present bless and comfort
  him!

The Enduring Ruler

Firm is the sky, firm is the earth, and firm is all this living
  world;
Firm are these mountains on their base, and steadfast is
  this King of men.
Steadfast may Varuna the King, steadfast the God Brihaspati,
Steadfast may Indra, steadfast, too, may Agni keep thy
  steadfast reign.
Firm, never to be shaken, crush thy foemen, under thy
  feet lay those who strive against thee.
One-minded, true to thee be all the regions: faithful to
  thee, the firm, be this assembly!

(from *Atharva Veda*, VI:86,87,88, in Griffith, I, pp. 292-
293, revised)

EARTH AS MOTHERLAND

One of the most enduring and vital features of the Hindu
tradition is the concept of the earth as motherland. Hinduism
is very firmly rooted in the Indian soil, and, unlike the other
great religions, has tended to be confined to the region of its
origin. The geography of the great myths and legends is the
actual geography of India, and almost every hill and river has
some association that is a constant reminder of the great deeds
of the gods. The importance of this "sacred geography" in
maintaining the tradition, and of continually renewing its
meaning to the people, can scarcely be overestimated. The
magnificent Hymn to Earth (or *Prithivī*) is one of the clearest
expressions of the conviction that the Earth is a fitting symbol
for the deepest of religious impulses.

Truth, high and potent Law, the Consecrating Rite, Fervour, Brahma, and Sacrifice uphold the Earth.

May she, the Queen of all that is and is to be, may Earth
make ample space and room for us.

Not over-crowded by the crowd of Manu's sons, she who
hath many heights and floods and level plains;

She who bears plants endowed with many varied powers,
may Earth for us spread wide and favour us.

In whom the sea, and the great river, and the waters, in
whom our food and corn-lands had their being,

In whom this all that breathes and moves is active, this
Earth assign us foremost rank and station!

She who is Lady of the earth's four regions, in whom our
food and corn-lands had their being,

Nurse in each place of breathing, moving creatures, this
Earth vouchsafe us kine with milk that fails not!

On whom the men of old before us battled, on whom the
Gods attacked the hostile demons,

The varied home of bird, and kine and horses, this Earth
vouchsafe us luck and splendour! . . .

O Earth, auspicious be thy woodlands, auspicious be thy
hills and snow-clad mountains.

Unslain, unwounded, unsubdued, I have set foot upon the
Earth,

On earth, brown, black, ruddy and every-coloured, on the
firm earth that Indra guards from danger.

O Earth, thy centre and thy navel, all forces that have
issued from thy body—

Set us amid those forces; breathe upon us. I am the son of
Earth, Earth is my Mother. The Rain God is my Sire;
may he promote me.

Earth on whose surface they enclose the altar, and all-
performers spin the thread of worship;

In whom the stakes of sacrifice, resplendent, are fixed and
raised on high before the oblation, may she, this Earth,
prospering, make us prosper.

The man who hates us, Earth! who fights against us, who

threatens us with thought or deadly weapon, make him our thrall as thou hast done aforetime.

(from *Atharva Veda*, XII:1, in Griffith, II, pp. 93-101, revised)

CHAPTER III

THE CROWN OF
THE VEDIC AGE:
THE UPANISHADS

≈≈≈≈≈≈≈

The designation of the Upanishads as "the end of the Veda" (Vedānta) indicates both their place in the temporal sequence of the Vedic literature and their position within the canon of Hindu scripture as the summation of the truth contained in all the previous works. Over a hundred works are given the name of "Upanishad" but only about thirteen of these can be dated with assurance as belonging to the Vedic Age. They do not present any consistent religious or philosophical system, and even within a single work there may be contradictions; nor do they claim to present new truths. It is sometimes suggested that the Upanishads are the product of a religious revolt, a turning away from the rigid ritualistic formulations of the past, but there actually is little within the works themselves to suggest any such origin. There is no attack on the old ways, no demand for reform; at most, there is an indifference to some features of the older Vedic sacrificial tradition. In general, the ideas of the Upanishads can be traced to developments which had already made their appearance in the older texts.

Yet having emphasized their continuity with the tradition, it must be recognized that the spirit and temper of the Upanishads is remarkably different from that of the earlier literature. New questions were asked, and their form determined the answers given to them. One of the most notable transformations that took place in this direction related to the understanding of sacrifice. The interest in ritualistic performance, with fantastic attention to details, was replaced by an interest in attaining the same goals through meditation and concentration, with the physical materials of the old sacrifices being treated in a symbolic fashion. Related to this was a turning inward to examine the nature of reality, rather than studying the external world. The aim of this examination of the self was not, however, psychological understanding; it was motivated by the conviction that "underlying the exterior world of change there is an unchangeable reality which is identical with that which underlies the essence of man." [1]

The Vedic thinkers had been inclined to identify some particular phenomenon—wind or water, for example—as a god, and to see this as the ultimate source of the universe. In the Upanishads this unifying principle is seen to be not a deity or any physical property but brahman, *that mysterious principle that even in early thought is regarded as forming the substratum of the universe. At the same time, the basis of human selfhood was understood to be the* āt-man, *the self or soul. One conclusion that the sages of the Upanishads reached was that these two principles,* brah-man *and* ātman, *were identical, and that the essence of being underlying both the self and the external was absolutely undifferentiated. This doctrine is summed up in the famous formula,* tat tvam asi, *"that art thou," with "that" standing for the universal* brahman, *"thou" for the individual* ātman. *An exposition of this is given in the selection below entitled "The Identity of Brahman and Ātman."*

Although this assertion of the ultimate identity of brah-man *and* ātman *seems to be the dominating theme of the Upanishads, there are other interpretations of the nature of the relationship between the two principles. One of the*

[1] S. N. Dasgupta, *A History of Indian Philosophy* (Cambridge: 1922), I, p. 42.

Upanishads, Śvetaśvatara, *speaks of* brahman *as God, making a distinction between this and the external world. In addition to this theistic interpretation, there is also a movement towards pantheism, a tendency to think of the natural universe and the individual soul as* God.

These varying interpretations could exist side by side because the sages and teachers were not seeking to formulate a statement of belief but something entirely different, "a radical alteration in the mode of consciousness . . . with a view to gaining intuitive knowledge of reality." [2] They defined this reality in terms of the brahman-ātman equation, but their quest can probably also be understood in western terminology as an attempt to experience a sense of the immortality of the soul, to find a self more permanent than the ego immediately known to consciousness. At this level of the Indian tradition, therefore, the religious concern is not with a relationship between man and God, but with the realization of the nature of the self. This is brought out in the selection, "Ātman: the Real Self."

Underlying much of the speculation of the *Upanishads* are the two closely related concepts, karma *and transmigration.* Karma, *literally "action,"* is the belief that every act produces an effect which inevitably finds fruition. One of the great unquestioned assumptions of the Indian tradition, this doctrine may have its roots in the idea of rita, the cosmic principle that the early Vedic peoples saw as ordering the whole universe. The prominence of the idea of sacrifice must also have been a contributing factor in the development of the belief in karma, for sacrifice was the supreme action that men could perform, and the performance of the ritual led inevitably to certain results.

Indissolubly linked with the concept of karma is the other great characteristic feature of Indian thought, the belief in transmigration. The idea that the human soul on death finds lodging in another body is widespread, but by being linked with the doctrine of karma it took on special

[2] R. C. Zaehner, *At Sundry Times* (London: Faber and Faber, 1958), p. 37.

significance. Since every act carries with it an inevitable result, the span of one lifetime may not suffice as a field for the working out of all the implications of action. Transmigration makes possible, therefore, a belief in the strict justice of the universe, with each action reaping its due reward of good or evil fruit. Conversely, the two concepts can be used to explain the seeming injustices and inequities of the world.

The concepts of karma and transmigration have had enormous influence on every aspect of the Indian tradition, and were accepted in some form not only by Hinduism but also by Jainism and Buddhism, both of which rejected the Vedic scriptures. Readings to illustrate them have been included in this section because they are accepted without question as part of the structure of the universe.

THE NEW MEANING
OF SACRIFICE

While the Upanishadic thinkers turned to new concepts of religion, they did not abandon the old ritual forms, but transformed what had been actual physical acts into symbolic representations. One of the best examples of this is the elaborate allegorization of the Horse Sacrifice, the greatest of the Vedic rituals. Involving large numbers of priests and great preparations, it exemplified the extreme development of external ritual. Basically, it was the act whereby a king proclaimed his intention to become a "world ruler," or, more prosaically, to extend his territory, and the horse represented such qualities as virility, power, and majesty. To the Upanishadic thinker, the significance of the sacrifice was in the identities he saw between the great sacrificial animal and the cosmos. Through this process of symbolic identification the sage moved towards a statement of the unity of the disparate parts of the universe and also linked his meditations with the sacrificial ritual, whose

power and potency had long been accepted as a fundamental
feature of existence.

Dawn verily is the head of the sacrificial horse. The sun is
his eye; the wind, his breath; the universal sacrificial fire,
his open mouth; the year is the body (ātman) of the sacrificial horse. The sky is his back; the atmosphere, his belly;
the earth, his underbelly; the directions, his flanks; the
intermediate directions, his ribs; the seasons, his limbs;
the months and half-months, his joints; days and nights,
his feet; the stars, his bones; the clouds, his flesh. Sand is
the food in his stomach; rivers, his entrails; mountains, his
liver and lungs; plants and trees, his hair; the rising sun, his
forepart; the setting sun, his hindpart. When he yawns,
then it lightnings; when he shakes himself, then it thun-
ders; when he urinates, then it rains. Speech (vāc) is actually his neighing (vāc).

(from *Brihad Āranyaka*, I:1:1, in *Sources of Indian Tradition*,
pp. 27-28)

BRAHMAN: THE SEARCH FOR
THE GROUND OF THE UNIVERSE

In their quest for some ultimate ground for the world of
natural phenomena, of time and space, and of human existence, the Upanishadic sages came to the conception of *brahman*, an undefinable, impersonal, unknowable power. One of
the most interesting discussions of this absolute principle is
given in the form of a dialogue between Gārgī, a woman
philosopher, and Yājnavalkya, a great sage. Although in the
preceding dialogues Gārgī had been warned not to ask too
many questions, lest her head fall off, she persisted, and was
rewarded with answers to her questions.

Yājñavalkya said: 'Ask, Gārgī.'

She said: 'That, O Yājñavalkya, which is above the sky, that which is beneath the earth, that which is between these two, sky and earth, that which people call the past and the present and the future—across what is that woven, warp and woof?'

He said: 'That, O Gārgī, which is above the sky, that which is beneath the earth, that which is between these two, sky and earth, that which people call the past and the present and the future—across space is that woven, warp and woof.'

She said: 'Adoration to you, Yājñavalkya, in that you have solved this question for me. Prepare yourself for the other.'

'Ask, Gārgī.'

She said: 'That, O Yājñavalkya, which is above the sky, that which is beneath the earth, that which is between these two, sky and earth, that which people call the past and the present and the future—across what is that woven, warp and woof?'

He said: 'That, O Gārgī, which is above the sky, that which is beneath the earth, that which is between these two, sky and earth, that which people call the past and the present and the future—across space alone is that woven, warp and woof.'

'Across what then, pray, is space woven, warp and woof?'

He said: 'That, O Gārgī, Brāhmans call the Imperishable (*akṣara*). It is not coarse, not fine, not short, not long, not glowing [like fire], not adhesive [like water], without shadow and without darkness, without air and without space, without stickiness, (intangible), odorless, tasteless, without eye, without ear, without voice, without wind, without energy, without breath, without mouth, (without personal or family name, unaging, undying, without fear, immortal, stainless, not uncovered, not covered), without measure, without inside and without outside.

> *It consumes nothing soever.*
> *No one soever consumes it.*

Verily, O Gārgī, at the command of that Imperishable the sun and the moon stand apart. Verily, O Gārgī, at the command of that Imperishable the earth and the sky stand apart. Verily, O Gārgī, at the command of that Imperishable the moments, the hours, the days, the nights, the fortnights, the months, the seasons, and the years stand apart. Verily, O Gārgī, at the command of that Imperishable some rivers flow from the snowy mountains to the east, others to the west, in whatever direction each flows. Verily, O Gārgī, at the command of that Imperishable men praise those who give, the gods are desirous of a sacrificer, and the fathers [are desirous] of the Manes-sacrifice.

Verily, O Gārgī, if one performs sacrifices and worship and undergoes austerity in this world for many thousands of years, but without knowing that Imperishable, limited indeed is that [work] of his. Verily, O Gārgī, he who departs from this world without knowing that Imperishable is pitiable. But, O Gārgī, he who departs from this world knowing that Imperishable is a Brāhman.

Verily, O Gārgī, that Imperishable is the unseen Seer, the unheard Hearer, the unthought Thinker, the ununderstood Understander. Other than It there is naught that sees. Other than It there is naught that hears. Other than It there is naught that thinks. Other than It there is naught that understands. Across this Imperishable, O Gārgī, is space woven, warp and woof.'

She said: 'Venerable Brāhmans, you may think it a great thing if you escape from this man with [merely] making a bow. Not one of you will surpass him in discussions about Brahman.'

Thereupon [Gārgī] held her peace.

(from *Brihad Āranyaka*, III:8:2-12, in Hume, *The Thirteen Principal Upanishads*, pp. 118-19)

ĀTMAN: THE REAL SELF

Over against the questions concerning the ground of the external world are to be set those that probe inward, asking what is meant by the concept of the Self. The Self could be identified with the physical body, or "food," as some of the Upanishadic thinkers were inclined to say. But consciousness, breath, will, all had claims to be regarded as the Self, and all were unsatisfactory as final definitions. What was needed was something that could be identified as being beyond change, something that was in fact immortal. This was found in the conception of the *ātman* as given in the following parable. Here the Self is, as another *Upanishad* says, "the shining, immortal Person." The search for this permanent and unchanging reality found expression in the famous prayer, in the *Brihad Āranyaka*:

> From the unreal lead me to the real;
> From darkness lead me to the light;
> From death lead me to deathlessness.

"The Self (ātman) who is free from evil, free from old age, free from death, free from grief, free from hunger, free from thirst, whose desire is the Real, whose intention is the Real—he should be sought after, he should be desired to be comprehended. He obtains all worlds and all desires, who, having found out that Self, knows him." Thus, indeed, did the god Prajāpati speak. Verily, the gods and the demons both heard this. They said among themselves: "Aha! Let us seek after that Self—the Self, having sought after whom one obtains all worlds and all desires." Then Indra from among the gods went forth unto Prajāpati, and Virochana from among the demons. Indeed, without communicating with each other, those two came into the presence of Prajāpati with sacrificial fuel in hand [i.e., as students willing to serve their preceptor]. For thirty-two years the two lived under Prajāpati the disci-

plined life of a student of sacred knowledge. Then Prajāpati asked them: "Desiring what have you lived the disciplined life of a student of sacred knowledge under me?"
They said: " 'The Self, who is free from evil, free from old
age, free from death, free from grief, free from hunger,
free from thirst, whose desire is the Real, whose intention
is the Real—he should be sought after, he should be
desired to be comprehended. He obtains all worlds and all
desires, who, having found out that Self, knows him.'
These, people declare to be the venerable master's words.
Desiring him [the Self] have we lived the student's life under you." Prajāpati said to them: "That Purusha who is
seen in the eye—he is the Self (ātman)," said he. "That is
the immortal, the fearless; that is Brahman." "But this
one, Sir, who is perceived in water and in a mirror—who is
he?" Prajāpati replied: "The same one, indeed, is perceived in all these." "Having looked at yourself in a pan of
water, whatever you do not comprehend of the Self, tell
that to me," said Prajāpati. They looked at themselves in
the pan of water. Prajāpati asked them: "What do you
see?" They replied: "We see here, Sir, our own selves in
entirety, the very reproduction of our forms, as it were,
correct to the hairs and the nails." Then Prajāpati said to
them: "Having become well ornamented, well dressed,
and refined, look at yourselves in a pan of water." Having
become well ornamented, well dressed, and refined, they
looked at themselves in a pan of water. Thereupon Prajāpati asked them: "What do you see?" They replied: "Just
as we ourselves here are, Sir, well ornamented, well
dressed, and refined. . . ." "That is the Self," said he.
"That is the immortal, the fearless; that is Brahman."
Then they went away with a tranquil heart. Having looked
at them, Prajāpati said to himself: "They are going away
without having realized, without having found out the
Self. Whosoever will accept this doctrine as final, be they
gods or demons, they shall perish." Then Virochana, verily, with a tranquil heart, went to the demons and declared
to them that doctrine, namely: One's self [one's bodily

self] alone is to be made happy here; one's self is to be served. Making oneself alone happy here, serving oneself, does one obtain both worlds, this world and the yonder. Therefore, here, even now, they say of one who is not a giver, who has no faith, who does not offer sacrifices, that he is, indeed, a demon; for this is the doctrine of the demons. They adorn the body of the deceased with perfumes, flowers, etc., which they have begged, with dress and with ornaments, for they think they will thereby win the yonder world.

But then Indra, even before reaching the gods, saw this danger: "Just as, indeed, the bodily self becomes well ornamented when this body is well ornamented, well dressed when this body is well dressed, and refined when this body is refined, even so that one becomes blind when this body is blind, lame when this body is lame, and maimed when this body is maimed. The bodily Self, verily, perishes immediately after the perishing of this body. I see no good in this." With sacrificial fuel in hand, he again came back to Prajāpati. [Indra states his objection to Prajāpati, who admits its truth and asks him to live as a student under him for another thirty-two years.] Indra lived a student's life under Prajāpati for another thirty-two years. Then, Prajāpati said to him: "He who moves about happy in a dream —he is the Self," said he. "That is the immortal, the fearless; that is Brahman." Thereupon, with a tranquil heart, Indra went away.

But then, even before reaching the gods, he saw this danger: "Now, even though this body is blind, the Self in the dream-condition does not become blind; even though this body is lame, he does not become lame; indeed, he does not suffer any defect through the defect of this body. He is not slain with the slaying of this body. He does not become lame with the lameness of this body. Nevertheless, they, as it were, kill him; they, as it were, unclothe him. He, as it were, becomes the experiencer of what is not agreeable; he, as it were, even weeps. I see no good in this." [Again Indra returns to Prajāpati with his objection.

The latter admits its truth but asks Indra to be his student for another thirty-two years.] Then Prajāpati said to him: "Now, when one is sound asleep, composed, serene, and knows no dream—that is the Self," said he. "That is the immortal, the fearless; that is Brahman." Thereupon, with a tranquil heart, Indra went away.

But then, even before reaching the gods, he saw this danger: "Assuredly, this Self in the deep sleep condition does not, indeed, now know himself in the form: 'I am he'; nor indeed does he know these things here. He, as it were, becomes one who has gone to annihilation. I see no good in this." [Indra once more returns to Prajāpati, who promises to tell him the final truth after another five years of studentship.] Indra lived a student's life under Prajā-pati for another five years. The total number of these years thus came to one hundred and one; thus it is that people say that, verily, for one hundred and one years Maghavan [Indra, the Rewarder] lived under Prajāpati the disci-plined life of a student of sacred knowledge. Then Prajā-pati said to him: "O Maghavan, mortal, indeed, is this body; it is taken over by death. But it is the basis of that deathless, bodiless Self. Verily, the Self, when embodied, is taken over by pleasure and pain. Verily, there is no free-dom from pleasure and pain for one who is associated with the body. The wind is bodiless; cloud, lightning, thunder—these are bodiless. Now as these, having risen up from yonder space and having reached the highest light, appear each with its own form, even so this serene Self, having risen up from this body and having reached the highest light, appears with its own form. That Self is the Supreme Person."

(from *Chāndogya*, VIII:7-12, in *Sources of Indian Tradition*, pp. 30-33)

THE IDENTITY OF
BRAHMAN AND ĀTMAN

In the macrocosm of the universe, the sages saw *brahman*; in the microcosm of their own being they saw the *ātman*. The realization that there is no distinction between the two, that the ground of one's own being is identical with the ground of the universe, is the great discovery of the Upanishadic thinkers. "Whoever thus knows, 'I am *brahman*,'" declares the sage, "becomes this all. Even the gods have not the power to prevent him from becoming thus, for he thus becomes the self." The best-known statement of this identity of individual self and universal self is given here. It should be carefully noted that this is not described as merging with the divine or union between God and man or reaching a state of unity. It is rather a recognition that there is no "divine" as distinct from the individual, no being over against the self, no process of becoming what once was not, but only the knowledge of the truth that always existed.

There, verily, was Shvetaketu, the son of Uddālaka Āruni. To him his father said: "O Shvetaketu, live the disciplined life of a student of sacred knowledge (brahmacharya). No one, indeed, my dear, belonging to our family, is unlearned in the Veda and remains a brāhman only by family connections as it were." He, then, having approached a teacher at the age of twelve and having studied all the Vedas, returned at the age of twenty-four, conceited, thinking himself to be learned, stiff. To him his father said: "O Shvetaketu, since, my dear, you are now conceited, think yourself to be learned, and have become stiff, did you also ask for that instruction whereby what has been unheard becomes heard, what has been unthought of becomes thought of, what has been uncomprehended becomes comprehended?" "How, indeed, Sir, is that instruction?" asked Shvetaketu. "Just as, my dear, through the comprehension of one lump of clay all that is made of clay would become comprehended—for the modification is occasioned only on account of a convention of speech, it is only a name; while clay as such alone is the reality. Just as, my dear, through the comprehension of one ingot of iron all that is made of iron would become comprehended—for the modification is occasioned only on account of a convention of speech, it is only a name; while iron as such alone is the reality. . . . So, my dear, is that instruction." "Now, verily, those venerable teachers did not know this; for, if they had known it, why would they not have told me?" said Shvetaketu. "However, may the venerable sir tell it to me." "So be it, my dear," said he.

"In the beginning, my dear, this world was just being, one only, without a second. Some people, no doubt, say: 'In the beginning, verily, this world was just nonbeing, one only, without a second; from that nonbeing, being was produced.' But how, indeed, my dear, could it be so?" said he. "How could being be produced from nonbeing? On the contrary, my dear, in the beginning this world was being alone, one only, without a second. Being thought to itself: 'May I be many; may I procreate.' It produced fire. That fire thought to itself: 'May I be many, may I procreate.' It produced water. Therefore, whenever a person grieves or perspires, then it is from fire [heat] alone that water is produced. That water thought to itself: 'May I be many; may I procreate.' It produced food. Therefore, whenever it rains, then there is abundant food; it is from water alone that food for eating is produced. . . . That divinity (Being) thought to itself: 'Well, having entered into these three divinities [fire, water, and food] by means of this living Self, let me develop names and forms. Let me make each one of them tripartite.' That divinity, accordingly, having entered into those three divinities by means of this living Self, developed names and forms. . . . It made each one of them tripartite. . . .

"Bring hither a fig from there." "Here it is, sir." "Break it." "It is broken, sir." "What do you see there?" "These extremely fine seeds, sir." "Of these, please break one." "It is broken, sir." "What do you see there?" "Nothing at all, sir." Then he said to Shvetaketu: "Verily, my dear, that subtle essence which you do not perceive—from that very essence, indeed, my dear, does this great fig tree thus arise. Believe me, my dear, that which is the subtle essence—this whole world has that essence for its Self; that is the Real; that is the Self; that subtle essence art thou, Shvetaketu." "Still further may the venerable sir instruct me." "So be it, my dear," said he.

"Having put this salt in the water, come to me in the morning." He did so. Then the father said to him: "That salt which you put in the water last evening—please bring it hither." Even having looked for it, he did not find it, for it was completely dissolved. "Please take a sip of water from this end," said the father. "How is it?" "Salt." "Take a sip from the middle," said he. "How is it?" "Salt." "Take a sip from that end," said he. "How is it?" "Salt." "Throw it away and come to me." Shvetaketu did so thinking to himself: "That salt, though unperceived, still persists in the water." Then Āruni said to him: "Verily, my dear, you do not perceive Being in this world; but it is, indeed, here only: That which is the subtle essence—this whole world has that essence for its Self. That is the Real. That is the Self. That art thou, Shvetaketu." "Still further may the venerable sir instruct me." "So be it, my dear," said he.

"Just as, my dear, having led away a person from Gandhāra with his eyes bandaged, one might then abandon him in a place where there are no human beings; and as that person would there drift about toward the east or the north or the south: 'I have been led away here with my eyes bandaged, I have been abandoned here with my eyes bandaged'; then as, having released his bandage, one might tell him: 'In that direction lies Gandhāra; go in that direction.' Thereupon he, becoming wise and sensible, would, by asking his way from village to village, certainly reach Gandhāra. Even so does one who has a teacher here know:

'I shall remain here [in this phenomenal world] only as long as I shall not be released from the bonds of nescience. Then I shall reach my home.' "

(from *Chāndogya*, VI:1-14, *passim*, in *Sources of Indian Tradition*, pp. 33-36)

KARMA AND TRANSMIGRATION

The conviction that *karma*, the law of cause and effect, worked so that every action must have a result, was well-established when the earliest *Upanishads* were written. The fruits of action—which included thoughts and desires as well as actual deeds—are inexorably fulfilled and according to necessity built into the structure of the universe. The idea of rebirth of the soul may well have been an older idea, but in any case the two concepts fitted together, with actions in one life determining the conditions of future existences, and producing an endless cycle of rebirths. In this conception there is no thought of punishment and reward given by some deity external to man; indeed, many schools of thought which explicitly reject belief in gods accept the doctrine of *karma*. The system is one of perfect justice—a man reaps precisely what he sows. Nor is there anything inherently pessimistic about the scheme, since man is master of his fate.

According as one acts, according as one conducts himself, so does he become. The doer of good becomes good. The doer of evil becomes evil. One becomes virtuous by virtuous action, bad by bad action.

But people say: "A person is made not of acts, but of desires only." In reply to this I say: As is his desire, such is his resolve; as is his resolve, such the action he performs; what action (*karma*) he performs, that he procures for himself.

On this point there is this verse:—

Where one's mind is attached—the inner self
Goes thereto with action, being attached to it alone.

> *Obtaining the end of his action,*
> *Whatever he does in this world,*
> *He comes again from that world*
> *To this world of action.*

—So the man who desires.

Now the man who does not desire.—He who is without desire, who is freed from desire, whose desire is satisfied, whose desire is the Soul—his breaths do not depart. Being very Brahman, he goes to Brahman.

(from *Brihad Āranyaka*, IV:4:5-6, in Hume, pp. 140-41)

Accordingly, those who are of pleasant conduct here—the prospect is, indeed, that they will enter a pleasant womb, either the womb of a Brahman, or the womb of a Kshatriya, or the womb of a Vaishya. But those who are of stinking conduct here—the prospect is, indeed, that they will enter a stinking womb, either the womb of a dog, or the womb of a swine, or the womb of an outcaste (*candāla*).

(from *Chāndogya*, V:10:7, in Hume, p. 233)

By the delusions of imagination, touch, and sight,
And by eating, drinking, and impregnation there is birth
    and development of the self.
According unto his deeds (*karma*) the embodied one suc-
    cessively
Assumes forms in various conditions.

(from *Śvetāśvatara*, V:11-12, in Hume, p. 407)

EMANCIPATION
FROM KARMA

In some of the *Upanishads* the problem of emancipation or salvation is closely related to the concepts of *karma* and rebirth, and of the statement of the identity of individual self with the world self. On the one hand, *karma* stresses recurrence, continual renewal and rebirth; but this very emphasis leads to a discussion of what is reborn and renewed in the cyclical process. On the other hand, the doctrine of the identity of *ātman* and *brahman* stresses the permanent and unchanging. This seeming contradiction between the two concepts was solved by the understanding that the cycle of rebirth is caused by ignorance of the true nature of the Self and the failure to realize that it never changes or alters. Emancipation becomes, therefore, a process of coming to an awareness of that state of being that is beyond process, the identity of *ātman* and *brahman*. To have this intuitive knowledge is to become immortal, for "knowing All, he becomes All." While in one sense it is true to say that this search is defined in terms of escape from the cycle of rebirth, on a higher level it is to be understood as the realization of the soul's true nature.

The wise one [the Self] is not born, nor dies.
This one has not come from anywhere, has not become
    anyone.
Unborn, constant, eternal, primeval, this one
Is not slain when the body is slain. . . .
He, however, who has not understanding,
Who is unmindful and ever impure,
Reaches not the goal,
But goes on to reincarnation.
He, however, who has understanding,
Who is mindful and ever pure,
Reaches the goal
From which he is born no more. . . .

When are liberated all the desires that lodge in one's
   heart,
Then a mortal becomes immortal!
Therein he reaches Brahman!
When are cut all the knots of the heart here on earth,
Then a mortal becomes immortal!

(from *Katha*, II, III, and VI, selected verses, in Hume, pp.
349, 352, and 360)

PART TWO

THE GROWTH OF
THE TRADITION

〜〜〜〜〜

(550 B.C. – 300 A.D.)

INTRODUCTION

Few cultural stereotypes are less acceptable than that
which sees Indian civilization as static and unchanging.
While it is true that there is an unquestionable continuity
linking the remote past in an unbroken line with the present, there have been numerous transformations within the
general cultural pattern. These have not involved a rejection of the past or a break with historic traditions, but they
have led to a culture of extraordinary richness and diversity. It was this possibility for inward transformation that
led the modern Indian thinker Sri Aurobindo to speak of
India's "stupendous vitality, her inexhaustible power of
life and joy of life, her almost unimaginable prolific crea-
tiveness." [1]

The sixth century B.C. saw the beginning of one such
period of creativity, and the force of this outburst of energy altered many features of Indian life. To this time belong many of the great achievements of the Indian mind,
and at the end of the age—the first and second centuries
of the Christian era—remarkable changes had taken place
in the social and religious life of India. By that time, almost all the great themes of the tradition can be clearly

[1] Sri Aurobindo, *The Renaissance in India* (Calcutta: Ayra Publishing House, 1946), p. 11.

discerned, and the form and style of the great classical Hindu civilization that reached its zenith after the fourth century A.D have been foreshadowed.

As we have seen, the Vedic Age provided the Hindu tradition with attitudes and values which have in large measure become unquestioned assumptions. One of these was the cluster of ideas around the belief in *karma* and rebirth; another was the acceptance of the divinely-ordained class structure. Related to both of these, and supporting them while being in turn fortified by them, was the concept of *dharma*, one of the most pervasive of all Hindu ideas. In the earliest Vedic literature the concept of an unalterable moral law underlying the universe had made possible the creation of a coherent world-view, and as *dharma* this was transformed into a definition of the duties and obligations of social life. *Dharma* received its most explicit formulations in the great law books that outlined the nature of the social order, especially as it was exemplified in the class structure.

Historically, the period from about 550 B.C. to 300 A.D. is marked by the rise to prominence of two great religious movements, Jainism and Buddhism, and by the emergence of great empires that attempted for the first time to create governmental authorities that would bring most of the area of India under the rule of one dynasty. The center of both the religious and political movements was the area south and north of the Ganges River now known as Bihar. Here Magadha, the first Indian state of which we have any certain knowledge, began a career of expansion shortly after 600 B.C. By the end of the century, under Bimbisāra, it had become the strongest state of North India and it retained this position for over three hundred years. Of the history of South India at this time we know very little, but probably there were no kingdoms as strong as those of the Magadha rulers.

It was during the reign of Bimbisāra that Gautama (died about 483 B.C.), the founder of Buddhism, and Mahāvira (died about 468 B.C.), the founder of Jainism, flourished. Both were members of the warrior class who left their homes in search of salvation. They were also alike in rejecting the Vedic literature as the revealed truth from which there could be no dissent; having gathered followers, they taught doctrines that bear many resemblances to each other. But there is no real evidence that either influenced the other; their lives and teachings must be seen as part of the intellectual ferment that characterized the age. Although both Buddhism and Jainism are closely related to the main Hindu tradition, no attempt will be made to present their doctrines here, except insofar as they illumine certain features of the main cultural movement. The particular emphasis in Jain thought that had a considerable influence on general Indian thinking was the belief that all matter possessed living souls, and that therefore killing and violence of all kinds were evil. The belief in *ahimsa*, or non-killing, became a common belief and was finally given political implications by Mahatma Gandhi in our own time. Buddhism, with its analysis of the human condition as characterized by suffering occasioned by desire or attachment, has had a profound influence on all Indian thought. Its influence is especially seen in art; most of the early examples of Indian sculpture and architecture are Buddhist in origin.

At the end of the fourth century B.C. the Maurya family, under Chandragupta (c. 322 to 298 B.C.), established themselves at Magadha, and they quickly expanded their power over most of North India and into what is now modern Afghanistan. His capital city was at Pātaliputra, a very large city on a tributary of the Ganges. According to Greek visitors, his palace was the most magnificent in the world. Under his grandson, the famous Ashoka (c. 269-232 B.C.), the Mauryan Empire reached its greatest extent, and it was not until the time of Aurangzīb (1658-1707) that one ruler again controlled so much territory in India.

Knowledge of Ashoka's reign comes mainly from the edicts he had carved on rocks and pillars throughout his extensive dominions. These inscriptions were not precisely laws, but rather statements of policy and, in some cases, homilies addressed to his officials. Ashoka's reign had enduring consequences, for he appears to have been the first Indian king to patronize Buddhism in a significant way. Because of this, Buddhism spread not only throughout India but beyond its borders, most notably to Ceylon. This meant that although India was never a Buddhist country in the sense that the majority of the people were Buddhists, the values of Buddhism permeated very deeply the fabric of Indian life. Ashoka gave India an ideology that, even when it was forgotten, still influenced the life of the people.

The downfall of Ashoka's empire in the generation after his death was the result of causes that can be generalized to explain the failure of successive Indian dynasties. Problems of communication, rebellious governors, intrigues within the palace, foreign invasions, all played a part. Various attempts were made by other rulers, including invaders from Central Asia, to create new empires, but none had any lasting success until the Guptas established their dynasty in the fourth century A.D. The history of India from about 150 B.C. to 200 A.D. is marked by invasions and internal turmoil.

During this period of dynastic struggles the Brahmanical religion of the Vedic Age transformed itself into the Hinduism of the later ages. Again it must be stressed that there had never been a period when the Vedas had not been the living scriptures of probably the majority of the people, but partly in response to the challenge of the great heretical movements of Jainism and Buddhism the guardians of the ancient tradition reformulated and redefined many of the old concepts in a new class of religious literature. These were the *dharmashāstra* texts which, by incorporating many practices which had grown up since the completion of the Vedic literature and by reinterpreting Vedic customs which had fallen into disuse, made it possible for the ancient tradition to survive in a changing soci-

ety. These texts, by providing both meticulous directions
for all of the contingencies of life and at the same time,
many examples of exceptions to the general rules, became
the guide for the ordering of social life. An important feature of these texts is that they underwent revision and
change over a long period, thus making it possible for
them to reflect changing conditions and needs of society.
One of the most famous of the texts, the *Manu Smriti*, for
example, probably originated in the third century B.C. but
it did not receive its final form until the fourth century
A.D.

The growth of theism as an integral part of the Hindu
tradition was another important element in the religious
life of the period. This theistic movement, taking the form
of devotion to a particular god, may have its roots in the
worship of the ancient Vedic gods or it may reflect influence from non-Aryan religions of India, but it is probably
true that some form of worship in which the devotees
looked to a god for help and protection was the most widespread form of religious expression among the common
people. Two gods that emerge are of particular importance—Vishnu and Shiva. Henceforth they dominate the
religious scene. The *Bhagavad Gītā*, the most famous of
the religious works of the period, is associated with Vishnu
in that its central figure, Krishna, is later identified as an
incarnation of Vishnu. While there is no comparable literary monument to Shiva, his cult was apparently widespread. Here as elsewhere in this period one senses the passionate intensity and surging creativity of Indian life.

CHAPTER IV

THE EXPOSITION
OF LIFE'S DUTIES

〰〰〰

One of the most important aspects of the Hindu tradition is the emphasis placed on the performance of social duties and obligations according to carefully formulated codes of behavior. These codes find their most vivid expression in three great ideal structures: the four classes, the four stages of life, and the four ends of man. While it is clear that these idealized constructions were never fully realized within Indian society at any time, nevertheless they provided the background for social life, and still exercise a powerful appeal to all those who live within the Hindu milieu. Very briefly, what is involved in the three idealizations is, first of all, that society is grouped by nature and divine law into four classes; secondly, that each man in each class passes in his lifetime through four carefully marked stages; and, thirdly, that there are certain ends of life which are legitimate and proper for the virtuous man to pursue. The element common to the three structures is the assumption that there are fundamental differences in men that make it necessary for different men to be controlled by norms of behavior appropriate for their station in life, and that the same standards cannot be made applicable to all men. In every situation the guiding factor is dharma, that protean word already noted in the introduc-

*tion. This means that man applies to problems of social
and moral behavior the understanding of his duty or obligation as a member of a particular group in a particular
situation. <u>The resolution of moral decisions does not take
place in the context of the individual making choices
through private appeal to conscience but rather through a
knowledge of what is suitable in the context of one's
membership in a group</u>. This ideal has implications for
ethical theory and practice which will frequently be illustrated in the selections.*

*The fundamental social ideal is that of the four-fold di-
vision of society, already briefly noted in Chapter II. In the
accounts of the division of society into four classes (<u>varna</u>)*   Varna
*in the sacred texts it is emphasized that <u>the origin of the
class structure is divine, not human</u>, the implication being
that the right ordering of society is ultimately a religious,
not a secular, concern. In other words, the social law, even
in its ordering of the most commonplace concerns, is co-
terminous with the law of the universe.*

*The theory was that all people were divided into four
classes. <u>The first class were the</u> Brāhmans, *the priestly
order, the possessors and guardians of the great tradition.
No priestly class in any other civilization, perhaps, has ever
made such claims for its sanctity as did the Brāhmans; but
neither has any other received such willing recognition of
that sanctity. Not all Brāhmans were priests, since there
were too many of them to be absorbed into ritual functions, and they filled many occupations, most notably in
government service. <u>The second class, the</u> kshatriyas, or
warriors, supplied the rulers and soldiers, but probably at
no time, certainly not after 600 B.C., did the class supply all
the soldiers or even all the kings. <u>The vaishy</u>as were the
merchants, traders and farmers. These three classes were
the "<u>twice-born</u>," signifying that they underwent a
religious ceremony of initiation. This was the dividing line
between them and <u>the fourth class, the</u> shūdras, to whom
were allotted the menial and unpleasant tasks of society.
The shūdras had a dharma, however, just as did the twice*

born classes. This was not true of those groups completely
outside the class structure, the "outcastes"; they were considered beyond the pale of the laws of class and society.

The actual origin of the class ideal is obscure, although
it reflects a fairly natural and widespread classification of
functions within society. Probably its origin is in the most
primitive levels of Aryan social organization, the product
of a life dependent upon agriculture and the skill of warriors to protect life, with a religion that was characterized
by a complex ritual needing skilled performers. Com-
pounding the difficulty of any discussion of the origin of
the class structure is the fact that it is the statement of an
ideal and not the description of the actual condition of
society; the actual social framework of the Hindu tradition
is the immensely complex web of castes. For Hindu society
what is important in everyday living is not so much the
four great classes as the multitudinous exclusive social
groupings that have proliferated throughout the centuries.
There are thousands of these groups, with boundaries defined by many restrictions, the most important of which
relate to marriage and the eating of food, and, to a lesser
extent, by occupation. The relation of these castes to the
four great classes is much disputed, although the explanation of the sacred texts is definite enough—they are seen as
subdivisions brought about by miscegenation. Historically,
the origin of the castes is probably to be found in many
other factors, such as invasions by foreign groups, numerous and quite distinct indigenous peoples, the emphasis of
the religious tradition on ritual purity, and geographic separation. What is important is that the ideal of the four
divinely ordained classes gave religious sanction to the
whole structure of caste and class, and that each caste lives
by its own dharma.

The second great ideal that undergirded the social and
religious structure was the conception of four stages
(āshrams) of life. Just as society as a whole was understood to be divided into classes performing mutually exclusive functions that came together under the general work-

ing of dharma, so *each individual life was divided into stages that were distinct but in the end produced a harmonious totality*. These stages, it should be noted, were taken to be *applicable mainly to members of the three "twice-born" classes*, and only to men and boys. After initiation, the boy became a celibate student, living in the house of his teacher or guru. Then he married, and observed the obligations and enjoyed the pleasures of the life of a householder. This placing of family life at the heart of the ideal value system is of immense significance for the Hindu tradition, for it means that the most basic of actual groupings within the society is unequivocally invested with all the sanctions that religion can give. The family that is pictured in the texts, and that in fact dominates the Hindu cultural pattern, is *the joint family, with all the sons bringing their wives into the parental home*. It is that large family unit that is the center of religious rites and all social customs, and its role in preserving and transmitting the values and traditions of the Hindu culture cannot be overemphasized.

Following the fulfillment of his duties as a householder, and having assured the continuance of his family, a man next becomes a hermit in the forest, meditating and studying the scriptures. Then finally comes the fourth stage when, abandoning all earthly ties, he wanders about unhindered by family, home, or possessions. Here, as everywhere, the assumption is that dharma is not the same at every stage of life, just as it is not the same for all men. While it cannot be supposed that this ideal pattern was ever followed by a majority of men, even by all Brāhmans, the values that it enshrines have made a potent appeal throughout Indian history, coloring the imagination and guiding responses to life even when the four stages were not followed in their entirety.

The third ideal construct, *the four ends of life*, related the religious understanding of the nature of human existence to the conduct of everyday life. The four legitimate ends to be pursued were *dharma, or duty; material gain* (artha); *the pleasures of physical sense* (kāma); *and salvation* (moksha).[1] *Since it was assumed that not only did men differ in their needs and capabilities according to their class but also according to their stage of life, these legitimate ends were defined in terms appropriate for one's particular station.* Kāma, physical pleasure, was defined very differently for a Brāhman student, for example, than it was for a mature member of the warrior class. Overarching all the ends was dharma, the essential element that made them all work together for the right ordering of society.

This social understanding of the implication of religion, especially the emphasis on the dharma of class and caste, goes a long way to explain how the old Vedic traditions were not only able to survive but actually to provide sources for change and growth in the vital centuries from 600 B.C. to 300 A.D. That external invasions and internal strife, as well as the rise of Buddhism and Jainism, did not destroy the ancient religious culture is probably due in large measure to the great encompassing social ideals of class, the stages of life, and the ends of man. They permitted a wide diversity of expression in a genuinely plural society but they maintained a coherent framework of actual institutional life and ideal statement.

THE CLASS STRUCTURE

The Statement of the Ideal

The following description of the class structure is taken from the *Manu Smriti*, the famous text that gives detailed descriptions of the duties of each class and prescribes penalties for the transgression of the customary laws. The verses given here are preceded by a genealogy of all creation that goes back to

[1] In some texts, only three ends are given, with *dharma* including salvation.

the time when "this universe existed in the shape of darkness," and the "Self-existent . . . appeared with irresistible creative power, dispelling darkness."

But in the beginning he assigned their several names, actions, and conditions to all (created beings), even according to the words of the Veda.

He, the Lord, also created the class of the gods, who are endowed with life, and whose nature is action; and the subtile class of the Sādhyas, and the eternal sacrifice.

But from fire, wind, and the sun he drew forth the threefold eternal Veda, called Rik, Yajus, and Sāman, for the due performance of the sacrifice.

Time and the divisions of time, the lunar mansions and the planets, the rivers, the oceans, the mountains, plains, and uneven ground,

Austerity, speech, pleasure, desire, and anger, this whole creation he likewise produced, as he desired to call these beings into existence. . . .

Whatever he assigned to each at the (first) creation, noxiousness or harmlessness, gentleness or ferocity, virtue or sin, truth or falsehood, that clung (afterwards) spontaneously to it.

As at the change of the seasons each season of its own accord assumes its distinctive marks, even so corporeal beings (resume in new births) their (appointed) course of action.

But for the sake of the prosperity of the worlds, he created the Brāhman, the Kshatriya, the Vaishya, and the Shūdra to proceed from his mouth, his arms, his thighs, and his feet. . . .

To Brāhmans he assigned teaching and studying (the Veda), sacrificing for their own benefit and for others, giving and accepting (of alms).

The Kshatriya he commanded to protect the people, to bestow gifts, to offer sacrifices, to study (the Veda), and to abstain from attaching himself to sensual pleasures;

The Vaishya to tend cattle, to bestow gifts, to offer sacrifices, to study (the Veda), to trade, to lend money, and to cultivate land.

One occupation only the lord prescribed to the Shūdra, to serve meekly even these (other) three castes.

(from *Manu Smriti*, I and X, *passim*, in *Sacred Books of the East*, XXV, pp. 12-13, 24)

Mutual Dependence of the Classes

For the Brāhman authors of the religious texts one validation of the class structure was the empirical evidence of a harmonious social structure. A hierarchical system, where each was aware of the boundaries of his duties and obligations, reflected the fundamental order of the universe, and peace and prosperity in this and future existences was assured by obedience to customary laws. This emphasis on the importance of the correct fulfillment of the proper duties of one's class underlies two features of the social codes. On the one hand it explains the high privileges accorded the Brāhman as the keystone of the social structure; on the other, it makes understandable the severity with which breaches of *dharma* were treated. The first selection, which is taken from the great epic poem, the *Mahābhārata*, emphasizes the harmony that results from following one's own *dharma*. The speaker is Bhīsma, one of the great heroic figures of the poem. The second selection is from the *Bhagavad Gītā*; here the consequence of failing to follow one's class obligations is depicted.

Bhīsma said: "I shall discourse on duties that are eternal. The suppression of wrath, truthfulness of speech, justice, forgiveness, begetting children upon one's own wedded wives, purity of conduct, avoidance of quarrel, simplicity, and maintenance of dependents,—these nine duties belong to all the four orders (equally). Those duties, however, which belong exclusively to Brāhmanas, I shall now tell thee! Self-restraint, O king, has been declared to be the first duty of Brāhmanas. Study of the Vedas, and patience in undergoing austerities, (are also their other duties). By practising these two, all their acts are accomplished. If while engaged in the observance of his own duties, without doing any improper act, wealth comes to a peaceful Brāhmana possessed of knowledge, he should then marry and seek to beget children and should also practise charity and perform sacrifices. It has been declared by the wise that wealth thus obtained should be enjoyed by distributing it (among deserving persons and relatives). By his study of the Vedas all the pious acts (laid down for the Brāhmana) are accomplished. Whether he does or does not achieve anything else, if he devotes himself to the study of the Vedas he becomes (by that) known as a Brāhmana or the friend of all creatures. I shall also tell thee, O Bhārata, what the duties are of a Kshatriya. A Kshatriya, O king, should give but not beg, should himself perform sacrifices but not officiate as a priest in the sacrifices of other's. He should never teach (the Vedas) but study (them with a Brāhmana preceptor). He should protect the people. Always exerting himself for the destruction of robbers and wicked people, he should put forth his prowess in battle. Those among Kshatriya rulers who perform great sacrifices, who are possessed of a knowledge of the Vedas, and who gain victories in battle, become foremost of those that acquire many blessed regions hereafter by their merit. Persons conversant with the old scriptures do not applaud that Kshatriya who returns unwounded from battle. This has been declared to be the conduct of a wretched Kshatriya. There is no higher duty for him than the suppression of robbers. Gifts, study, and sacrifices, bring prosperity to kings. Therefore, a king who desires to acquire religous merit should engage in battle. Establishing all his subjects in the observance of their respective duties, a king should cause all of them to do everything according to the dictates of righteousness. Whether he does or does not do any other act, if only he protects his subjects, he is regarded to accomplish all religious acts and is called a Kshatriya and the foremost of men. I shall now tell thee, O Yudhishthira, what the eternal duties of the Vaishya are. A Vaishya should make gifts, study the Vedas, perform sacrifices, and acquire wealth by fair means. With proper attention he should also protect and rear all (domestic) animals as a sire protecting his sons. Anything else that he will do will be regarded as improper for him. By protecting the (domestic) animals he would obtain great happiness. The Creator, having created the (domestic) animals, bestowed their care upon the Vaishya. Upon the Brāhmana and the Kshatriya he conferred (the care of) all creatures. I shall tell thee what the Vaishya's profession is and how he is to earn the means of his sustenance. If he keeps (for others) six kine, he may take the milk of one cow as his remuneration; and if he keeps (for others) a hundred kine, he may take a single pair as such fee. If he trades with other's wealth, he may take a seventh part of the profits (as his share). A seventh also is his share in the profits arising from the trade in horns, but he should take a sixteenth if the trade be in hoofs. If he engages in cultivation with seeds supplied by others, he may take a seventh part of the yield. This should be his annual remuneration. A Vaishya should never desire that he should not tend cattle. If a Vaishya desires to tend cattle, no one else should be employed in that task. I should tell thee, O Bhārata, what the duties of a Shudra are. The Creator intended the Shudra to become the servant of the other three orders. For this, the service of the three other classes is the duty of the Shudra. By such service of the other three, a Shudra may obtain great happiness. He should wait upon the three other classes according to their order of seniority. A Shudra should never amass wealth, lest, by his wealth, he makes the numbers of the three superior classes obedient to him. By this he would incur sin. With the king's permission, however, a Shudra, for performing religious acts, may earn wealth. I shall now tell thee the profession he should follow and the means by which he may earn his livelihood. It is said that Shudras should certainly be maintained by the (three) other orders. <u>Worn out umbrellas, turbans, beds and seats, shoes, and fans, should be given to the Shudra servants</u>. <u>Torn clothes, which are no longer fit for wear, should be given away by the regenerate classes unto the Shudra</u>. These are the latter's lawful acquisitions. Men conversant with morality say that if the Shudra approaches any one belonging to the three regenerate orders from desire of doing menial service, the latter should assign him proper work. Unto the sonless Shudra his master should offer the funeral cake. The weak and the old amongst them should be maintained. The Shudra should never abandon his master whatever the nature or degree of the distress into which the latter may fall. If the master loses his wealth, he should with excessive zeal be supported by the Shudra servant. A Shudra cannot have any wealth that is his own. Whatever he possesses belongs lawfully to his master. Sacrifice has been laid down as a duty of the three other orders. It has been ordained for the Shudra also, O Bhārata! <u>A Shudra, however, is not competent to utter *swāhā* and *sadhā* or any other Vedic *mantra*</u>. <u>For this reason, the Shudra, without observing the vows laid down in the Vedas, should worship the gods in minor sacrifices called *Pāka-yajnas*</u>. . . . Sacrifice (as has been already said), O Bhārata, is as much laid down for the Shudra as for the three other classes. Of all sacrifices, devotion has been laid down to be the foremost. Devotion is a high deity. It cleanses all sacrificers.

(from *Mahābhārata* XII:60, *passim*, in P. C. Roy, *The Mahābhārata*)

When a family decays, the immemorial religious laws of that family are destroyed. When the religious laws of the family are destroyed, then lawlessness destroys the whole family. Because lawlessness prevails, the women of the family become corrupted, and when women are corrupt, intermingling of caste follows. <u>Intermingling of caste leads to hell both those who destroy the family as well as the</u>

family itself. The ancestors also fall into hell for they are deprived of the offerings of food made to them.

(from *Bhagavad Gītā*, I:40-42)

THE FOUR STAGES OF LIFE

The Student

Following the rites of initiation, of which the visible symbol was the wearing of a sacred cord around the chest, a boy of the three upper classes went to live and study in the house of his teacher. The relationship that developed between pupil and teacher is a constant theme of Indian literature and one of the unifying features of the whole tradition. Respect was given to the teacher that did not differ essentially from that paid to parents, while the pupil's development was regarded as a sacred charge by his teacher. The main subject of study was the memorization of Vedic texts but archery, the science of war, medicine, astrology, and music were all included within the sacred texts. This system of education ensured the transmission of the tradition and meant that a common culture and common language existed throughout India for the members of the upper classes. It also exalted the power and prestige of the teachers, the Brāhmans.

The selection given here is taken from a text prescribing proper norms of behavior written possibly in the fifth century B.C.

He who has been initiated shall dwell as a religious student in the house of his teacher . . .

Twelve years (should be) the shortest time (for his residence with his teacher).

A student who studies the sacred science shall not dwell with anybody else than his teacher.

Now (follow) the rules for the studentship.

He shall obey his teacher, except when ordered to commit crimes which cause loss of caste.

He shall do what is serviceable to his teacher, he shall not contradict him.

He shall always occupy a couch or seat lower than that of his teacher.

He shall not eat food offered at a sacrifice to the gods or the Manes,

Nor pungent condiments, salt, honey, or meat.

He shall not sleep in the day-time.

He shall not use perfumes.

He shall preserve chastity.

He shall not embellish himself by using ointments and the like.

He shall not wash his body with hot water for pleasure.

But, if it is soiled by unclean things, he shall clean it with earth or water, in a place where he is not seen by a Guru.

Let him not sport in the water whilst bathing; let him swim motionless like a stick. . . .

Let him not look at dancing.

Let him not go to assemblies for gambling, &c., nor to crowds assembled at festivals.

Let him not be addicted to gossiping.

Let him be discreet.

Let him not do anything for his own pleasure in places which his teacher frequents.

Let him talk with women so much only as his purpose requires.

Let him be forgiving.

Let him restrain his organs from seeking illicit objects.

Let him be untired in fulfilling his duties;

Modest;

Possessed of self-command;

Energetic;

Free from anger;

And free from envy.

Bringing all he obtains to his teacher, he shall go begging with a vessel in the morning and in the evening, and
he may beg from everybody except low-caste people unfit
for association with Aryas.

(from *Apastamba Dharma Sūtra*, I:1,2,3, and 6, *passim*, in
Sacred Books of the East, II, pp. 7-8, 10-11.

The Householder and Family Life

As one of the texts points out, the householder is the source
of all the other stages of life "because the others do not produce offspring." As the selections given here indicate, the centrality of marriage and the family in the social system was
clearly recognized. Three functions of family life were singled
out for particular attention: the maintenance of the tradition
through the performance of certain rituals that only a householder could perform; begetting of offspring to ensure the
continuance of the rites; and the enjoyment of the pleasures
of physical love as a legitimate end of human life.

Closely related to the status of the householder was the
attitude towards women revealed in the texts. Perhaps no
other literature shows such an ambivalence at this point as
does the Indian, for on one level woman was seen as a lustful
temptress, the occasion of sin for men who would otherwise
remain chaste, while on another level, that of wife and mother,
she is praised almost to excess. It may be that the literature
is the product of a class of men who, valuing asceticism, resented the passions aroused in them by women, or it may be
that the complexity of the Indian attitude represents a true
understanding of human nature.

Monogamy was the normal marital arrangement, although
a man might take a second wife in certain circumstances, as
when his first wife was barren. Divorce was impossible for the
twice-born castes, since the marriage rite was a sacrament that
could not be revoked.

One should first examine the family [of the intended
bride or bridegroom], those on the mother's side and on
the father's side. . . . One should give his daughter in
marriage to a young man endowed with intelligence. One

should marry a girl who possesses the characteristics of intelligence, beauty, and good character, and who is free from disease. . . .

(from *Āśvalāyana Grihya Sūtra*, I:5, *passim*, in *Sources of Indian Tradition*, p. 230)

A householder should perform every day a Smriti rite [i.e., a domestic rite prescribed by the Sacred Law, Smriti] on the nuptial fire or on the fire brought in at the time of the partition of ancestral property. He should perform a Vedic rite on the sacred fires.

Having attended to the bodily calls, having performed the purificatory rites, and after having first washed the teeth, a twice-born [Aryan] man should offer the morning prayer.

Having offered oblations to the sacred fires, becoming spiritually composed, he should murmur the sacred verses addressed to the sun god. He should also learn the meaning of the Veda and various sciences. . . .

He should then go to his lord for securing the means of maintenance and progress. Thereafter having bathed he should worship the gods and also offer libations of water to the manes.

He should study according to his capacity the three Vedas, the *Atharva Veda*, the Purānas, together with the Itihāsas [legendary histories], as also the lore relating to the knowledge of the Self, with a view to accomplishing successfully the sacrifice of muttering prayers.

Offering of the food oblation, offerings with the proper utterance, performance of Vedic sacrifices, study of the sacred texts, and honoring of guests—these constitute the five great daily sacrifices dedicated respectively to the spirits, the manes, the gods, the Brahman, and men.

He should offer the food oblation to the spirits [by throwing it in the air] out of the remnant of the food offered to the gods. He should also cast food on the ground for dogs, untouchables, and crows.

Food, as also water, should be offered by the house-holder to the manes and men day after day. He should continuously carry on his study. He should never cook for himself only.

Children, married daughters living in the father's house, old relatives, pregnant women, sick persons, and girls, as also guests and servants—only after having fed these should the householder and his wife eat the food that has remained. . . .

Having risen before dawn the householder should ponder over what is good for the Self. He should not, as far as possible, neglect his duties in respect of the three ends of man, namely, virtue, material gain, and pleasure, at their proper times.

Learning, religious performances, age, family relations, and wealth—on account of these and in the order mentioned are men honored in society. By means of these, if possessed in profusion, even a shūdra deserves respect in old age.

(from *Yājnavalkya Smriti*, I:97-116, *passim*, in *Sources of Indian Tradition*, pp. 231-32)

I will now propound the eternal laws for a husband and wife who keep to the path of duty, whether they be united or separated.

Day and night must women be kept in dependence by the males of their families, and, if they attach themselves to sensual enjoyments, they must be kept under one's control.

Her father protects her in childhood, her husband protects her in youth, and her sons protect her in old age; a woman is never fit for independence.

Reprehensible is the father who gives not his daughter in marriage at the proper time; reprehensible is the husband who approaches not his wife in due season, and reprehensible is the son who does not protect his mother after her husband has died.

Women must particularly be guarded against evil inclinations, however trifling they may appear; for, if they are not guarded, they will bring sorrow on two families.

Considering that the highest duty of all castes, even weak husbands must strive to guard their wives.

He who carefully guards his wife, preserves the purity of his offspring, virtuous conduct, his family, himself, and his means of acquiring merit. . . .

No man can completely guard women by force; but they can be guarded by the employment of the following expedients:

Let the husband employ his wife in the collection and expenditure of his wealth, in keeping everything clean, in the fulfilment of religious duties, in the preparation of his food, and in looking after the household utensils.

Women, confined in the house under trustworthy and obedient servants, are not well guarded; but those who of their own accord keep guard over themselves, are well guarded.

Drinking spirituous liquor, associating with wicked people, separation from the husband, rambling abroad, sleeping at unseasonable hours, and dwelling in other men's houses, are the six causes of the ruin of women. . . .

Thus has been declared the ever pure popular usage which regulates the relations between husband and wife; hear next the laws concerning children which are the cause of happiness in this world and after death.

Between wives who are destined to bear children, who secure many blessings, who are worthy of worship and irradiate their dwellings, and between the goddesses of fortune who reside in the houses of men, there is no difference whatsoever.

The production of children, the nurture of those born, and the daily life of men, of these matters woman is visibly the cause.

Offspring, the due performance of religious rites, faithful service, highest conjugal happiness and heavenly bliss for the ancestors and oneself, depend on one's wife alone.

She who, controlling her thoughts, speech, and acts, violates not her duty towards her lord, dwells with him after death in heaven, and in this world is called by the virtuous a faithful wife.

(from *Manu Smriti* IX:1-7, 10-13, 25-29, *Sacred Books of the East,* XXV, pp. 328-29, 332)

The Hermit

Indicative of the movement of life from one position to another that adds to the richness and complexity of the Indian tradition, the householder turns his back upon family life and becomes a hermit. In this stage of life he seeks to fulfill his *dharma* through performing rituals and studying the scriptures, particularly the *Upanishads.* He is not entirely cut off from the world, however, but is available to those who seek his counsel.

Asceticism, which is often associated with the whole of the Indian tradition, is the appropriate mode of life in this stage. It is possible that the stress on asceticism as the characteristic feature of the religious life was an attempt to institutionalize a growing tendency within Indian society towards renunciation of the world. For Buddhism and Jainism, the monastic existence was the normal state, and the appeal of these rival faiths may have seemed a threat to those aspects of the social structure, especially family life, which were so highly valued by the ancient tradition.

The goal of Indian asceticism is self-control and the acquisition of spiritual power, and it has little relation to the idea of "mortifying the flesh." That the power gained through austerities of the most rigorous kind was so great that even the gods grew fearful and sought to prevent the continuance of the sage's meditation is a very common theme in Indian literature.

When a householder sees his skin wrinkled, and his hair white, and the sons of his sons, then he may resort to the forest.

Abandoning all food raised by cultivation, and all his

belongings, he may depart into the forest, either committing his wife to his sons, or accompanied by her.

Taking with him the sacred fire and the implements
required for domestic sacrifices, he may go forth from the
villages into the forest and reside there, duly controlling
his senses.

Let him offer those five great sacrifices according to the
rule, with various kinds of pure food fit for ascetics, or
with herbs, roots, and fruit.

Let him wear a skin or a tattered garment; let him bathe
in the evening or in the morning; and let him always wear
his hair in braids, the hair on his body, his beard, and his
nails being unclipped.

Let him perform the food offering with such food as he
eats, and give alms according to his ability; let him honour
those who come to his hermitage with alms consisting of
water, roots, and fruit.

Let him be always industrious in privately reciting the
Veda; let him be patient of hardships, friendly towards all,
of collected mind, ever liberal and never receiver, and
compassionate toward all beings. . . .

He should live without a fire, without a house, a silent
sage subsisting on roots and fruit. . . .

(from *Manu Smriti* VI:2-8, 25, in *Sacred Books of the East*,
XXV, pp. 198-200)

The Homeless Wanderer

Having gained the knowledge that led to salvation, the hermit
cuts off all earthly ties, even to his hut in the forest, and becomes a homeless wanderer. He no longer performs the rituals,
for he has passed beyond needing the results they bring. Desiring neither to live or die, he wanders about until death claims
him.

But having thus passed the third part of a man's natural
term of life in the forest, he may live as an ascetic during

the fourth part of his existence, after abandoning all attachment to worldly objects.

He who after passing from order to order, after offering sacrifices and subduing his senses, becomes, tired with giving alms and offerings of food, an ascetic, gains bliss after death.

When he has paid the three debts, let him apply his mind to the attainment of final liberation; he who seeks it without having paid (his debts) sinks downwards.

Having studied the Vedas in accordance with the rule, having begat sons according to the sacred law, and having offered sacrifices according to his ability, he may direct his mind to the attainment of final liberation.

A twice-born man who seeks final liberation, without having studied the Vedas, without having begotten sons, and without having offered sacrifices, sinks downwards. . . .

Departing from his house fully provided with the means of purification, let him wander about absolutely silent, and caring nothing for enjoyments that may be offered to him.

Let him always wander alone, without any companion, in order to attain final liberation, fully understanding that the solitary man, who neither forsakes nor is forsaken, gains his end.

He shall neither possess a fire, nor a dwelling, he may go to a village for his food, (he shall be) indifferent to everything, firm of purpose, meditating and concentrating his mind on Brahman.

A potsherd instead of an alms-bowl, the roots of trees for a dwelling, coarse worn-out garments, life in solitude and indifference towards everything, are the marks of one who has attained liberation.

Let him not desire to die, let him not desire to live; let him wait for his appointed time, as a servant waits for the payment of his wages.

Let him put down his foot purified by his sight, let him

drink water purified by straining with a cloth, let him utter speech purified by truth, let him keep his heart pure.

Let him patiently bear hard words, let him not insult anybody, and let him not become anybody's enemy for the sake of this perishable body.

Against an angry man let him not in return show anger, let him bless when he is cursed, and let him not utter speech, devoid of truth, scattered at the seven gates.

Delighting in what refers to the Soul, sitting in the postures prescribed by the Yoga, independent of external help, entirely abstaining from sensual enjoyments, with himself for his only companion, he shall live in this world, desiring the bliss of final liberation.

(from *Manu Smriti*, VI, *passim*, in *Sacred Books of the East*, XXV, pp. 204-07)

THE RECOGNITION
OF LIFE'S LIMITATIONS

The statement of the ideal expression of the fulfillment of *dharma* through adherence to the proper duties of class and stage of life was adjusted to actual human conditions and possibilities by many discussions within the texts of the appropriate action for a situation when the strict formulas could not be applied. Special provision was made for "times of distress," when a man might have to improvise a moral response. These exceptions to the general rules made the social structure much less rigid in practice than it was in theory.

Among the several occupations the most commendable are, teaching the Veda for a Brâhmaṇa, protecting the people for a Kshatriya, and trade for a Vaishya.

But a Brâhma*n*a, unable to subsist by his peculiar occupations just mentioned, may live according to the law applicable to Kshatrivas; for the latter is next to him in rank.

If it be asked, 'How shall it be, if he cannot maintain himself by either of these occupations?' the answer is, he may adopt a Vaishya's mode of life, employing himself in agriculture and rearing cattle.

But a Brâhma*n*a, or a Kshatriya, living by a Vaishya's mode of subsistence, shall carefully avoid the pursuit of agriculture, which causes injury to many beings and depends on others.

Some declare that agriculture is something excellent, but that means of subsistence is blamed by the virtuous; for the wooden implement with iron point injures the earth and the beings living in the earth.

But he who, through a want of means of subsistence, gives up the strictness with respect to his duties, may sell, in order to increase his wealth, the commodities sold by Vaishyas, making however the following exceptions.

He must avoid selling condiments of all sorts, cooked food and sesamum, stones, salt, cattle, and human beings,

All dyed cloth, as well as cloth made of hemp, or flax, or wool, even though they be not dyed, fruit, roots, and medical herbs;

Water, weapons, poison, meat, Soma, and perfumes of all kinds, fresh milk, honey, sour milk, clarified butter, oil, wax, sugar, Kusa-grass;

All beasts of the forest, animals with fangs or tusks, birds, spirituous liquor, indigo, lac, and all one-hoofed beasts. . . .

A Kshatriya who has fallen into distress, may subsist by all these means; but he must never arrogantly adopt the mode of life prescribed for his betters.

A man of low caste who through covetousness lives by the occupations of a higher one, the king shall deprive of his property and banish.

It is better to discharge one's own appointed duty incompletely than to perform completely that of another;

for he who lives according to the law of another caste is
instantly excluded from his own.

A Vaishya who is unable to subsist by his own duties,
may even maintain himself by a Shûdra's mode of life,
avoiding however acts forbidden to him, and he should
give it up, when he is able to do so.

But a Shûdra, being unable to find service with the
twice-born and threatened with the loss of his sons and
wife through hunger, may maintain himself by handi-
crafts.

Let him follow those mechanical occupations and those
various practical arts by following which the twice-born are
best served.

(from *Manu Smriti* X:80-100, *passim*, in *Sacred Books of
the East*, XXV, pp. 420-23)

THE POSSIBILITY
OF GROWTH AND CHANGE

A further indication that the tradition was not static but
allowed for growth is shown in the discussions of the sources
of *dharma*. One source was scriptural, and while injunctions
drawn from the sacred texts would always carry a special sanctity, the distinction made between the two classes of scripture,
shruti, the works that are revealed, and *smriti*, the works that
belong to the tradition, that preserve customary usage, made
possible the entry of new ideas and new interpretations. Another source of *dharma* was the prompting of one's conscience,
which itself had been formed through obedience to the appropriate obligations and duties. These aspects of *dharma* are
touched upon in the following selection.

The whole Veda is the first source of the sacred law, next
the tradition and the virtuous conduct of those who know

the Veda further, also the customs of holy men, and finally self-satisfaction.

Whatever law has been ordained for any person by Manu, that has been fully declared in the Veda: for that sage was omniscient.

But a learned man after fully scrutinising all this with the eye of knowledge, should, in accordance with the authority of the revealed texts, be intent on the performance of his duties.

For that man who obeys the law prescribed in the revealed texts and in the sacred tradition, gains fame in this world and after death unsurpassable bliss.

But by Shruti (revelation) is meant the Veda, and by Smriti (tradition) the Institutes of the sacred law: those two must not be called into question in any matter, since from those two the sacred law shone forth.

Every twice-born man, who, relying on the Institutes of dialectics, treats with contempt those two sources of the law, must be cast out by the virtuous, as an atheist and a scorner of the Veda.

The Veda, the sacred tradition, the customs of virtuous men, and one's own pleasure, they declare to be visibly the fourfold means of defining the sacred law.

The knowledge of the sacred law is prescribed for those who are not given to the acquisition of wealth and to the gratification of their desires; to those who seek the knowledge of the sacred law the supreme authority is the revelation, Shruti.

But when two sacred texts (Shruti) are conflicting, both are held to be law; for both are pronounced by the wise to be valid law.

(from *Manu Smriti* II:6-14, in *Sacred Books of the East*, XXV, pp. 30-32)

LIFE AS SACRAMENT

A potent force in maintaining the tradition was the scheme of sacraments that provided a religious sanction to each important step in life. The following enumeration of the forty sacraments suggests how impressive and solemn rituals bounded human existence with a reminder of the individual's relation to society and the moral order. Many of these are no longer observed, but the chief ones, such as marriage, are still performed according to the ancient rites.

1) The ceremony relating to the conception of the embryo; 2) the ceremony relating to the desired birth of a male child; 3) the parting of the pregnant wife's hair by the husband [to ward off evil spirits]; 4) the ceremony relating to the birth of the child; 5) the naming of the child; 6) the first feeding; 7) the tonsure of the child's head; 8) the initiation; 9-12) the four vows taken in connection with the study of the Veda; 13) the ceremonial bath [graduation]; 14) the union with a mate who could practice dharma together with him [i.e., marriage]; 15-19) the daily performance of the five sacrifices to gods, manes, men, spirits, and the Brahman; 20-26) and the performance of the following sacrifices, that is, of the seven cooked-food sacrifices . . . ; 27-33) the seven kinds of oblation sacrifices . . . ; 34-40) the seven kinds of soma sacrifices . . . these are the forty sacraments.

Now follow the eight good qualities of the soul, namely, compassion to all beings, forbearance, absence of jealousy, tranquillity, goodness, absence of meanness, and absence of covetousness. He who is sanctified by these forty sacraments but is not endowed with the eight good qualities of the soul does not become united with the Brahman, nor does he even reach the abode of the Brahman. On the other hand, he who is, verily, sanctified by a few only of the sacraments but is endowed with the eight good qualities of the soul becomes united with the Brahman, he dwells in the abode of the Brahman.

(from *Gautama Dharma Sūtra*, VIII:14-26, in *Sources of Indian Tradition*, p. 235)

A WIDOW'S
ACT OF DEVOTION

One striking witness to the Hindu conviction that marriage was a sacramental rite that endured beyond death was the custom observed in many areas, particularly in North India, of a widow burning herself on her husband's funeral pyre. The practice was condemned by European travellers as inhuman, but it was regarded by Hindus as an act of the greatest spiritual merit, even though, as this passage shows, they frequently tried to persuade women not to follow their husbands into the flames. This description of the preparation of a Queen about to die, and the attempt of her son to dissuade her, is taken from the account of the reign of Harsha written by the poet Bāna in the seventh century A.D. The woman who died on her husband's funeral pyre was known as a *satī*, meaning a "virtuous woman," and this word is often applied to the act itself. Not all Indian widows cremated themselves with their husbands; the action seems to have been really widespread only among the upper classes. It was common, however, from the eighth century, and was not suppressed until the nineteenth century.

It is not, my dear, [the Queen said to her son, who was seeking to persuade her not to enter the fire], that you are unloved, without noble qualities, or deserving to be abandoned. With my very bosom's milk you drank up my heart. If at this hour my regard is not towards you, it is that my lord's great condescenscion comes between us. Furthermore, dear son, I am not ever craving for the sight of another lord. I am the lady of a great house, born of a stainless ancestry, one whose virtue is her dower. Have you forgotten that I am the lioness mate of a great spirit, who like a lion had his delight in a hundred battles? Daughter, spouse, mother of heroes, how otherwise could such a woman as I, whose price was valour, act? This hand has been clasped by even such a hero, thy father, a chief among princes, peer of Bharata and other great kings. Upon this head have the subservient wives of countless feudatories poured coronation water from golden ewers. This forehead, in winning the honourable fillet of chief-queen, has enjoyed a thing scarce accessible to desire. These breasts have worn robes swayed by the wind of fans waved by captive wives of foes; they have been sucked by sons like you. Upon the heads of rival wives have these feet been set; they have been adored with diamond-wreaths of diadems by the bending matrons of a whole capital. Thus every limb has fulfilled its mission: I have spent my store of good works, what more should I look to? I would die while still unwidowed. I cannot endure, like the widowed Rati, to make unavailing lamentations for a burnt husband. Going before, like the dust of your father's feet, to announce his coming to the heavens, I shall be high esteemed of the hero-loving spouses of the gods. Nay, what will the smoke-bannered one burn of me, who am already on fire with the recent sight of his heart-rending pains? Not to die, but to live at such a time would be un-feeling. Compared with the flame of wifely sorrow, whose fuel is imperishable love, fire itself is chilly cold. How suits it to be parsimonious of a life light as a bit of rotten straw, when that life's lord, majestic as Kailāsa, is passing away? Even should I live, yet after the mortal sin of slighting the king's death the joys, my son, of my son's rule will touch me not. In those that are consumed by grief felicity is ominous, accursed, and unavailing. Not in the body, dear son, but in the glory of loyal widows would I abide on earth. Therefore dishonour me no more, I beseech you, beloved son, with opposition to my heart's desire.

So saying she fell at his feet. But the prince hastily drew them away, and bending down, held her in both his arms, and raised her prostrate form. Pondering the inevitableness of grief, deeming that act to be the better part befitting a lady of rank, recognizing her fixed resolution, he stood in silence with downcast looks.

True is it that, even when made timorous by affection, a noble nature resigns itself to what accords with place and time. Having embraced her son and kissed his head, the queen went forth on foot from the women's quarter, and, though the heavens, filled with the citizens' lamentations, seemed to block her path, proceeded to the Sarasvatī's banks. Then, having worshipped the fire with the blooming red lotus posies of a woman's timorous glances, she plunged into it, as the moon's form enters the adorable sun.

(from Bāna, *Harsacarita*, in E. B. Cowell and F. W. Thomas, pp. 153-55)

CHAPTER V

THE MAINTENANCE OF
THE SOCIAL FABRIC

∽∽∽∽∽

The importance of the great social ideals—class, stages of life, the ends of man—were discussed in the previous chapter; in the selections in this chapter the significance of political ideas within the tradition will be explored. One feature that emerges at once is that while the texts make a formal distinction between the study of morals (dharma-shāstra) and the art of government (arthashāstra), in practice no real separation was made. This was so partly because of the deeply ingrained belief that the social order was a divine construction, and partly because of what may be called the horizontal and vertical divisions of human life within the Hindu system. The horizontal structure was that of class, with duties defined in terms of one's particular station in life, leading to a way of life that tended to be self-contained. To lead a good life within this framework meant the fulfilling of functions that were both secular and religious, and the texts make little distinction between instructions on the conduct of business and on the performance of the sacrifices. These horizontal divisions of life, with their tendency to stratify society, were cut across by vertical social divisions—such as the stages of life and the legitimate ends of man—that worked against a completely rigid social order.

In such a society a fusion of spiritual and temporal power would seem inevitable, but priest-kings did not arise in Indian history. Instead, the ordering of society took place through a mutual exaltation of the powers and functions of the priestly and warrior classes. Since the authors of the texts were priests it is not surprising that the superiority of this class is emphasized, but it is significant that temporal power is rarely claimed. The admission of the temporal rights of rulers involved, however, the acceptance by kings of the responsibility of maintaining the laws of class. The king was not thought of as a law-giver; his task was the preservation of existing orders to prevent "the confusion of caste and class." State power entered ordinary life only when the internal regulations of groups broke down, and the assumption was that the ruler acted to restore a relationship, not to take an active part in creating the social order.

This view of the ruler's function was enormously important for the development of Hindu civilization, for it meant that life within the social units could become almost autonomous. Rulers were generally content, as long as taxes were paid, to leave the people to their own devices. This meant that dynasties could rise and fall without touching the fabric of social life. But this did not mean a static society, for particularly with the rise of the great Mauryan Empire new political practices and concepts received religious sanction and became part of the general tradition. One of the most significant of these was an increased emphasis on the divinity of the king. Here as elsewhere it should be noted that "king" in the tradition becomes a kind of short-hand designation for all the functions of political power, and "government" would often be a more accurate term.

The clearest expression of the emphasis on royal prerogative is given in the work associated with Kautilya, the minister of Chandragupta Maurya, known as the Artha-shāstra, or "Treatise on Material Gain." This book exalts the power of the king and extends government control to *almost every aspect of life. Here Kautilya seems to be in conflict with the tendency, noted above, for Indian social groups to lead an autonomous existence, without interference by the king. It might be argued, however, that the attempt to control all social relationships does not conflict with the laws of class and caste, but merely makes them more explicit by emphasizing the king's role in society. Even Kautilya's assertion that material advantage is the chief end of life, since the others depend upon it, can be understood as an elaboration of the usual statement of the duty of kings to maintain the whole social order.*

Another important source for the political thought of the period is the great series of edicts carved on rocks and pillars by the Emperor Ashoka (c. 269-232 B.C.). Behind the edicts, with their many fervent appeals for righteousness, can be seen the authority of a king willing to compel his people to be virtuous insofar as this is possible.

Other sources drawn upon in this chapter to illustrate the understanding of the role of the king within the Hindu tradition are the Mahābhārata, *the great epic poem, and the* Manu Smriti, *the statement of ideal law already frequently drawn upon. All of these sources underline Kautilya's sentiment that "the king shall never allow people to swerve from their duties . . . for whoever upholds his own duty, following the rules of class . . . will surely be happy both here and hereafter" (I:3).*

KINGSHIP AS A REMEDY
FOR AN EVIL SOCIETY

In the twelfth book of the *Mahābhārata* there are numerous discussions of duties and functions of kings. These are generally cast in the form of dialogues between Bhīsma, the elder statesman of the Kuru clan, and Yudhishthira, the oldest of the five brothers who are struggling to regain the throne which is rightfully theirs. In the selection given here, Bhīshma is asked a crucial question: why does a king, who is merely a man, have the right to dominate other human beings? Human history, he suggests by way of answer, is rightly understood only when one realizes the vast cycles through which human existence has passed. The greatest of these cycles is almost unimaginably long—billions of years—but the four smallest cycles are of immediate concern to man. Each of these cycles is marked by a decline in virtue; the one in which we are living marks the nadir of human virtue. In every cycle the rulers are the embodiment of the proper *dharma* or values for the time, and in this age, the characteristic of kings is that they are protectors of the laws of class and caste. Their instrument for fulfilling this function is punishment, and "the science of chastisement" occupies a large place in the political thought of the age. But as the passage suggests, sternness alone was not enough; it had to be combined with justice. In the search for a suitable ruler to become the founder of the true line of kings, it was not until the birth of Prithi, the seventh in the order of succession, that a ruler was found who fulfilled the requirements.

Yudhishtira asked, "Subject like others to the same kinds of grief and joy, . . . resembling others in birth and death, in fact, similar to others in respect of all the attributes of humanity, for what reason does one man, the king, govern the rest of the world numbering many men possessed of great intelligence and bravery? . . . There cannot but be a grave reason for this since the whole world bows down to one man as to a god!" . . .

Bhīshma said, "Listen in detail how sovereignty first began in the Krita age. At first there was no sovereignty, no king, no chastisement, and no chastiser. All men used to protect one another righteously. As they thus lived, O Bhārata, righteously protecting one another, they found the task (after sometime), to be painful. Error then began to assail their hearts. Having become subject to error, the perceptions of men, O prince, came to be clouded, and thence their virtue began to decline. When their perceptions were dimmed and when men became subject to error, all of them became covetous, O chief of the Bhāratas! And because men sought to obtain objects which they did not possess, another passion called lust (of acquisition) got hold of them. When they became subject to lust, another passion, named wrath, soon soiled them. Once subject to wrath, they lost all consideration of what should be done and what should not. Unrestrained sexual indulgence set in. Men began to utter what they chose. All distinctions between food that is clean and unclean and between virtue and vice disappeared. When this confusion set in amongst men, the Vedas disappeared. Upon the disappearance of the Vedas, righteousness was lost. When both the Vedas and righteousness were lost, the gods were possessed by fear. Overcome with fear, O tiger among men, they sought the protection of Brahman. Having gratified the divine Grandsire of the universe, the gods, afflicted with grief, said unto him, with joined hands;—O god, the eternal Vedas have been afflicted in the world of men by covetousness and error! For this, we have been struck with fear. Through loss of the Vedas, O Supreme Lord, righteousness also has been lost! For this, O Lord of the three worlds, we are about to descend to the level of human beings! In consequence, however, of the cessation of all pious rites among men, great distress will be our lot. Do thou then, O Grandsire, think of that which would benefit us, so that the universe, created by thy power, may not meet with destruction!—Thus addressed, the Self-born and divine Lord said unto them,—I shall think of what will do good to all! Ye foremost of gods, let your fears be dispelled!—The Grandsire then composed by his own intelligence a treatise consisting of a hundred thousand lessons. In it were treated the subjects of Virtue, Profit, and Pleasure. The Self-born designated them as the three ends of man. The diverse means of acquisition, the desire for diverse kinds of wealth, the methods of agriculture and other operations that form the chief source of revenue, and the various means for producing and applying illusions, the methods by which stagnant water is rendered foul, were laid down in it. All those means, O tiger among kings, by which men might be prevented from deviating from the path of righteousness and honesty, were all described in it. Having composed that highly beneficial treatise, the divine Lord cheerfully said unto the deities having Indra for their head, these words:—For the good of the world and for establishing the three ends of man (Virtue, Profit, and Pleasure), I have composed this science representing the very essence of speech! Assisted by chastisement, this science will protect the world. Dealing rewards and punishments, this science will operate among men. And because men are led (to the acquisition of the objects of their existence) by chastisement, or, in other words, chastisement leads or governs every thing, therefore will this science be known in the three worlds as *Dandaniti* (science of chastisement). . . .

(from *Mahābhārata*, XII:59, *passim* in P. C. Roy, X, pp. 180-87)

THE DANGER OF ANARCHY

Some writers have seen in the horror of anarchy which characterizes ancient Indian thought a reflection of social disorder that followed the breakup of the Mauryan Empire, but whatever the cause, the emphasis is very plain. In the natural state of society, it is said, "the law of the fish" is dominant—the big one eats the smaller. According to legend, the people promised Manu, the mythical lawgiver pictured here as the first king, that they would give him a share of their produce in return for protection. Kingship is thus the result of a "social contract," although the aim of the relationship—the protection of the laws of class—is part of the framework of the universe.

Yudhishthira said,—'Thou hast said what the duties are of the four modes of life and of the four orders. Tell me now, O grandsire, what are the principal duties of a kingdom.'

Bhīshma said,—'The (election and) coronation of a king is the first duty of a kingdom. A kingdom in which anarchy prevails becomes weak and is soon afflicted by robbers. In kingdoms torn by anarchy, righteousness cannot dwell. The inhabitants devour one another. An anarchy is the worst possible of states. The *Shrutis* declare that in crowning a king, it is Indra that is crowned (in the person of the king). A person who is desirous of prosperity should worship the king as he should worship Indra himself. No one should dwell in kingdoms torn by anarchy. Agni does not convey (to the gods) the libations that are poured upon him in kingdoms where anarchy prevails. If a powerful king approaches kingdoms weakened by anarchy, from desire of annexing them to his dominions, the people should go forward and receive the invader with respect. Such conduct would be consistent with wise counsels. There is no evil greater than anarchy. If the powerful invader be inclined to equity, everything will be right. If, on the other hand, he be enraged, he may exterminate all. That cow which cannot be easily milked has to suffer much torture. On the other hand, that cow which is capable of being easily milked, has not to suffer any torture whatever. The wood that bends easily does not require to be heated. The tree that bends easily, has not to suffer any torture (at the hands of the gardener). Guided by these instances, O hero, men should bend before those that are powerful. The man that bends his head to a powerful person really bends his head to Indra. For these reasons, men desirous of prosperity should (elect and) crown some person as their king. They who live in countries where anarchy prevails cannot enjoy their wealth and wives. During times of anarchy, the sinful man derives great pleasure by robbing the wealth of other people. When, however, his (ill-got) wealth is snatched by others, he wishes for a king. It is evident, therefore, that in times of anarchy the very wicked even cannot be happy. The wealth of one is snatched away by two. That of those two is snatched away by many acting together. He who is not a slave is made a slave. Women, again, are forcibly abducted. For these reasons the gods created kings for protecting the people. If there were no king on Earth for wielding the rod of chastisement, the strong would then have preyed on the weak after the manner of fishes in the water. It hath been heard by us that men, in days of old, in consequence of anarchy, met with destruction, devouring one another like stronger fishes devouring the weaker ones in the water. . . .

'Thus, O Yudhishthira, those men on Earth who desire prosperity should first elect and crown a king for the protection of all! Like disciples humbling themselves in the presence of preceptors or the gods in the presence of Indra, all men should humble themselves before the king. One that is honored by his own people becomes an object of regard with his foes also, while one that is disregarded by his own is overridden by foes. If the king be overridden by his foes, all his subjects become unhappy. Therefore, umbrellas and vehicles and outward ornaments, and viands, and drinks, and mansions, and seats, and beds, and all utensils for use and show, should be assigned to the king. By such means the king will succeed in discharging his duties of protection (the better) and become irresistible. . . .

'In the absence of royal protection, all things, inspired with fear and anxiety and becoming senseless and uttering cries of woe, would meet with destruction in no time. No sacrifices extending for a year and completed with presents according to the ordinances would occur if the king did not exercise the duty of protection. In the absence of royal protection Brāhmanas would never study the four Vedas or undergo austerities or be cleansed by knowledge and rigid vows. In the absence of royal protection, the slayer of a person guilty of the slaughter of a Brāhmana would not obtain any reward; on the other hand, the person guilty of

Brāhmanicide would enjoy perfect immunity. In the absence of royal protection, men would snatch other people's wealth from their very hands, and all wholesome barriers would be swept away, and everybody, inspired with fear, would seek safety in flight. In the absence of royal protection, all kinds of injustice would set in; an intermixture of castes would take place; and famine would ravage the kingdom. In consequence again of royal protection, men can everywhere sleep fearlessly and at their ease without shutting their houses and doors with bolts and bars. Nobody would bear the evil speeches of others, far less actual assaults, if the king did not righteously protect the Earth. If the king exercises the duty of protection, women decked with every ornament may fearlessly wander everywhere without male relatives to attend upon them. Men become righteous and without injuring serve one another because the king exercises the duty of protection. In consequence of royal protection the members of the three orders are enabled to perform high sacrifices and devote themselves to the acquisition of learning with attention. The world depends upon agriculture and trade and is protected by the Vedas. All these again are duly protected by the king exercising his principal duty. Since the king, taking a heavy load upon himself, protects his subjects with the aid of a mighty force, it is for this that the people are able to live in happiness. Who is there that will not worship him in whose existence the people exist and in whose destruction the people are destroyed? That person who does what is agreeable and beneficial to the king and who bears (a share of) the burthen of kingly duties that strike every caste with fear, conquers both this and the other world. That man who even thinks of doing an injury to the king, without doubt meets with grief here and goes to hell hereafter. No one should disregard the king by taking him for a man, for he is really a high divinity in human form.'

(from *Mahābhārata*, XII:67, *passim*, as in P. C. Roy, X, pp. 215-17)

WAR AND PEACE

In dealing with political problems, the ancient Indian writers tended to solve them either by constructing a mythological framework, as in the previous passage, or by analyzing all possibilities in a system of minute classifications, as in the following selection from Kautilya's *Arthashāstra*, the most famous work on statecraft. The assumption underlying the argument of the passage is that war is the natural occupation of kings. One possible result of this aspect of the tradition may have been that refusal to recognize the sovereignty of other kings led to a constant state of war. Another result may have been that the common people regarded war as the concern of the king and his fighting men, and lived out their lives unmoved by the strife around them. This was probably what Megasthenes, the Greek ambassador to the Mauryan court, had in mind when he wrote that during a battle "the tillers of the soil . . . are undisturbed . . . for the combatants make carnage of each other, but allow those engaged in husbandry to remain quite unmolested."

If a king thinks:

"That by making peace with one, I can work out my own resources, and by waging war with another, I can destroy the works of my enemy," then he may adopt that double policy and improve his resources. . . .

When the advantages derivable from peace and war are of equal character, one should prefer peace; for disadvantages, such as the loss of power and wealth, sojourning, and sin, are ever attending upon war.

The same holds good in the case of neutrality and war.

Of the two (forms of policy), double policy and alliance, double policy (*i.e.* making peace with one and waging war with another) is preferable; for whoever adopts the double policy enriches himself, being ever attentive to his own works, whereas an allied king has to help his ally at his own expense.

One shall make an alliance with a king who is stronger than one's neighbouring enemy; in the absence of such a king, one should ingratiate oneself with one's neighbouring enemy, either by supplying money or army or by ceding a part of one's territory and by keeping oneself aloof; for there can be no greater evil to kings than alliance with a king of considerable power, unless one is actually attacked by one's enemy.

A powerless king should behave as a conquered king (towards his immediate enemy); but when he finds that the time of his own ascendancy is at hand, due to a fatal disease, internal troubles, increase of enemies, or a friend's calamities that are vexing his enemy, then under the pretence of performing some expiatory rites to avert the danger of his enemy, he may get out (of the enemy's court); or if he is in his own territory, he should not go to see his suffering enemy; or if he is near to his enemy, he may murder the enemy when opportunity affords itself.

A king who is situated between two powerful kings shall seek protection from the stronger of the two; or from one of them on whom he can rely; or he may make peace with both of them on equal terms. Then he may begin to set one of them against the other by telling each that the other is a tyrant causing utter ruin to himself, and thus cause dissension between them. When they are divided, he may put down each separately by secret or covert means. Or, throwing himself under the protection of any two immediate kings of considerable power, he may defend himself against an immediate enemy. Or, having made an alliance with a chief in a stronghold, he may adopt the double policy (*i.e.* make peace with one of the two kings and wage war with another). Or, he may adapt himself to circumstances, depending upon the causes of peace and war in order. Or, he may make friendship with traitors, enemies, and wild chiefs who are conspiring against both the kings. Or, pretending to be a close friend of one of them, he may strike the other at the latter's weak point by employing enemies and wild tribes. Or, having made friendship with

both, he may form a Circle of States. Or, he may make an
alliance with the Madhyama or the neutral king; and with
this help he may put down one of them or both. Or when
hurt by both, he may seek protection from a king of righteous character among the Madhyama king, the neutral
king, and their friends or equals, or from any other king
whose subjects are do disposed as to increase his happiness
and peace, with whose help he may be able to recover his
lost position, with whom his ancestors were in close intimacy or blood relationship, and in whose kingdom he can
find a number of powerful friends.

Of two powerful kings who are on amicable terms with
each other, a king shall make alliance with one of them
who likes him and whom he likes; this is the best way of
making alliance.

(from Kautilya, *Arthaśāstra* VII:1, in Shamasastry, pp. 296-
297)

ASHOKA'S VISION
OF TRUE CONQUEST

One of the most persistent desires of Indian rulers was to become a "Universal Emperor," a semi-divine figure who would
conquer the whole world. Imbued with this ideal, many rulers
sought to extend their power over all of India. One of the few
who nearly succeeded was Ashoka (c. 269-232 B.C.), who,
having inherited a vast empire, sought to extend it still farther.
But, according to tradition, he was filled with horror in the
moment of conquest at the cost of his victory, and accepted
the teachings of Buddha, with their emphasis on peace, as his
guide.

The record of Ashoka's attempts to spread the Rule of
Righteousness is contained in the edicts he had engraved on
pillars and rocks. His insistence that he was the father and

protector of his people is in keeping with traditional theories of Indian kingship, and he sought to use the machinery of the state to encourage virtuous living. As these selections from the Edicts suggest, Ashoka was especially anxious to end the killing of animals and to encourage his officials to administer strict justice. His injunction to his people to practice religious tolerance is especially noteworthy. It is possible that this emphasis reflects to some extent his recognition that the Brāhman priesthood resented his support of Buddhism, which was the religion of a minority of the population.

When the king, Beloved of the Gods and of Gracious Mien, had been consecrated eight years Kalinga was conquered, 150,000 people were deported, 100,000 were killed, and many times that number died. But after the conquest of Kalinga, the Beloved of the Gods began to follow Righteousness (Dharma), to love Righteousness, and to give instruction in Righteousness. Now the Beloved of the Gods regrets the conquest of Kalinga, for when an independent country is conquered people are killed, they die, or are deported, and that the Beloved of the Gods finds very painful and grievous. And this he finds even more grievous—that all the inhabitants—brāhmans, ascetics, and other sectarians, and householders who are obedient to superiors, parents, and elders, who treat friends, acquaintances, companions, relatives, slaves, and servants with respect, and are firm in their faith—all suffer violence, murder, and separation from their loved ones. Even those who are fortunate enough not to have lost those near and dear to them are afflicted at the misfortunes of friends, acquaintances, companions, and relatives. The participation of all men in common suffering is grievous to the Beloved of the Gods. Moreover there is no land, except that of the Greeks, where groups of brāhmans and ascetics are not found, or where men are not members of one sect or another. So now, even if the number of those killed and captured in the conquest of Kalinga had been a hundred or a thousand times less, it would be grievous to the Beloved of the Gods. The Beloved of the Gods will forgive as far as he can, and he even conciliates the forest tribes of his dominions; but he warns them that there is power even in the remorse of the Beloved of the Gods, and he tells them to reform, lest they be killed.

For all beings the Beloved of the Gods desires security, self-control, calm of mind, and gentleness. The Beloved of the Gods considers that the greatest victory is the victory of Righteousness; and this he has won here (in India) and even five hundred leagues beyond his frontiers in the realm of the Greek king Antiochus, and beyond Antiochus among the four kings Ptolemy, Antigonus, Magas, and Alexander. Even where the envoys of the Beloved of the Gods have not been sent men hear of the way in which he follows and teaches Righteousness, and they too follow it and will follow it. Thus he achieves a universal conquest, and conquest always gives a feeling of pleasure; yet it is but a slight pleasure, for the Beloved of the Gods only looks on that which concerns the next life as of great importance.

I have had this inscription of Righteousness engraved that all my sons and grandsons may not seek to gain new victories, that in whatever victories they may gain they may prefer forgiveness and light punishment, that they may consider the only [valid] victory the victory of Righteousness, which is of value both in this world and the next, and that all their pleasure may be in Righteousness. . . .

(from the Thirteenth Rock Edict in *Sources of Indian Tradition*, pp. 146-47)

Here no animal is to be killed for sacrifice, and no festivals are to be held, for the king finds much evil in festivals, except for certain festivals which he considers good.

Formerly in the Beloved of the God's kitchen several hundred thousand animals were killed daily for food; but now at the time of writing only three are killed—two peacocks and a deer, though the deer not regularly. Even these three animals will not be killed in future.

(from the First Rock Edict in *Sources of Indian Tradition*, p. 148)

The Beloved of the Gods . . . honors members of all sects, whether ascetics or householders, by gifts and various honors. But he does not consider gifts and honors as important as the furtherance of the essential message of all sects. This essential message varies from sect to sect, but it has one common basis, that one should so control one's tongue as not to honor one's own sect or disparage another's on the wrong occasions; for on certain occasions one should do so only mildly, and indeed on other occasions one should honor other men's sects. By doing this one strengthens one's own sect and helps the others, while by doing otherwise one harms one's own sect and does a disservice to the others. Whoever honors his own sect and disparages another man's, whether from blind loyalty or with the intention of showing his own sect in a favorable light, does his own sect the greatest possible harm. Concord is best, with each hearing and respecting the other's teachings. It is the wish of the Beloved of the Gods that members of all sects should be learned and should teach virtue. . . . Many officials are busied in this matter . . . and the result is the progress of my own sect and the illumination of Righteousness.

(from the Twelfth Rock Edict in *Sources of Indian Tradition*, p. 151)

In the past kings sought to make the people progress in Righteousness but they did not progress. . . . And I asked myself how I might uplift them through progress in Righteousness. . . . Thus I have decided to have them instructed in Righteousness, and to issue ordinances of Righteousness, so that by hearing them the people might conform, advance in the progress of Righteousness, and themselves make great progress. . . . For that purpose many officials are employed among the people to instruct them in Righteousness and to explain it to them. . . .

Moreover I have had banyan trees planted on the roads to give shade to man and beast; I have planted mango groves, and I have had ponds dug and shelters erected along the roads at every eight kos. Everywhere I have had wells dug for the benefit of man and beast. But this benefit is but small, for in many ways the kings of olden time have worked for the welfare of the world; but what I have done has been done that men may conform to Righteousness.

(from the Seventh Pillar Edict in *Sources of Indian Tradition*, p. 152)

CHAPTER VI

THE SEARCH FOR

SALVATION

~~~~~~~~~~

During the period that we have characterized as the Age of Growth, the older Vedic religion was reinterpreted and, to some extent, transformed, but the sacred texts remained the source of revealed truth. At the same time, certain other ideas had become so firmly fixed in the tradition that they were the unquestioned assumptions of almost all schools of thought. The most fundamental of these, the doctrine of karma, the idea that each act carried with it a necessary result, and belief in the transmigration of the soul, as we have seen, had already been accepted when the Upanishads were written, and with the passing of time they had been woven more deeply into the fabric of Indian life. It is against the background of these assumptions, as well as of the ancient Vedic inheritance, that the religious developments of the Age of Growth took place.

One of the most important features of the religious life of the period was the rise of sects or cults which have remained ever since an essential feature of Hinduism. These sects were marked by two features which were of great significance for the spiritual life of India. One was bhakti, an attitude of devotion and adoration towards some particular god; the other was an emphasis on the grace of this deity in freely granting salvation to his devotees. The *deities that were the object of devotion seem, in general, to have been of two kinds: either folk heroes who were deified (or, conceivably, deities who were made culture heroes), or personifications of some natural force. Krishna and Rama are examples of the first class, Shiva of the second, although Krishna and Rama are not strictly comparable to Shiva, since they are regarded as incarnations of Vishnu. In any case, it is around Vishnu, in one of his incarnations, or Shiva that the sectarian cults are mainly centered. Both deities were widely worshipped in some form by about 300 A.D., and it is quite possible that by then most of the people would have classed themselves as followers of one or the other. Thus the distinction between the Vaishnavite, or follower of Vishnu, and the Shaivite, became a basic feature of Hinduism.*

The devotees of Vishnu picture their deity, either in his own person or in that of his incarnations, as beneficent and loving. Symbols denoting light and the life-giving sun are frequently associated with him, and his grace in offering salvation to his followers is stressed. This aspect of the Vishnu cult is prominent in the Bhagavad Gītā, *the greatest literary monument of the cults that emphasized worship of an individual god. This famous work forms a part of the* Mahābhārata, *but is probably a separate composition. It exalts Krishna as supreme deity, but endeavors to bring all of the main trends of religious experience into a harmonious whole. Partly because it offers something to seekers of all kinds, partly because it synthesizes the ethical and religious insights of the Hindu tradition into a coherent statement, the* Gītā *has played an important role in the life of India.*

Shiva is almost certainly one of the most ancient of Indian gods, dating back before the physical and spiritual conquest of India by the Aryans. Images found at the sites of the prehistoric Indus Valley civilization bear a striking resemblance to later representations of Shiva, and his cult is strongest in South India, the area where Aryan influences were latest in coming. He is a god of fertility and power, but he is also pictured as an ascetic, covered with ashes and with snakes garlanded around his neck. Most frequently worshipped through a phallic symbol, a reminder of his origin as a god of fertility, he is also the Lord of the Dance, maintaining the cosmic order through his energy and power.

A characteristic feature of the Hindu tradition, the use of images in worship, is associated with the rise to prominence of the great cults. Images of the gods seem to have been unknown in Vedic times, but probably the emphasis on devotion offered to one particular deity fostered the use of plastic representations. Whatever the cause, images of all kinds became one of the most obvious marks of Hinduism, with carving becoming one of the most highly developed of the arts. The religious life of the people was thus nourished on a visual statement unmatched, perhaps, in the history of any civilization.

The Buddhist and Jain movements which flourished in the centuries when Vaishnavism and Shaivism were also taking hold can only be mentioned in passing, although they influenced the Hindu tradition at many points. The interpenetration of the various movements was an extremely complex process, which, because of the lack of detailed historical data, cannot be analyzed with any certainty. The use of images in Buddhism, for example, might seem to be a clear case of the influence of the sectarian cults, but the very widespread and early use of images by Buddhism suggests the possibility that the influence was the other way around.

MAN'S TRUE NATURE

As we have already seen, for Indian religion salvation is understood in terms of the fundamental beliefs in *karma* and rebirth. On one level, the search for salvation is related to an attempt to improve one's *karma*, the fruit of one's actions, in order to improve one's future existence; on another and higher level, salvation is understood as the finding of a mode of existence that is beyond the changing flux of time and circumstance. This concept was directly linked to the ancient message of the *Upanishads* that there is an identity between man's spirit and the universal spirit, and that salvation consisted in an intuitive realization of this truth. To come to this state of knowledge is to realize man's true nature.

A description of man's nature is placed near the beginning of the *Bhagavad Gītā*, where Arjuna, the great warrior, is filled with horror at the consequences that will follow from the fratricidal war in which he is engaged. Krishna, who is acting as his charioteer, insists that the first prerequisite for facing this and all other problems is an understanding of the true nature of human existence. Krishna's statement is one of the *Bhagavad Gītā's* most famous passages.

The Blessed Lord said:

You grieve for those who should not be mourned, and yet you speak words of wisdom! The learned do not grieve for the dead or for the living.

Never, indeed, was there a time when I was not, nor when you were not, nor these lords of men. Never, too, will there be a time, hereafter, when we shall not be.

As in this body, there are for the embodied one [i.e., the soul] childhood, youth, and old age, even so there is the taking on of another body. The wise sage is not perplexed thereby.

Contacts of the sense-organs, O son of Kuntī, give rise to cold and heat, and pleasure and pain. They come and go, and are not permanent. Bear with them, O Bhārata.

That man, whom these [sense-contacts] do not trouble, O chief of men, to whom pleasure and pain are alike, who is wise—he becomes eligible for immortality.

For the nonexistent there is no coming into existence; nor is there passing into nonexistence for the existent. The ultimate nature of these two is perceived by the seers of truth.

Know that to be indestructible by which all this is pervaded. Of this imperishable one, no one can bring about destruction.

These bodies of the eternal embodied one, who is indestructible and incomprehensible, are said to have an end. Therefore fight, O Bhārata.

He who regards him [i.e., the soul] as a slayer, and he who regards him as slain—both of them do not know the truth; for this one neither slays nor is slain.

He is not born, nor does he die at any time; nor, having once come to be will he again come not to be. He is unborn, eternal, permanent, and primeval; he is not slain when the body is slain.

Whoever knows him to be indestructible and eternal, unborn and immutable—how and whom can such a man, O son of Prithā, cause to be slain or slay?

Just as a man, having cast off old garments, puts on other, new ones, even so does the embodied one, having cast off old bodies, take on other, new ones.

Weapons do not cleave him, fire does not burn him; nor does water drench him, nor the wind dry him up.

He is uncleavable, he is unburnable, he is undrenchable, as also undryable. He is eternal, all-pervading, stable, immovable, existing from time immemorial.

He is said to be unmanifest, unthinkable, and unchangeable. Therefore, knowing him as such, you should not grieve [for him].

And even if you regard him as being perpetually born and as perpetually dying, even then, O long-armed one, you should not grieve for him.

For, to one who is born death is certain and certain is birth to one who has died. Therefore in connection with a thing that is inevitable you should not grieve. . . .

Unmanifest in their beginnings are beings, manifest in the middle stage, O Bhārata, and unmanifest, again, in their ends. For what then should there be any lamentation?

Someone perceives him as a marvel; similarly, another speaks of him as a marvel; another, again, hears of him as a marvel; and, even after hearing of him, no one knows him.

The embodied one within the body of everyone, O Bhārata, is ever unslayable. Therefore, you should not grieve for any being. . . .

When one renounces all the desires which have arisen in the mind, O son of Prithā, and when he himself is content within his own Self, then is he called a man of steadfast wisdom.

He whose mind is unperturbed in the midst of sorrows and who entertains no desires amid pleasures; he from whom passion, fear, and anger have fled away—he is called a sage of steadfast intellect.

He who feels no attachment toward anything; who, having encountered the various good or evil things, neither rejoices nor loathes—his wisdom is steadfast.

When one draws in, on every side, the sense-organs from the objects of sense as a tortoise draws in its limbs from every side—then his wisdom becomes steadfast.

(from *Bhagavad Gītā*, II:11-30, 55-59, in *Sources of Indian Tradition*, pp. 284-85, 298)

The Way of Salvation: Duty

Having stated the goal, Krishna proceeds to show how it may be obtained. His definition of the end of life as a state beyond any attachment, including concern for the results of action, raises the problem of how action can be performed without motivation, that is, without being involved in its result. He gives the answer in terms of performance of *dharma*, the duties appropriate to one's particular class. This fulfillment of one's obligations as defined by life is known as *karma yoga*, the discipline of action, but it must be carefully distinguished from what is known in western thought as "salvation by works." *Karma yoga*, the way of obedience to the demands imposed by a particular existence, is a necessity for all those who seek to escape from the involvement in the fruits of actions, or, in other words, in rebirth.

Not by nonperformance of actions does a man attain freedom from action; nor by mere renunciation of actions does he attain his spiritual goal.

For no one, indeed, can remain, for even a single moment, unengaged in activity, since everyone, being powerless, is made to act by the dispositions of matter.

Whoever having restrained his organs of action still continues to brood over the objects of senses—he, the deluded one, is called a hypocrite.

But he who, having controlled the sense-organs by means of the mind, O Arjuna, follows without attachment the path of action by means of the organs of action—he excels.

Do you do your allotted work, for action is superior to nonaction. Even the normal functioning of your body cannot be accomplished through actionlessness.

Except for the action done for sacrifice, all men are under the bondage of action. Therefore, O son of Kunti, do you undertake action for that purpose, becoming free from all attachment. . . .

But the man whose delight is in the Self alone, who is content with the Self, who is satisfied only within the Self—for him there exists nothing that needs to be done.

He, verily, has in this world no purpose to be served by action done nor any purpose whatsoever to be served by action abnegated. Similarly, he does not depend on any beings for having his purpose served.

Therefore, without attachment, always do the work that has to be done, for a man doing his work without attachment attains to the highest goal. . . .

Better is one's own dharma [class duties] which one may be able to fulfill but imperfectly, than the dharma of others which is more easily accomplished. Better is death in the fulfillment of one's own dharma. To adopt the dharma of others is perilous. . . .

The fourfold class system was created by Me in accordance with the varying dispositions and the actions [resulting from them]. Though I am its creator, know Me, who am immutable, to be a non-doer.

Actions do not cling to Me, for I have no yearning for their fruit. He who knows Me thus [and himself acts in that spirit] is not bound by actions.

So knowing was action done even by men of old who sought liberation. Therefore do the same action [i.e., your class duties] which was done by the ancients in ancient times.

What is action? What is inaction?—as to this even the wise sages are confounded. I will expound action to you, knowing which you will be liberated from evil.

One has to realize what is action; similarly, one has to realize what is wrong action; and one has also to realize what is inaction. Inscrutable, indeed, is the way of action.

He who sees inaction in action and action in inaction, he is discerning among men, expert in the technique of karma-yoga, the doer of the entire action [enjoined by his dharma].

He whose undertakings are all devoid of motivating desires and purposes and whose actions are consumed by the fire of knowledge—him the wise call a man of learning.

Renouncing all attachment to the fruits of actions, ever content, independent—such a person even if engaged in action, does not do anything whatever.

(from *Bhagavad Gītā*, III:3-9, 17-19, IV:13-20, in *Sources of Indian Tradition*, pp. 286-87, 289)

The Way of Salvation: Knowledge

The second way commended by Krishna for a realization of the true nature of man is the path of knowledge. This does not mean the gaining of information or even of wisdom—although it includes knowledge of the scriptures and the teachings of the sages—but rather the acquisition of truth that comes through meditation. In the following selection both the fruits and techniques of this way, or *yoga*, are strikingly delineated.

To him who has subjugated his self by his self, his self is a friend; but to him who has not restrained his self, his own self behaves inimically, like an enemy. The self of one who has subjugated his self and is tranquil, is absolutely concentrated on itself, in the midst of cold and heat, pleasure and pain, as well as honour and dishonour. The devotee whose self is contented with knowledge and experience, who is unmoved, who has restrained his senses, and to whom a sod, a stone, and gold are alike, is said to be devoted. And he is esteemed highest, who thinks alike about well-wishers, friends, and enemies, and those who are indifferent, and those who take part with both sides, and those who are objects of hatred, and relatives, as well as about the good and the sinful. A devotee should constantly devote his self to abstraction, remaining in a secret place, alone, with his mind and self restrained, without expectations, and without belongings. Fixing his seat firmly in a clean place, not too high nor too low, and covered over with a sheet of cloth, a deerskin, and blades of Kusa grass,—and there seated on that seat, fixing his mind exclusively on one point, with the workings of the mind and senses restrained, he should practice devotion for purity of self. Holding his body, head, and neck even and unmoved, remaining steady, looking at the tip of his own nose, and not looking about in all directions, with a tranquil self, devoid of fear, and adhering to the rules of chastity, he should restrain his mind, and concentrate it on me, and sit down engaged in devotion, regarding me as his final goal. Thus constantly devoting his self to abstraction, a devotee whose mind is restrained, attains that tranquillity which culminates in final emancipation, and assimilation with me. Devotion is not his, O Arjuna! who eats too

much, nor his who eats not at all; not his who is addicted
to too much sleep, nor his who is ever awake. That devotion which destroys all misery is his, who takes due food
and exercise, who toils duly in all works, and who sleeps
and awakes in due time. When a man's mind well restrained becomes steady upon the self alone, then he being
indifferent to all objects of desire, is said to be devoted. As
a light standing in a windless place flickers not, that is declared to be the parallel for a devotee, whose mind is restrained, and who devotes his self to abstraction.

(from *Bhagavad Gītā*, VI:7-19, in *Sacred Books of the East*,
VIII, pp. 68-69)

The Way of Salvation: Devotion

Throughout all the discussions of the ways of salvation in the
Bhagavad Gītā is the implicit assumption that transcending
and completing the disciplines of work and knowledge is the
way of devotion to Krishna as Supreme Lord. Through surrender to him, men find the final end they seek—the realization of their true self. It is this emphasis on devotion that has
made the *Gītā* the scripture that appeals most directly to the
heart of the Indian people. The verses given here describe the
glorious vision of Krishna that comes to Arjuna, overwhelming
his senses with the splendor and power of the god who has
sought through his love and mercy to bring him to a realization of the truth.

ARJUNA:
                              Fain would I see,
As thou Thyself declar'st it, Sovereign Lord!
The likeness of that glory of Thy Form
Wholly revealed. O Thou Divinest One!
If this can be, if I may bear the sight,
Make Thyself visible, Lord of all prayers!
Show me Thy very self, the Eternal God!

KRISHNA:

Gaze, then, thou Son of Prithâ! I manifest for thee
Those hundred thousand thousand shapes that clothe
my Mystery:
I show thee all my semblances, infinite, rich, divine,
My changeful hues, my countless forms. See! in this face
of mine . . .
Wonders unnumbered, Indian Prince! revealed to none
save thee.
Behold! this is the Universe!—Look! what is live and
dead
I gather all in one—in Me! Gaze, as thy lips have said,
On GOD ETERNAL, VERY GOD! See ME! see what thou
prayest!

.   .   .   .

Thou canst not!—nor, with human eyes, Arjuna! ever
mayest!
Therefore I give thee sense divine. Have other eyes, new
light!
And, look! This is My glory, unveiled to mortal sight!

ARJUNA:

I mark Thee strike the skies
With front in wondrous wise
Huge, rainbow-painted, glittering; and thy
mouth
Opened, and orbs which see
All things, whatever be,
In all Thy worlds, east, west, and north and
south.

O Eyes of God! O Head!
My strength of soul is fled,
Gone is heart's force, rebuked is mind's desire!
When I behold Thee so,
With awful brows a-glow,
With burning glance, and lips lighted with fire,

Fierce as those flames which shall
Consume, at close of all,
Earth, Heaven! Ah me! I see no Earth and
Heaven!
Thee, Lord of Lords! I see,
Thee only—only Thee!
Ah! let Thy mercy unto me be given! . . .

How, in the wide worlds three
Should any equal be?
Shall any other share Thy majesty?

Therefore, with body bent
And reverent intent,
I praise, and serve, and seek Thee, asking grace.
As father to a son,
As friend to friend, as one
Who loveth to his lover, turn Thy face

In gentleness on me!
Good is it I did see
This unknown marvel of Thy Form! But fear
Mingles with joy! Retake,
Dear Lord! for pity's sake
Thine earthly shape, which earthly eyes may bear!

Be merciful, and show
The visage that I know;
Let me regard Thee, as of yore, arrayed
With disc and forehead-gem,
With mace and anadem,
Thou who sustainest all things! Undismayed

Let me once more behold
The form I loved of old,
Thou of the thousand arms and countless eyes!
My frightened heart is fain
To see restored again
The Charioteer, my Krishna's kind disguise. . . .

KRISHNA:

Yea! it was wonderful and terrible
To view me as thou didst, dear Prince! The gods
Dread and desire continually to view!
Yet not by Vedas, nor from sacrifice,
Nor penance, nor gift-giving, nor with prayer
Shall any so behold, as thou hast seen!
Only by fullest service, perfect faith,
And uttermost surrender am I known
And seen, and entered into, Indian Prince!
Who doeth all for Me; who findeth Me
In all; adoreth always; loveth all
Which I have made, and Me, for Love's sole end,
That man, Arjuna! unto Me doth wend.

(from *Bhagavad Gītā*, XI, selected verses, as in Sir Edwin,
Arnold, *The Song Celestial*)

INCARNATION: THE RESPONSE
TO HUMAN NEED

One of the most vital aspects of the Hindu tradition is the
belief in the numerous incarnations of the great divinities,
especially of Vishnu. The *Bhagavad Gītā* presents this in a
striking manner with the assertion that whenever the world
is threatened by disorder then Krishna appears to restore order
to human affairs. While in the *Gītā* itself it is not explicitly
stated that Krishna is an incarnation of Vishnu, later religious
thought interpreted him as such and around him gathered an
enormous literature describing his loving care for mankind.

KRISHNA:

Manifold the renewals of my birth
Have been, Arjuna! and of thy births, too!
But mine I know, and thine thou knowest not,

O Slayer of thy Foes! Albeit I be
Unborn, undying, indestructible,
The Lord of all things living; not the less—
By Maya, by my magic which I stamp
On floating Nature-forms, the primal vast—
I come, and go, and come. When Righteousness
Declines, O Bharata! when Wickedness
Is strong, I rise, from age to age, and take
Visible shape, and move a man with men,
Succoring the good, thrusting the evil back,
And setting Virtue on her seat again.
Who knows the truth touching my births on earth
And my divine work, when he quits the flesh
Puts on its load no more, falls no more down
To earthly birth: to Me he comes, dear Prince!

(from *Bhagavad Gītā*, IV:5-9, in Arnold, *The Song Celestial*)

ADORATION OF SHIVA

While the early devotees of Shiva did not leave a literary
monument comparable to the *Bhagavad Gītā*, it is quite certain that he is one of the most ancient of the gods of the
Indian people. One indication of this, apart from the existence
of images from the Indus Valley civilization that bear a striking resemblance to Shiva, are the references in one of the
later *Upanishads*, *Śvetāśvatara*. There Shiva seems to be identified with Rudra, the storm-god of the Vedic hymns. The hymn
given here shows how closely theism, especially in terms of
worship of one supreme God, was related to the great tradition.

The One spreader of the net, who rules with his ruling
    powers,
Who rules all the worlds with his ruling powers,
The one who alone stands in their arising and in their con-
    tinued existence—

They who know That, become immortal.
For truly, Rudra (the Terrible) is the One—they stand
    not for a second—
Who rules all the worlds with his ruling powers.
He stands opposite creatures. He, the Protector,
After creating all beings, merges them together at the end
    of time.
Having an eye on every side and a face on every side,
Having an arm on every side and a foot on every side,
The One God forges together with hands, with wings,
Creating the heaven and the earth.
He who is the source and origin of the gods,
The ruler of all, Rudra, the great seer,
Who of old created the Golden Germ,
May He endow us with clear intellect!
The form of thine, O Rudra, which is kindly (*śiva*),
Unterrifying, revealing no evil—
With that most benign form to us
Appear, O dweller among the mountains!
O dweller among the mountains, the arrow
Which thou holdest in thy hand to throw
Make kindly (*śiva*), O mountain protector!
Injure not man or beast!
Higher than this is Brahma. The Supreme, the Great,
Hidden in all things, body by body,
The One embracer of the universe—
By knowing Him as Lord men become immortal.
I know this mighty Person
Of the color of the sun, beyond darkness.
Only by knowing Him does one pass over death.
There is no other path for going there.
Than whom there is naught else higher,
Than whom there is naught smaller, naught greater,
The One stands like a tree established in heaven.
By Him, the Person, this whole world is filled.
    That which is beyond this world
    Is without form and without ill.
They who know That, become immortal;

But others go only to sorrow.
Who is the face, the head, the neck of all,
Who dwells in the heart of all things,
All-pervading is He, and bountiful;
Therefore omnipresent, and kindly (*śiva*).
A mighty lord is the Person,
The instigator of the highest being
Unto the purest attainment,
The ruler, a light imperishable!
A Person of the measure of a thumb is the inner soul,
Ever seated in the heart of creatures.
He is framed by the heart, by the thought, by the mind.
They who know That, become immortal.

> The Person has a thousand heads,
> A thousand eyes, a thousand feet;
> He surrounds the earth on all sides,
> And stands ten fingers' breadth beyond.
> The Person, in truth, this whole world is,
> Whate'er has been and whate'er will be;
> Also ruler of immortality,
> [And] whatever grows up by food.
> It has a hand and foot on every side,
> On every side an eye and head and face,
> It has an ear everywhere in the world.
> It stands encompassing all.

(from *Śvetāśvatara Upanishad*, III:1-16, in Hume, pp. 399-401)

THE GREAT HERESIES
OF THE TRADITION

All great religious traditions give rise to movements that are closely related in fundamental ideas and value structures to the parent stock but which historically have stood in opposition to the main lines of the development. Within the general context of Indian civilization, Buddhism and Jainism were both formidable rivals for the allegiance of the people and both had a far-reaching influence on many aspects of the Hindu tradition, but all that can be attempted here, however, is to indicate two important emphases of the great heretical movements that arose in the sixth century B.C. The first selection is traditionally regarded as the first sermon of Gautama, or Buddha, the Enlightened One. Here is sounded a note that comes to be associated, not very accurately, with the Hindu tradition itself: the supposition that the characteristic mark of the human condition is misery. According to this diagnosis, the suffering of mankind is caused by attachment, by the error of supposing that there is anything—including the Self —that is permanent in this world of perpetual change. The remedy was the Middle Way, a refusal to be concerned with anything that did not serve to cut the bonds of attachments of all kinds.

The second selection expresses the important Jain doctrine that all matter is possessed of life which differs in quality but not in kind in different objects. The logical extension of this belief was that no form of life should be injured in any way. The emphasis is perhaps not so much on compassion for all life as for the fundamental vision of an integrated universe. There is also the suggestion that the passion involved in killing and the taking of life binds one to existence. This Jain doctrine undoubtedly played a part in the general Indian belief in nonviolence.

Buddha's First Sermon

Thus I have heard. Once the Lord was at Vārānasī, at the deer park called Isipatana. There he addressed the five monks:

There are two ends not to be served by a wanderer. What are these two? The pursuit of desires and of the pleasure which springs from desire, which is base, common, leading to rebirth, ignoble, and unprofitable; and the pursuit of pain and hardship, which is grievous, ignoble, and unprofitable. The Middle Way of the Tathāgata

avoids both these ends. It is enlightened, it brings clear
vision, it makes for wisdom, and leads to peace, insight,
enlightenment, and Nirvāna. What is the Middle Way?
. . . It is the Noble Eightfold Path—Right Views, Right
Resolve, Right Speech, Right Conduct, Right Livelihood,
Right Effort, Right Mindfulness, and Right Concentration. This is the Middle Way. . . .

And this is the Noble Truth of Sorrow. Birth is sorrow,
age is sorrow, disease is sorrow, death is sorrow; contact
with the unpleasant is sorrow, separation from the pleasant
is sorrow, every wish unfulfilled is sorrow—in short all the
five components of individuality are sorrow.

And this is the Noble Truth of the Arising of Sorrow. It
arises from craving, which leads to rebirth, which brings
delight and passion, and seeks pleasure now here, now
there—the craving for sensual pleasure, the craving for
continued life, the craving for power.

And this is the Noble Truth of the Stopping of Sorrow.
It is the complete stopping of that craving, so that no passion remains, leaving it, being emancipated from it, being
released from it, giving no place to it.

And this is the Noble Truth of the Way which Leads to
the Stopping of Sorrow. It is the Noble Eightfold Path—
Right Views, Right Resolve, Right Speech, Right Conduct, Right Livelihood, Right Effort, Right Mindfulness,
and Right Concentration.

(from *Samyutta Nikāya*, V:421 ff., in *Sources of Indian Tradition*, pp. 101-02)

The Jain Vision of Life

From clubs and knives, stakes and maces, breaking my
   limbs,
An infinite number of times I have suffered without hope.
By keen-edged razors, by knives and shears,
Many times I have been drawn and quartered, torn apart
   and skinned.

Helpless in snares and traps, a deer,
I have been caught and bound and fastened, and often I
  have been killed.
A helpless fish, I have been caught with hooks and nets;
An infinite number of times I have been killed and
  scraped, split and gutted.
A bird, I have been caught by hawks or trapped in nets,
Or held fast by birdlime, and I have been killed an infinite
  number of times.
A tree, with axes and adzes by the carpenters
An infinite number of times I have been felled, stripped of
  my bark, cut up, and sawn into planks.
As iron, with hammer and tongs by blacksmiths
An infinite number of times I have been struck and
  beaten, split and filed. . . .
Ever afraid, trembling, in pain and suffering,
I have felt the utmost sorrow and agony. . . .
In every kind of existence I have suffered
Pains which have scarcely known reprieve for a moment.

(from *Uttarādhyayana*, XIX, selections, in *Sources of Indian
Tradition*, pp. 59-60)

CHAPTER VII

THE UNIVERSE OF
THE GREAT EPICS

〰〰〰〰〰

The culture and civilization that had been developing in India for nearly two thousand years is reflected in two great poems, the Mahābhārata *and the* Rāmāyana, *that are different in texture and theme from the religious texts. These two works are usually referred to as epics, but the implied comparison with the* Odyssey *and* Iliad *is not altogether apt. Simply in terms of authorship, the* Mahābhārata *is the product of many hands, and hundreds of years must have elapsed between the first and the last compositions. The original materials have been so worked over that it is now quite impossible to separate any kernel and show it to be the most ancient. At the same time, despite the continuous reworking of the poem, the heterogeneous elements have been woven into an extraordinarily complex structure with all the parts related. But the most important difference between the Indian epics and their western counterparts is the place the* Mahābhārata *and the* Rāmāyana *have held for two millennia in the life of the Indian people. While probably originally secular in origin, insofar as that term has any meaning within the Indian tradition, by about 200 A.D. both poems had become scripture, accepted as* smriti, *the part of the texts which are regarded as dependent upon tradition, not divine revela-*

tion, for their truth. The vast storehouse of myths, legends, and moral teaching has provided the Indian people with the material for artistic productions of every kind as well as coloring every aspect of their lives. They have thus given Indian society a basis of common ideas and ideals as well as a common treasury of stories known to all. This inheritance from the epics cannot be overstressed in any attempt to explain the unity and endurance of Hindu life. Although the peoples of India differ widely in language and race, they share a history that is half human, half divine, but that has been lived out on Indian soil.

The Mahābhārata tells the story of the great war that took place for the control of the kingdom of the Kurus, an area near modern Delhi. The occasion of the war was a struggle for the succession between two branches of the family. The succession had devolved on Dhritarāshtra, but since he was blind his brother Pāndu ruled in his place. When Pāndu, because of a curse, had to go into exile, he left his five sons in Dhritarāshtra's care, with the expectation that the oldest, Yudhishthira, would succeed. The other four brothers—Arjuna, Nakula, Bhīma, and Sahadeva—all play important parts in the story, but Arjuna is in many ways the hero of the poem. Civil war began when Dhritarāshtra's hundred sons, led by the oldest, Duryodhana, refused to give up the kingdom. The long story that follows is filled with many digressions and embellishments, but the rivalry of the cousins is the central theme, and it provides the unifying thread for the introduction of the most diverse materials, including lengthy discussions on statecraft.

The Rāmāyana, ascribed to Sage Valmīki, tells the story of how Rāma, heir apparent to the kingdom of Ayodhya, went into exile with his wife, Sītā, and his brother Lakshman, because of the promise made by his father to his stepmother to let her son succeed to the throne. The heart of the poem is the capture of Sītā by Rāvan, the demon king of Ceylon, and the long struggle to free her, with the assistance of Hanumān and his fellow monkeys, provides op-

portunity for stirring battle scenes as well as praise for Rāma's and Sītā's incomparable virtue.

In the selections given here no attempt has been made to tell the long and complex story, but only to indicate the way in which the epics reinforce the values that are particularly prized within the Hindu tradition. Throughout the selections there are continual reminders of the themes already mentioned—the duties of class, the role of a king, and the nature of a true marital relationship.

THE MAHĀBHĀRATA:
THE FOUNDING OF
THE ROYAL LINE

The central theme of the *Mahābhārata* is the great war between the sons of the two royal brothers, Dhritarāshtra and Pāndu, and the following selection traces the strange origin of the hundred sons of the one and of the five sons of the other. The story is told in the form of a dialogue between a descendant of the family and a great sage. Interwoven into the narrative are many familiar elements of the Hindu tradition: the importance of sons, the character of the gods, the power of asceticism, and the nature of kingship. All these form a complex pattern of grotesque fantasy and historical possibility that takes the reader into a self-contained universe quite different from the ordinary structure of reality. No doubt part of the secret of the appeal of the stories of the great poem to the people of India is the success of the authors in creating a new order of life, where the people are recognizably human but the conventions of action and behavior are not those familiar in everyday life.

Janamejaya asked: 'O best of Brahmanas, how did Ghandhari have a hundred sons? And how were the five sons of Pandu born of the Gods?'

Vaisampayana continued: 'Bhishma, the grandfather of the Kurus, heard that Ghandhari, the daughter of King Suvala, had obtained as a boon from Hari a promise that she should have a hundred sons. Bhishma sent to ask for her as a wife to Dhritarashtra, but Suvala hesitated because of Dhritarashtra's blindness. Eventually he consented, and the chaste Ghandhari agreed; but she blindfolded herself so that she should not be different from her husband. Her brother Sakuni brought her to the Kurus by whom she was received with great honour. Ghandhari, after her marriage, pleased everyone with her behaviour. . . . After Ghandhari conceived, she bore the burden for two years. But she was so beside herself with suffering because of the load in her womb that she struck herself and thereupon was delivered of a ball of hard flesh. She was about to destroy it when Dwaipayana appeared before her. She said: "O Rishi, you granted me the boon of a hundred sons. See what I have!"

'The Rishi told her to sprinkle the ball with water and bring a hundred pots of clarified butter. The ball was divided into a hundred parts the size of a thumb and each was put into a pot, and the pots were left for two years.

'The first to be born was Duryodhana, who began to cry and bray like an ass; and at the sound vultures and crows also began to utter cries, winds began to blow and fires broke out. . . .

'At once jackals and other beasts began to howl, and hearing these frightful omens the wise Vidura said: "It is evident that this your son shall be the destroyer of your race. The prosperity of all depends on his being abandoned. If you keep him calamities will surely follow. O King, you will still have ninety-nine sons; if you wish for the good of your race and of the world, cast this child away. It has been said that for the sake of a family one member should be cast off; for the sake of a village, a family; for the sake of a country, a village; and for the sake of a soul the whole world!"

'But Dhritarashtra had not the heart to do so.

'After Duryodhana the other ninety-nine sons were born in succession; also a daughter named Dussala.'

Janamejaya said: 'O tongue of Brahma, now that you have told me about the birth of the hundred sons and one daughter of Dhritarashtra, I wish to hear how the Pandavas, the sons of Pandu, were born.'

Vaisampayana said: Among the Yadavas was a king named Sura, who had a beautiful daughter named Pritha. It happened that Pritha once pleased the terrible Brahmana, Durvasa, by the way she carried out her duties. The sage, having foreknowledge that Pandu, her future husband, would not be able to have children, imparted to her a mantra, whereby she could summon what God she wished, to give her sons.

'But instead of waiting as she should have done, she, out of curiosity, wished to see if the mantra would work, and though a maiden, she invoked Surya, the Sun God, who at once appeared. She was overcome with confusion, but he approached and asked her: "O black-eyed one, what do you wish?"

'Pritha said: "O Bharata, a Brahmana gave me the mantra and I used it only to test its power. I ask your forgiveness. A woman, whatever her offence, deserves to be forgiven."

'Surya said: "I know all that Durvasa has said. Do not be afraid, but grant me the happiness of embracing you. And you know that my embraces are always fruitful. Having summoned me you are bound to fulfil the purpose of the summons, otherwise you will be guilty of a grave sin."

'He talked with her for a long time in order to allay her anxiety, but from fear of her relatives she would not consent. At length he said: "O Princess, I promise that you shall not suffer on my account," and so saying he took her. At once a son, Karna, was born from their union, encased in natural armour and wearing ear-rings. As soon as he was born Surya restored her virginity, and ascended to heaven. But she, from shame, threw Karna into a river; he was, however, rescued by Radha and her husband, who brought him up. Later on Indra, to benefit his son Arjuna, asked Karna for his armour; Karna agreed and was given in return a dart with power to kill one person, whether God, man, or Rakshasa.

'Although the large-eyed Pritha, daughter of Kuntibojha, was beautiful and accomplished, no king had asked for her, so her father invited kings and princes from many countries to visit him. And when they were all seated he bade his daughter select a husband from among them. The intelligent Pritha entered the hall and looking down on that great gathering, her eyes rested on Pandu, proud as a lion, with the strength of a bull. At once she began to tremble with emotion; then, walking modestly, she went to him and placed the marriage garland round his neck. Seeing that she had made her choice, the rest of the princes and kings returned to their homes on elephants and horses and in chariots.

'After the marriage ceremonies Pandu returned to his capital with Pritha, his queen.

'In due course, according to custom, Pandu chose a second wife, Madri, the daughter of the King of Madra. And on an auspicious day, he married her. For some time, he gave himself up to his wives and to the enjoyment of them and of their company.

'He then determined to subdue the robber tribes and the kings who had in the past taken the Kuru lands; and with the permission of Bhishma and his elders set out. He consumed all who came against him, so that the kings of the world paid tribute to him.

'Pandu, one day, while hunting on the slopes of Himavat saw in the forest a huge stag coupling with his doe. Letting fly five arrows, Pandu pierced both the deer. They fell to the ground and the stag began to weep bitterly, like a man. For he was no deer, but the son of a great Rishi, and had been enjoying his wife in the form of a deer.

'He spoke to Pandu and said: "O King, even wicked men do not do this that you have done. You belong to a virtuous race. How is it then that you have forgotten yourself and done such a cruel deed?" Pandu replied: "When kings go out to hunt deer they kill them as they do their enemies when chasing them. Even Rishis hunt deer and sacrifice them to the Gods. Why do you reproach me?"

'The deer said: "Virtuous kings do not attack their enemies when they are unprepared, but first declare war. I do not blame you for killing deer, but to kill any creature in the act of copulation is a great sin. When male and female join together it is agreeable to every creature; it is ordained by the Gods, and is productive of good to all. You should have waited until the act had been completed. You yourself have known the pleasures of sexual union, and you are also acquainted with morality. I am a Muni, existing on fruits and roots, and I have lived in peace with all. Sometimes I assume the form of a deer and roam through the woods with my mate. We had gone to a secluded spot in the forest and you came upon us and killed us. For this I shall curse you—not for killing a Brahmana (for you were not aware of this), but for killing a deer at such a time. So then, when you wish to have your wives, and you join with them, as soon as you do this you shall go to the world of Spirits, and your wife shall follow you. As you brought grief to me whilst I was enjoying happiness, so shall the same happen to you."

'So saying, the deer died, and Pandu was dismayed and sorrowful. He wept bitterly, and said: "Oh, the Gods have forsaken me. There is only one thing for me to do. I will give up my kingdom, my family, my friends; I will shave my head and wander alone over the earth and by enduring severe penances free myself from all my sins. I shall seek nothing, neither will I mock anyone nor knit my brows at them. I will not harm the four orders of life—beasts, birds, worms and plants, but devote myself to the good of all creatures. I shall not desire either to live or to die, and shall regard impartially those who do me good or ill."

'Looking at his wives and sighing, he bade them go to his people and tell them what he intended to do. But they begged him to let them stay with him. So he delivered his jewels and robes to his attendants, ordering them to return to Hastinapura.

'Pandu, after reflection, called Pritha and said to her: "Strive to raise sons for me in this time of distress. You know that on account of my evil act I cannot have children, but the self-born Manu has said that a man who cannot beget children on his wife may have them through her by other men."

'Pritha said: "Do not speak like this. No man in the world is superior to you. Embrace me, let us have children, and I will die with you. Death is a friend to a woman without a husband."

'Pandu replied: "What you say is true. But I will tell you about the customs of old which were lauded by the great Rishis. In former times women were not kept at home dependent on husbands and relatives. They went about freely; nor did they keep to their husbands, and for this they were not regarded as wicked. And so it is today among the Northern Kurus. The custom of a woman having but one husband is quite recent. The Vedas have declared that a wife should obey her husband; and so, O woman of faultless beauty, joining my palms I place them on your head as an act of propitiation. I ask you to raise sons for me, for only thus shall I be able to tread the path that is reserved for those blest with children."

'Pritha said: "You know that in my youth, I was granted a boon by the Rishi—a mantra for invoking the Gods to help me. O foremost of men, tell me which of the Celestials I shall summon. I await your commands."

'Pandu replied: "First summon the God of Justice, the most virtuous of the Celestials. The son he begets on you shall be the first among the Kurus." '

Vaisampayana continued: 'In due time Pritha summoned the God of Justice, who appeared seated in his resplendent chariot. Smiling he asked,: "O Pritha, what do you wish of me?" Pritha, also smiling, said: "I wish you to give me a son!" The God joyfully granted her request, and from the union was born an excellent child, and a voice from the skies said: "This child shall be the first of men and the most virtuous, and he shall rule the earth. This first-born of Pandu shall be called Yudhisthira."

'Pandu again spoke to Pritha: "The wise have said that a Kshatriya must be endowed with great physical strength. Therefore ask for such a son." Thus commanded, Pritha summoned Vayu, the mighty God of the winds, who came to her riding on a deer. "What do you wish, O Pritha?" he asked. Smiling modestly, she said: "Give me, O Celestial Being, a son of great strength and large limbs, capable of humbling the pride of anyone." Vayu then possessed her, and when the child was born, a voice said: "This child shall be called Bhima, of mighty arms and fierce energy." And so it was. And once, while he was asleep on her lap, a tiger frightened his mother, so that she leapt up, and the child falling on to a great rock, the rock was smashed into a hundred pieces. On the very day that Bhima was born, Duryodhana also was born.

'After the birth of Bhima, Pandu began to consider how he might have a son who would achieve great fame. "Everything in the world," he thought, "depends on destiny and effort. But destiny cannot be actualised without timely effort. Indra is the chief of the Gods, of immeasurable might and glory. If I gratify him I shall obtain a son who shall be capable of overcoming men and Rakshasas."

'He then stood on one leg for a whole year, his mind fixed in meditation. At last Indra, gratified, said: "I will give you a son who will be celebrated over the three worlds and who will cherish the welfare of Brahmanas, men and cows. He will be the despair of the wicked and the delight of the good—the embodiment of Kshatriya virtues."

'Pandu told all this to Pritha, who went away and invoked Sakra Indra, the ruler of the Gods, who came to her and got a child on her. As soon as the child was born, a voice loud and deep as the clouds, filling the welkin, said: "This child, O Pritha, shall be equal in energy to Siva himself; he shall increase your joy and uphold the prosperity of the Kuru race; he shall overcome the enemies of the Gods and become famous in his own generation and those that succeed him." '

Vaisampayana continued: 'After the birth of Pandu's sons and the hundred sons of Dhritarashtra, Pandu's second wife, Madri, said to him: "O sinless one, I do not complain that Pritha, though inferior to me in birth, is above me as your first wife; neither do I grudge Ghandhari her hundred sons, but it grieves me that I have no children of my own. I do not like to ask Pritha if she would object to my having children, but I beg you to ask her for me."

'Pandu replied: "O Madri, I have often thought about this. Now that you tell me you wish for children I will approach Pritha and I know she will not refuse." When Pandu spoke to Pritha about Madri's wish for children, she agreed to use the mantra, and said to Madri, "Which of the Gods do you wish to be the father of your children? Tell me, and I will invoke him." Madri, after reflecting, thought of the twin Aswins. They came to her, and by them she had twin sons, Nakula and Sahadeva; and a voice was heard saying: "These children shall transcend in energy and beauty even their fathers, the Aswins."

'The eldest of Pritha's sons was Yudhisthira, the second Bhimasena, the third Arjuna; of Madri's, the first-born twin was Nakula and the next Sahadeva, and they all grew up in beauty, accomplishments and courage equal almost to the Gods.

'When Pandu saw his five handsome sons growing up in the forest on the slopes of the mountain, he felt his sexual force returning, and one day, accompanied by Madri, he went out to wander in the woods. It was the time of Spring, the season that causes unrest in all born creatures. Flowers bloomed everywhere filling the woods with gentle perfume, and the pools were full of lotus-blossoms. Pandu in the midst of all this sat down to rest with the youthful Madri, gazing at her beauty; and his desire for her flared up like a forest fire. Unable to restrain himself, he put his arms around her, while she, knowing that his death would be the result, endeavoured to restrain him. But intoxicated

with desire, and as if he wished to put an end to his life, he
united himself to her, and no sooner was this done than
his life left him, in accordance with the Rishi's curse.
Madri, clasping the body of her lord, began to weep. Then
she went to Pritha and told her what had happened.
Pritha at first reproached her; but afterwards said that she
at least was fortunate in that she had seen Pandu's face,
for a moment, suffused with happiness. They disputed as
to which of them should ascend the funeral pyre, each
wishing to be the one. At last it was agreed that Madri
should do so. The body of Pandu, having been brought
back to Hastinapura, was anointed with fragrant ointment
and sandal paste, and dressed in a white dress. When it
was placed on the pyre, Madri ascended and lay beside her
lord. A torch was put to the wood, and both the dead and
the living were soon burnt to ashes.

(from *Mahābhārata*, Adi Parva, as selected by S. C. Nott,
The Mahābhārata, pp. 54-67.

THE RĀMĀYANA:
THE DEFENCE OF DHARMA

The *Rāmāyana* tells how Rāma, most perfect of princes, was
banished from his kingdom for fourteen years because his
father, King Dasratha, made a vow to his stepmother, Kaikeyī,
that he would grant her whatever she asked. When Kaikeyī
asked that Rāma should be banished and her own son, Bharata,
should become heir, all of the main characters—the King,
Rāma, Bharata—were confronted with problems of conflicting
loyalties. Perhaps even more important than the working out
of the story are the statements on ideal conduct that follow
as these problems are resolved. In the following selection all
of Rāma's friends, including his father and finally even his
stepmother, urge him to disregard the vow, but Rāma insists
that his primary duty is as a son, and that the word his father

has spoken must be fulfilled, even though it means hardship for the kingdom. Rāma's arguments provide a valuable insight into the inner meaning of Hindu ethics.

The princes surrounded by relatives and friends passed the night sorrowing. The day having dawned, the brothers observed the fire sacrifice and performed the repetition of silent prayer on the banks of the river Mandakini, then entering the hermitage of Rama, they sat in profound silence, no one uttering a word, a great peace prevailing over all.

At length, Shri Bharata, in the midst of his friends, broke the silence and thus addressed Shri Rama: "O My Brother, our illustrious sovereign conferred the kingdom on me to satisfy my mother and fulfil the obligation of his former boons and my mother having given this kingdom to me, I now offer it to thee, enjoy it without hindrance. When the dam bursts in the rainy season, none can stem the tide, similarly none but thee can protect this vast dominion. O King, as an ass cannot equal the pace of a horse, nor an ordinary bird's flight that of an eagle, so am I unable to rule the kingdom without thee. . . .

The people hearing Shri Bharata's words applauded them saying, "Well said!" "Well said!"

Then the compassionate Rama perceiving Bharata afflicted and lamenting, consoled him saying: "O Bharata, man is not free, time drags him hither and thither. All objects perish, all individualised souls must depart when their merit is exhausted; sons, friends, wives, all who live must die one day. Hoarding and spending, prosperity and destitution, meeting and parting, life and death are all akin. When the ripe fruit falls, we are not surprised, thus a man being born should not fear when death claims him. . . .

"I cannot disregard the commands of my illustrious father, he is worthy to be obeyed by thee and me, being our parent and our ruler. O Son of Raghu, I shall, therefore, obey his will and dwell in the forest. O Chief of Men, those who desire felicity in a future state, and who are virtuous and benevolent should obey their elders. O Great One, bear in mind the behests of our father, a lover of truth, and return to the capital to rule over the kingdom!"

Rama, the lover of his people, having spoken, ceased; then the pious Bharata answered Rama, putting forth persuasive arguments of righteous purport, saying: "O Lord, who is there in this world like thee? Adversity does not move thee, nor does any agreeable thing touch thee. All look on thee as their superior, yet thou seekest counsel of thine elders!

"The man to whom the living and dead are one and who is indifferent as to what he possesses or loses, for what reason should he grieve? O Lord, those who like thee, know, as thou dost, what is the nature of the soul and its essence, are not moved in the hour of distress!

"O Prince of Raghu, like the gods, thou art magnanimous, thou art ever forbearing and faithful to thy vows. Thou art wise, thou knowest and seest all! Thou art aware of the motives of men's actions and the cause of their abandoning them, therefore, that distress which is insupportable to others, does not, in any wise, disturb thee."

Having spoken thus, Bharata continued: "O Rama, be gracious to me, though during my absence in a strange land, my mother committed those sins which cause my affliction. I am bound by the ties of duty, else would I have slain my wicked mother. What is evil and what is good is known to me, descended as I am from the righteous King Dasaratha, therefore I am unable to act contrary to virtue. I cannot speak evil in the assembly of my pious and aged father, who has passed away, and where is a man to be found so wholly acquainted with the law of righteousness as was the king, yet what person familiar with the moral law, would commit so great a wrong prompted by the desire to please a woman? There is an ancient saying that, at the approach of death, man loses the power of judgment! The king has verily justified this adage to the whole world!

Through fear of Queen Kaikeyi's wrath or her threat of self-imposed destruction, or through mental agitation, the king may have acted thus without consulting his subjects, but thou art not bound by such a deed. He who imputes the transgressions of his father to righteous motives is not considered a good son; as heir to the king, reveal not the errors of thy sire, but conceal this unjust deed from the world.

"O Hero, it is thy duty to save my mother Kaikeyi, my father, my relatives and myself from the consequences of this action condemned by all. O Brother, remember thy duty as a warrior and reflect on the outcome of thy sojourn in the forest as an ascetic, but do thou also consider the good of thy people. It becomes thee not to undertake this course of action. The first duty of a warrior is to be installed so that he may be able to protect his people. Say, why should a man giving up that which is an established duty, embrace that which is wretched, cheerless, visionary and undefined? If, O Blessed One, thou desirest to undertake this mortification, why dost thou not seek it through the arduous labour of ruling the four castes? It is said that the duty of the householder is the highest dharma, then, why dost thou abandon it?

"O Lord, hear me; I am but thy child in respect of learning, age and state, how should I be able to govern the kingdom? I, a child, void of understanding and virtue and in rank also thine inferior; how should I be able to live without thee much less rule in thy stead? Therefore, O Raghava, O Thou Virtuous One, do thou, with thy relatives govern the kingdom without opposition and acquire merit! The great sage, the Holy Vasishtha, is here present with the ministers and priests, permit thyself to be crowned and return with us to Ayodhya!

"As Indra, having conquered his foes, entered heaven attended by the Maruts, do thou enter Ayodhya, thereby discharging thy duties to the gods, the sages, and thine ancestors, gratifying the ambitions of thy friends! Regard me as thy servant and command me! O Noble One, let thy

friends to-day rejoice at thine enthronement and let the
evil doers flee to the uttermost ends of the earth! O Chief
of Men, wash away the taint of my mother's guilt and deliver our great parent from this heinous sin. With my head
bent in submission, I entreat thee; as Shri Vishnu shows
his compassion to all beings, do thou show mercy to us.
Shouldst thou however reject my prayer and go hence to
some other forest, then will I follow thee there!"

Shri Rama, thus entreated by Shri Bharata, who had
placed his head at the feet of his brother in humility, still
remained steadfast in his vow and did not waver or consent to return to Ayodhya. Beholding the constancy of
Shri Rama, all present rejoiced to see him so faithful to his
vow, yet bewailed his determination not to return to the
capital.

(from Valmiki, *Rāmāyana*, translated by Hari Prasad Shastri,
pp. 382-88)

PART THREE

THE FLOWERING OF
THE TRADITION

~~~~~~~~~~

(300-1200 A.D.)

INTRODUCTION

The fourth and fifth centuries A.D. are usually referred to as the Classical Age because the achievements in art and literature during these centuries provided the standards of excellence against which the more ancient as well as the later products of the culture are judged. This tendency to impose a style and form upon the imagination ultimately became a stultifying legacy, but for centuries it served to channel the exuberant streams of Indian creativity into an art that was both disciplined and vital. While it is obviously impossible to give terminal dates to this process of artistic and intellectual growth, political changes as well as observable cultural traits suggest those chosen for the selections in the section. The fourth century saw the establishment of the powerful Gupta dynasty (c. 320-540 A.D.), and by 1200 A.D. the Islamic invaders from the northwest had begun through their political hegemony to alter the direction of Indian social development.

The rise of the Gupta dynasty can be seen as a manifestation of the impulse to political unification, which is one of the characteristic motifs of Indian history. Like the Mauryan Empire of five centuries before, it was based on Magadha in modern Bihar, and gradually extended its control over most of North India. During the two hundred years that the Guptas maintained their power India quite possibly enjoyed the greatest period of material prosperity in its history, and this physical wellbeing, combined with political stability and self-confidence, is undoubtedly reflected in the flowering of art and culture. And as a corollary, the fall of the Empire in the sixth century must have hastened a decline in cultural achievement.

Poetry and drama were two areas of particular accomplishment during the Gupta Empire, and in general both appear to have been composed for a sophisticated, courtly audience. By this time Sanskrit had become a highly developed language, with a very scientific grammatical structure, and the poets, both in lyric and dramatic poetry, made full use of all its potentialities. While the Indian theater may have had its remote origins in temple rituals, in the hands of the dramatists of the Gupta period it mirrored the brilliant secular society that patronized it. An interesting feature of this poetic drama is that it does not know tragedy in the European understanding of the term, and the happy ending demanded by literary convention indicates, on one level, the emphasis and taste of the society. On a deeper level, the absence of tragedy is explainable in terms of the basic Indian belief in *karma*, with its insistence that man is responsible for the good or evil that befalls him. There is little place for the assertion of human will against any forces outside and beyond human control.

Perhaps the same temperament that demanded happy endings also accounts for the extraordinary vitality and energy shown in the painting and sculpture of the period. One particular feature of this vitality, the strongly sensuous and erotic element, has frequently been interpreted in a religious sense, as representing the longing of the soul for union with the divine, but this seems to be a forced interpretation. It is more likely that it is a reflection of the artists'—and the society's—awareness of the close relationship of the vitality of the imagination to the process of growth and change in nature.

Other areas of culture where there was considerable advance in this period were medicine, astronomy, and mathematics. While the modern Western tendency is to classify such fields as science, and to separate them from other cultural movements, in ancient India they were closely identified with religious concerns. For this reason alone it is difficult to identify ideas that are strictly comparable to Greek and Western science, but the difficulty is compounded by the fact that no one with the requisite breadth of scientific, religious, and linguistic skills has given his attention to the study of this aspect of the Hindu tradition. It is clear, nevertheless, that during the Gupta period Indians possessed mathematical concepts unknown to the Western world at that time. The most notable of these discoveries was the decimal system, a knowledge of which passed to Europe through the Arabs. Indian knowledge of medicine also seems to have been very advanced, as were surgical techniques. It was astronomy, however, that received the most attention in the texts. This interest had an extremely practical basis in the very highly developed practice of astrology, which occupies a unique place in the Hindu tradition. All the great events of life, such as marriage, were conducted in strict conformity with astrological data, and while this aspect of the tradition is one that arouses little sympathy in the outside observer it is important to recognize the extraordinary complexity of the study. It is probably no exaggeration to say that the precision needed in the study of horoscopes is comparable to that used in modern scientific reasoning.

In terms of literary works and of great movements the religious achievements of the era were perhaps less striking than in the preceding period, but as a time of synthesis the importance of the Gupta age cannot be overemphasized. Just as in the arts the imagination was disciplined into forms that have remained canonical for Indian taste, so in religion the disparate forms of experience were absorbed into the structure of orthodoxy. The resulting synthesis was not a new religion, since the *Vedas* still remained as the fundamental texts and the position of the

Brāhman priesthood was unchallenged, but the old rituals were largely replaced by forms of worship that emphasized devotion to a particular deity. Closely related to this was the use of images to represent the gods and the erection of temples as the center of their worship.

The synthesis of the devotional cults with the older Brahmanical tradition found literary expression in the *Purānas*. The word itself means "ancient," but the reference is not so much to the age of the books themselves as to the subjects they deal with—the origins and history of the gods, the creation of the world, the genealogies of kings. The *Purānas* are regarded as scripture, and it is through them that the legends and stories of the tradition have reached the common people. The almost endless variety of Indian religious experience that is given a place in them provides opportunity for the most varied temperaments to find something congenial, thus making it possible to bring the skeptical agnostic and the passionate theist, the profound philosopher and the illiterate peasant, under one encompassing roof.

The religious synthesis was strengthened, perhaps made possible, by philosophical developments that reached their height after the fourth century A.D. Philosophical speculation had, of course, a much more ancient beginning than this, but apparently the systemization and codification of the traditional "six systems" of Indian philosophy took place at this time. These systems are not philosophical statements comparable to Western models, nor are they really comparable to each other, but taken as a whole they provided an impressive intellectual framework for the Hindu tradition.

The great cultural, religious, and philosophical movements of the Classical Age coalesced to give Hinduism its distinctive characteristics. So deeply were these interwoven into the fabric of the social structure that the shocks administered to Indian life by the invasion of the Muslims in the eleventh and twelfth centuries did not destroy the essential unity that had been created.

CHAPTER VIII

THE LITERARY

REFLECTION

∽∽∽∽∽∽∽

Nowhere was the flowering of the Hindu tradition more conspicuous than in the literary arts, and in distinction to other ages of Indian civilization the particular glories of the period were secular, not sacred, works. Although this division can be made only with great qualification, since even the most secular of Indian works are integrated within a religious framework, nevertheless there is a great body of literature that served primarily to entertain and delight without apparently seeking to penetrate very deeply into the human condition.

For a variety of reasons the literary classics of India, as distinct from the religious texts, have not made a great impression upon Western readers. This is partly due to fundamental problems in aesthetics, since the canons of taste are very different, but translation difficulties have also contributed to the failure of Sanskrit literature to make a wide appeal. Not only does much of its charm depend upon sound, but within the tradition a value was placed on displays of ingenuity and virtuosity that are foreign to Western, especially English, literary conventions. Furthermore, the precision of Sanskrit vocabulary and grammar imposes restrictions on translators that have prevented the classics' being rendered into lively, modern English.

Yet if translation from the great age of Sanskrit literature cannot adequately convey its beauty, it can show a
pattern of life and the way that artists handled the materials that were available to them. The poets and dramatists
moved within the conventions of their tradition and neither questioned nor defended its values, but rather accepted them as the framework of the universe. This means
that there is remarkably little tension within the literature,
no striving to exalt personal will, no denunciation of fate
or of the gods. Instead, the great works of the period present a picture of man at peace with himself and with his
society.

The following selections illustrate various familiar
themes—the pains and pleasures of passionate human
love, the virtues and vices of women, the greatness of
kings, the beauty of nature, and, on a somewhat different
level, the need for worldly wisdom. While the treatment
of these themes is frequently idealized, the values and beliefs of the tradition stand out in clear relief, and while the
passages cannot convey much of the power of the originals
they serve to embody some aspects of the life of the Hindu
tradition.

The Pleasures of Love

One of the recognized ends of life within the Hindu tradition
was the enjoyment of physical love, and the poets were fond
of depicting the stirring of passionate emotion. One of the
most famous of these love scenes is contained in the play
Shakuntalā, where Kālidās, the greatest of Indian dramatists,
describes with great delicacy the meeting of King Dushyanta
and Shakuntalā, who is a hermit's daughter. As the scene
opens, the King, who has been hunting in the forest, hears
Shakuntalā complaining to her two companions that her dress
is becoming too tight for her. Through such statements, and
by combining references to nature with images of sexual desire—the vine clasping the tree, the opening flower, the bee

drinking nectar—the author creates a mood of expectancy and longing. The continuity between the life of man and that of the natural world suggested here is an important theme in Indian literature.

KING

This youthful form, whose bosom's swelling charms
By the bark's knotted tissue are concealed,
Like some fair bud close folded in its sheath,
Gives not to view the blooming of its beauty.
But what am I saying? In real truth, this bark-dress,
though ill-suited to her figure, sets it off like an ornament.
The lotus with mean plants entwined
Is not a whit less brilliant: dusky spots
Heighten the lustre of the cold-rayed moon:
This lovely maiden in her dress of bark
Seems all the lovelier. Yet the meanest garb
Gives to true beauty fresh attractiveness.

SHAKUNTALĀ   [*Looking before her.*

That Keshara-tree beckons to me with its young shoots, which, as the breeze waves them to and fro, appear like slender fingers. I will go and attend to it.

[*Walks towards it.*

PRIYAMVADĀ

Dear Shakuntalā, please rest in that attitude one moment.

SHAKUNTALĀ

Why so?

PRIYAMVADĀ

The Keshara-tree, whilst your graceful form bends about its stem, appears as if it were wedded to some lovely twining creeper.

SHAKUNTALĀ

Ah! saucy girl, you are most appropriately named Priyamvadā ("Speaker of flattering things").

KING

What Priyamvadā says, though complimentary, is nevertheless true. Verily,

Her ruddy lip vies with the opening bud;
Her graceful arms are as the twining stalks;
And her whole form is radiant with the glow
Of youthful beauty, as the tree with bloom.

ANASŪYĀ

See, dear Shakuntalā, here is the young jasmine, which you named "the Moonlight of the Grove," the self-elected wife of the mango-tree. Have you forgotten it?

SHAKUNTALĀ

Rather will I forget myself. [*Approaching the plant and looking at it.*] How delightful is the season when the jasmine-creeper and the mango-tree seem thus to unite in mutual embraces! The fresh blossoms of the jasmine resemble the bloom of a young bride, and the newly-formed shoots of the mango appear to make it her natural protector. [*Continues gazing at it.*

PRIYAMVADĀ [*Smiling.*

Do you know, my Anasūyā, why Shakuntalā gazes so intently at the jasmine?

ANASŪYĀ

No, indeed, I cannot imagine. I pray thee tell me.

PRIYAMVADĀ

She is wishing that as the jasmine is united to a suitable tree, so, in like manner, she may obtain a husband worthy of her.

SHAKUNTALĀ

Speak for yourself, girl; this is the thought in your own
mind.   [*Continues watering the flowers.*

KING

Would that my union with her were permissible! and
yet I hardly dare hope that the maiden is sprung from a
caste different from that of the Head of the hermitage.
But away with doubt:

That she is free to wed a warrior-king
My heart attests. For, in conflicting doubts,
The secret promptings of the good man's soul
Are an unerring index of the truth.

However, come what may, I will ascertain the fact.

SHAKUNTALĀ   [*In a flurry.*

Ah! a bee, disturbed by the sprinkling of the water, has
left the young jasmine, and is trying to settle on my face.

[*Attempts to drive it away.*

KING   [*Gazing at her ardently.*

Beautiful! there is something charming even in her re-
pulse.

Where'er the bee his eager onset plies,
Now here, now there, she darts her kindling eyes:
What love hath yet to teach, fear teaches now,
The furtive glances and the frowning brow.

[*In a tone of envy.*

Ah happy bee! how boldly dost thou try
To steal the lustre from her sparkling eye;
And in thy circling movements hover near,
To murmur tender secrets in her ear;
Or, as she coyly waves her hand, to sip
Voluptuous nectar from her lower lip!
While rising doubts my heart's fond hopes destroy,
Thou dost the fulness of her charms enjoy.

(from Kālidās, *Shakuntalā,* translated by Monier Williams,
pp. 14-17)

The Pain of Love

Bhavabhūti, a playwright who lived early in the eighth century A.D., wrote of the pains, as well as the pleasures, of love. In the following scene from *Mālati and Mādhava* the hero is telling his friends of his first sight of the beautiful Mālati. The emphasis of the play on the distress that comes from separation from one's beloved, and the anguish one feels as one longs to be reunited with her, is a common motif of Indian drama.

MĀDH. Led by her maidens to collect the flowers
   That thickly hung on my o'ershadowing tree,
   She neared the spot. Ah! then too plain I noted
   The signs of passion, for some happy youth
   Long entertained, the lovely maid revealed.
   As slender as the lotus stalk her shape;
   Her pallid cheeks, like unstained ivory,
   Rivalled the beauty of the spotless moon;
   And still her prompt compliance with the wishes
   Of her attendant damsels showed herself
   Indifferent to all. I scarce had gazed
   Upon her, but my eye felt new delight,
   As bathed with nectar, and she drew my heart
   As pow'rfully as attracts the magnet gem
   The unresisting ore, at once towards her.
   That heart, though causeless be its sudden passion,
   Is fixed on her for ever, chance what may,
   And though my portion be henceforth despair.
   The goddess destiny decrees at pleasure
   The good or ill of all created beings.
MAK. Nay, Mādhava, this cannot be, believe me,
   Without some cause. Behold! all nature's sympathies
   Spring not from outward form, but inward virtue.
   The lotus buds not till the sun has risen;
   Nor melts the moon-gem till it feels the moon.

What then ensued?

MĀDH. When her fair train beheld me, they exchanged
Expressive looks and smiles, and each to each,
As if they knew me, murmured—This is he!
The music of their tinkling zones was stilled,
Repressed the silver echo of their anklets
Sharp clanging to their undulating motion.
Hushed was the melody their bracelets made,
Whilst their fair lotus palms, in sportive mood,
Were beating measure to their merriment.
Silent they stood, and with extended fingers,
As if they said, "The fates have favoured us,
Lady, behold *him* here!" . . .

MAK. Proceed, my friend.

MĀDH. What words shall picture what those looks con-
            veyed;
The lore of love those lotus eyes revealed?
What firmness could resist the honest warmth
Of nature's mute expressiveness, nor fall
Before those orbs, that now like opening buds,
Beneath the creeper of the tremulous brow
Expansive bloomed, and now retiring shrunk
But half-averted from the answering gaze,
Then dropped the veiling lashes o'er their bright-
            ness?
I felt their influence, and those looks of love,
Beaming with mild timidity, and moist
With sweet abandonment, bore off my heart—
Nay plucked it from my bosom by the roots
All pierced with wounds.
Incredulous of my happiness, I sought
To mark her passion, nor display my own,
Though every limb partook the fond emotion.
Thence I resumed my task, and wove my wreath,
Seeming intent, till she at length withdrew
Attended by her maidens and a guard
Of eunuchs armed with staves and javelins.
A stately elephant received the princess

And bore her towards the city. Whilst they moved,
As winds the lily on its slender stalk,
So turned her head towards the grove of *Kāma*
   (the God of Love),
And from her delicate lids she shot retiring
Glances, with venom and ambrosia tipped.
My breast received the shafts. A mingled flame
And deathly chillness, since alternate spread
Throughout my form, and doom me to such agony
Words cannot paint, the world has never witnessed.
Perception dimly pictures present objects,
And past perceptions fade from recollection!
Vain were the lunar ray or gelid stream
To cool my body's fever, whilst my mind
Whirls in perpetual round, and knows not rest.

(from Bhavabhūti, *Mālati and Mādhava*, trans. by H. H. Wilson, *The Theatre of the Hindus*, II, pp. 22-24)

The Perils of Love

Bhartrihari, a poet who is said to have lived in the seventh century, wrote a cycle of one-stanza poems in which he displayed to a remarkable degree the ambiguous attitude to women and love so often found in the Hindu tradition. He feels, almost simultaneously, the attractions of physical love as well as of asceticism. Possibly he is suggesting that there are two ways of life, and one must choose one or the other; or he may be saying that both ways of life make such a powerful appeal that there is no use trying to separate them. Like Kalidās, he blends images from nature with symbols of erotic desire to create his effects.

No doubt sensual pleasures lead to no good result, and prevent us from properly renouncing the world. People may think and speak thus, but there is nevertheless something powerful and, indeed, indefinable, in sensuality; something that can even agitate the souls of those who have turned away from the world to devote themselves to meditation and the search for truth.

You, for your part, have found consolation in studying the divine Vedic writings, while we, on the other hand, are the disciples of poets whose words are always pleasing. You will therefore hold that there is nothing better on this earth than doing good to others, while we shall maintain that there is nothing better than lotus-eyed, beautiful women. . . .

It would have been an easy matter to pay for our passage over the ocean of existence if there had been no women with beautiful eyes to hinder our progress.

No one in this world, O king, has ever succeeded in crossing his ocean of desires. Of what use to us are abundant riches if we must let our youth slip away from us without the enjoyment of our wives whom we adore? Let us therefore hasten to our homes so that we may be able to reach them before the beauty of our loved ones has been withered by the approach of age. . . .

What greater calamity can a man suffer in this world than his own youth, which is at once the abiding-place of passion, the cause of dreadful agonies in hell, the seed of ignorance, the gatherings of clouds that hide the moon of knowledge, the great friend of the God of Love, and the chain that binds together innumerable sins.

Fortunate indeed is the person who can retain the mastery of his senses at the critical period of his youth—youth, this waterer of the tree of love, the rapid-flowing stream of sexual enjoyment, the dear friend of the God of Love, the full moon of the chakor-like eyes of women, and the treasury of happiness and wealth.

"Beautiful woman. What a divine expression! What a magnificent form!" cries the man who is blinded by passion; or, perhaps, "What a breast! What eye-brows!" In this way the sight of a beautiful woman delights him. He feels intoxicated with an excessive joy, and yet he may know very well that she is a woman whose impurity is known to the whole world.

How can we go on loving women when the thought of her warms our hearts, the sight of her intoxicates us, and a touch of her nearly drives us mad?

A woman is indeed the very incarnation of the purest ambrosia so long as we have her within sight; but no sooner is she beyond the range of our vision than she becomes worse even than poison.

Whatever young woman we may have in mind she is neither ambrosia nor poison—if she loves us she will be like an ambrosial creeper embracing us with its tendrils; but if she is indifferent she is like a poisonous plant.

A whirlpool of uncertainty, a palace of pride, a prison of punishment, a storehouse of sin, a fraud in a hundred different respects, an obstacle placed for us before the gates of paradise, the field of deceit, a basket of illusion, the open throat of hell: such are some of the features of women, who change nectar into poison and are as a chain by which man is attached to the chariot of folly.

It is certain enough that the face of a woman is not made up of the moon, that her eyes are not twin lotuses, and that her limbs are not really gold. Why, alas, have poets been led to deceive us in this manner? Men are capable of distinguishing; but nevertheless, deceived by the poets, they none the less adore those fawn-eyed women, even though they know well enough that their bodies are composed of nothing more than skin, flesh, and bone. . . .

We behold a young girl with a lotus-eyed face resembling the splendour of the moon, and we remark the ambrosia on her lips. Too soon this face, like a rotten piece of fruit, will lose all its flavour, and will begin to taste like bitter poison.

A young woman is like a river; for the lines of her body resemble the waves; her breasts represent the ducks swimming on the surface, the nymphs are seen in the brilliant colours of her face: but the bed of the river is dangerous, its course is difficult to perceive and leads rapidly to the ocean; so let men turn aside from it if they do not wish to be drowned.

(from Bhartrihari, *Sringāra Sataka,* stanzas 51-52, 68-77, 79-80, trans. by J. M. Kennedy)

A WIFE'S DEVOTION

By way of contrast to the passionate, demanding love of a young girl, the dramatists frequently picture the devotion offered by a wife to her husband. In the selection given here Shakuntalā is being advised by her father on the proper deportment of a wife, and, as one of the characters suggests, his words are a compendium of what the tradition understands to be the duties of a faithful wife. In this case the advice is made more meaningful to the audience by their knowledge that when Shakuntalā arrives at the palace of her husband he will reject her, denying that she is his wife and that he is the father of her child.

KANWA

Listen, then, my daughter. When thou reachest thy
husband's palace, and art admitted into his family,
    Honour thy betters; ever be respectful
    To those above thee; and, should others share
    Thy husband's love, ne'er yield thyself a prey
    To jealousy; but ever be a friend,
    A loving friend, to those who rival thee
    In his affections. Should thy wedded lord
    Treat thee with harshness, thou must never be
    Harsh in return, but patient and submissive.
    Be to thy menials courteous, and to all
    Placed under thee, considerate and kind:
    Be never self-indulgent, but avoid
    Excess in pleasure; and, when fortune smiles,

Be not puffed up. Thus to thy husband's house
Wilt thou a blessing prove, and not a curse.
What thinks Gautamī of this advice?

GAUTAMĪ

An excellent compendium, truly, of every wife's duties!
Lay it well to heart, my daughter.

KANWA

Come, my beloved child, one parting embrace for me
and for thy companions, and then we leave thee. . . .
Soon shall thy lord prefer thee to the rank
Of his own consort; and unnumbered cares
Befitting his imperial dignity
Shall constantly engross thee. Then the bliss
Of bearing him a son—a noble boy,
Bright as the day-star—shall transport thy soul
With new delights, and little shalt thou reck
Of the light sorrow that afflicts thee now
At parting from thy father and thy friends.

(from Kālidās, *Shakuntalā*, in Monier Williams, p. 100)

DIVINE AND HUMAN LOVE

Of all the legends about the gods, none has had a more
creative effect on the Indian imagination than the stories of
Krishna and his love for the milkmaids. While in modern
times there has been a tendency to allegorize these incidents,
with the milkmaids understood as the desire of the soul for
God, and Krishna's response symbolizing the generous response of God's love, it seems likely that originally the stories
were meant to be taken fairly literally. The Krishna who dallies
with endless beautiful maidens while his mistress Rādhā waits
for him consumed by passion can be understood as completing, not contradicting, the austere Krishna of the *Bhagavad
Gītā*. This aspect of Krishna's personality found its greatest

literary expression in the *Gītā Govinda,* a long poem written in Sanskrit by Jayadeva in the twelfth century. While this poem may appear to be a celebration of the joys and pains of physical desire, it is in fact widely sung as a religious lyric in praise of Krishna. Hari, lord, here refers to Krishna.

Sandal and garment of yellow and lotus garlands upon his body of blue,
In his dance the jewels of his ears in movement dangling over his smiling cheeks.
Hari here disports himself with charming women given to love!
The wife of a certain herdsman sings as Hari sounds a tune of love
Embracing him the while with all the force of her full and swelling breasts.
Hari here disports himself with charming women given to love!
Another artless woman looks with ardour on Krishna's lotus face
Where passion arose through restless motion of playful eyes with sidelong glances.
Hari here disports himself with charming women given to love!
Another comes with beautiful hips, making as if to whisper a word,
And drawing close to his ear the adorable Krishna she kisses upon the cheek.
Hari here disports himself with charming women given to love!
Another on the bank of the Jamna, when Krishna goes to a bamboo thicket,
Pulls at his garment to draw him back, so eager is she for amorous play.
Hari here disports himself with charming women given to love!
Hari praises another woman, lost with him in the dance of love,

The dance where the sweet low flute is heard in the
clamour of bangles on hands that clap.
Hari here disports himself with charming women given to
love!
He embraces one woman, he kisses another, and fondles
another beautiful one,
He looks at another one lovely with smiles, and starts in
pursuit of another woman.
Hari here disports himself with charming women given to
love!
May all prosperity spread from this, Shri Jayadeva's famed
and delightful
Song of wonderful Keshava's secret play in the forest of
Vrindāvana!
Hari here disports himself with charming women given to
love! . . .
With his limbs, tender and dark like rows of clumps of
blue lotus flowers,
By herd-girls surrounded, who embrace at pleasure, any
part of his body,
Friend, in spring beautiful Hari plays like Love's own self
Conducting the love sport, with love for all, bringing de-
light into being.

(from Jayadeva, *Gītā Govinda*, trans. by George Keyt)

THE CELEBRATION OF
A PRINCE'S BIRTH

The life of India during the classical age is reflected in the
works of Bāna, the chronicler of the deeds of the Emperor
Harsha (606-647 A.D.), who restored the political unity of
India for a short time in the seventh century. Bāna's descriptions frequently have a vivid mastery of detail that must owe

a good deal to actual observation of court life. One such passage is the account of the celebrations that followed the birth of Harsha. The lack of all restraints, which is in sharp contrast to the usual decorum of Indian life, is reminiscent of modern celebrations of such festivals as Holi. The exuberance shown in the scenes described here is quite in keeping, however, with the vitality and passion of much Hindu literature and art of the time.

Then the festal jubilation gradually blossomed forth. Here young people, of ancient noble houses and unused to dancing, showed by frolics their love for the king. There drunken slave women allured the favourites, while the monarch himself looked on with a secret smile. In one place respectable old feudatories were, much to his amusement, clasping the necks of the intoxicated bawds of the capital in a furious dance. In another place naughty slave boys, set on by a glance from the sovereign, betrayed in songs the secret amours of the ministers of state. Elsewhere wanton water-girls raised a laugh by embracing aged ascetics. Elsewhere again in the eagerness of ardent rivalry throngs of slaves carried on a war of foul language. In another place chamberlains knowing nothing of dancing were, to the entertainment of the maids, violently forced to dance by the king's women. The festival showed mountains of flower heaps, rum-booths like shower-baths, a hoar-frost of camphor dust, a booming of drums like Shiva's laugh, a hubbub like the ocean-churning, vortexes of dancing rings, a horripilation of rays from jewelled ornaments, a very tiara of sandal forehead marks, a never ceasing propagation of echoes, an endless efflorescence of tokens of favour.

Young men frolicked in thousands, prancing, like Kāmboja steeds, with garlands of flowers hanging upon their shoulders, leaping with dancing eyes like spotted antelopes, rending the earth with furious stamps. . . . Scarce could the earth sustain the tramp of troubadours dancing to time. Smash went the pearls in the ornaments of the young princes slapping each other in their play. Red powder crimsoned the earth in every part. . . . The heavens gleamed with clouds of perfume powder. . . . Yellowed with scattered scent dust, the daylight glowed, as though Brahmā's lotus, ground by the rocking world, had stained it with clouds of pollen from its filaments. Men tripped over heaps of pearls that fell from necklaces broken in collisions.

In this place and in that harlot-women danced to the accompaniment of instrumental music. Tambourines were slowly, slowly thumped; reeds sweetly piped, cymbals tinkled, string drums were belaboured, the low gourd lute sang, gently boomed the *kāhalas* with their brazen sounding boxes, while all the time a subdued clapping proceeded. Even the clank of jingling anklets kept time pace by pace, as if intelligent, with the clapping. Whispering softly, like cuckoos, in low passionate tones, they sang the words of vulgar mimes, ambrosia to their lovers' ears. Wreaths were about their brows, and chaplets round their ears, upon their foreheads sandal marks. With upraised creeper-like arms, vocal with rows of bracelets, they seemed to embrace the very sun. Like Kashmir colts, they leapt all aglow with saffron stains. Great garlands of amaranth hung down upon their round hips, as if they were ablaze with passion's flame. Their faces, marked with rows of vermilion spots, seemed to wear the rubric of the edict plates of Love, whose ordinances none may resist. Dusty were they with camphor and perfumes scattered in handfuls, like roads frequented by the desires of youth. Like women chamberlains of a children's festival, they lashed the young folk with great wreaths of flowers. With tossing forehead marks and earrings they swayed like creepers of Love's sandal tree. Like waves of passion's flood, they gleamed all resonant with the cries of anklets adding music to their steps. As to what was proper to be said or not, they were as void of discrimination as the childish play of happiness. While the rapid booming of the drums thrilled through their lithe frames, they cast off flower pollen. All day their faces were, like red lotuses, abloom; by night they slept no more than night lotuses. As if possessed, they were surrounded by throngs of princes. Like endearments, they stole away the heart; like songs, they kindled the flame of desire; like the symptoms of stoutness, they gave rise to joy. Adding passionateness to passion itself, a glow to love, a joy to joy, a dancing motion to dancing, festivity to festival, in ogling they seemed to drink with the white (shells) of their eyes, in scolding to imprison in cages of rays from their nails, in gestures of anger to lash with curling eyebrows, in making love to pour a rain of all (sweet) feelings, in deftly moving to scatter transformations.

In other places, where under the terror of chamberlains' wands the people had made room, the king's wives essayed the dance, a brilliant throng with a forest of white parasols held above them, as if they were wood nymphs roaming beneath trees of paradise. Some, wrapt in loose shawls hanging from both shoulders, swayed as if mounted on play swings. Some, with wavy robes torn by the edge of golden armlets, were like rivers lined by crossing ruddy-geese. Others, whose bright side glances were bounded by earrings entangled in tufts of white waving chowries, were like pools with swans plucking at forests of blue lotuses. Others, from whose tripping feet trickled a dew of lac-reddened sweat that besprinkled the palace swans, resembled moonlight nights when the twilight casts a glow upon the moon's disk. Others, with brows curved in derision at the contortions of chamberlains bending beneath golden girdles placed about their necks, seemed love-nets with outstretched arms for toils.

All womankind being thus set dancing, the earth, crimsoned by trickling lac from their feet, seemed rosy with the flush of love. Their round gleaming bosoms made the festival like a mass of auspicious pitchers. Their tossing arms caused the world to seem nought but rings of lotus roots. Their sparkling playful smiles created as it were a season all of lightning flashes. The days seemed dappled by the light of dancing eyes. Brilliant ear chaplets of flowers cast a green tint upon a daylight seemingly of parrots' tails. Dark hanging sprays of braided hair shed a blackness as of collyrium on the prospect. Uplifted tendril-like hands made all creation gleam like one red lotus-bed. The radiance of rainbow-tinted gems infused a colour of jays' wings into the sunlight. Echoing with clusters of tinkling ornaments, the heavens seemed nought but clanging bells. Even old ladies shouted like maniacs. Old men even lost all shame, as though bewitched. The wise forgot themselves, as if intoxicated. Even hermits' hearts were all agog for a dance. The king gave away all his fortune. Heaps of wealth were plundered by the folk on every side.

(from Bāna, *Harsacarita*, trans. by E. B. Cowell and F. W. Thomas, pp. 112-15)

THE SCIENCE OF PLEASURE

A distinctive mark of the Hindu tradition is the tendency to analyze and classify every aspect of human experience. One of the products of this is the *Kāmasūtra*, or *Aphorisms on Love*, by Vātsyāyana (c. 400 A.D.). The *Kāmasūtra* has an undeserved reputation in the West as a pornographic work, but it is in fact a rather pedantic classification of such things as ways of making love, the skills needed by a courtesan (including such rather surprising ones as metallurgy and architecture), and the daily routine of the cultured man-about-town. The following account of the way a young man should spend his time obviously bears little relation to the ordinary world, but it remains an ideal never quite forgotten by young men within the tradition.

After acquisition of learning, a person should with the help of the material resources obtained by him through gifts from others, personal gain, commerce or service, marry and set up a home, and then follow the ways of the man of taste and culture (*nāgaraka*).

He may make his abode, in accordance with the calling chosen by him, in a city, in a commercial center, or a town; any of these that he chooses should be inhabited by good people.

There he should make for himself a house, with water nearby, having a garden, provided with separate apartments for different activities, and having two retiring rooms.

In the retiring room in the forepart of the house, there shall be a fine couch, with two pillows, pliant at the center, having a pure white sheet; there shall be by its side another couch of lesser height [for lying down]; at the head, there shall be a wicker-seat [for doing his prayers] and a platform for the sandal paste left over after the night's use, a garland, a box for wax and scents, peelings of pomegranate fruit [a mouth deodorant] and betel leaves; a spittoon on the ground; a lute hanging on a bracket on the wall, a painting-board and box of colors, some books and garlands of flowers; not far away on the floor, different kinds of seats; a dice-board; outside the room, cages for the birds kept for playing with, and at a remote end [outside], things for private use.

In the garden a swing, well covered and under the shade of a tree, as also an earthen platform strewn with the falling flowers of the garden. Such is to be the layout of his residence.

He must get up early in the morning, answer the calls of nature, wash his teeth, smear his body with just a little fragrant paste, inhale fragrant smoke, wear some flower, just give the lips a rub with wax and red juice, look at his face in the mirror, chew betel leaves along with some mouth deodorants, and then attend to his work.

Every day he must bathe; every second day, have a massage; every third day, apply unguents to his legs; every fourth day have a partial shave and clipping of the nails;

every fifth or tenth day a more complete shave; he must frequently wipe off the perspiration in the armpit; have his food in the forenoon and afternoon.

After eating [in the forenoon] comes playing with parrots and myna birds and making them talk; and indulging in cock and ram fights and in other artistic activities; also attending to the work he has with his friends and companions. Then a little nap. In the forenoon still, he dresses and goes out for social calls and for enjoyment of the company of others. In the evening he enjoys music and dance. At the end of it, in his own apartments, decorated and fragrant with smoke, he awaits, along with his companions, his beloved who has given him an engagement, or else sends her a message and himself goes out to meet her. . . . Such is the daily routine.

He should arrange excursions in parties for attending festivals, salons for enjoying literature and art, drinking parties, excursions to parks, and group games. Once a fortnight or month, on the day sacred to particular deities, the actors and dancers attached to the temple of Sarasvatī [the Goddess of learning] gather and present shows [for the cultured citizens of the place]; or visiting actors and musicians from other places present their programs in the Sarasvatī temple.

(from Vātsyāyana, *Kamasūtra*, in *Sources of Indian Tradition*, pp. 260-61)

CAUTION AND COMMONSENSE

Over against the tendency within the Hindu tradition to go to extremes must be set an emphasis on moderation and commonsense found in much of the literature. The best known repository of such advice is the *Panchatantra*, a collection of stories whose ostensible purpose is to teach wisdom to kings but which must have always been intended for a wider audience. The original of this work is lost, but many versions were circulated. The one from which the story given below has been taken, the *Hitopadesha*, dates from the twelfth century in its present form. The stories were interlocked within a complicated framework of other stories, sometimes without any very obvious connection. The story used here, for example, of the Tiger and the Traveller, is told by Speckle-neck, King of the Pigeons, as a warning to be on guard against people who make generous offers. The story begins with a fowler setting a net for trapping pigeons.

Thus, replied Speckle-neck: I was pecking about one day in the Deccan forest, and saw an old tiger sitting newly bathed on the bank of a pool, like a Brahman, and with holy kuskus-grass in his paws.

"Ho! ho! ye travellers," he kept calling out, "take this golden bangle!"

Presently a covetous fellow passed by and heard him.

"Ah!" thought he, "this is a bit of luck—but I must not risk my neck for it either.

"Good things come not out of bad things; wisely leave a
*   longed-for ill.*
Nectar being mixed with poison serves no purpose but to
*   kill.*

"But all gain is got by risk, so I will see into it at least;" then he called out, "Where is thy bangle?"

The Tiger stretched forth his paw and exhibited it.

"Hem!" said the Traveller, "can I trust such a fierce brute as thou art?"

"Listen," replied the Tiger, "once, in the days of my cubhood, I know I was very wicked. I killed cows, Brahmans, and men without number—and I lost my wife and children for it—and haven't kith or kin left. But lately I met a virtuous man who counselled me to practise the duty of almsgiving—and, as thou seest, I am strict at ablutions and alms. Besides, I am old, and my nails and fangs are gone—so who would mistrust me? and I have so far conquered selfishness, that I keep the golden bangle for whoso comes. Thou seemest poor! I will give it thee. Is it not said,

"Give to poor men, son of Kūntī—on the wealthy waste
    not wealth;
 Good are simples for the sick man, good for nought to
    him in health.

"Wade over the pool, therefore, and take the bangle."
    Thereupon the covetous Traveller determined to trust him, and waded into the pool, where he soon found himself plunged in mud, and unable to move.
    "Ho! ho!" says the Tiger, "art thou stuck in a slough? stay, I will fetch thee out!"
    So saying he approached the wretched man and seized him—who meanwhile bitterly reflected—

"Be his Scripture-learning wondrous, yet the cheat will be
    a cheat;
 Be her pasture ne'er so bitter, yet the cow's milk will be
    sweet."

And on that verse, too—

"Trust not water, trust not weapons; trust not clawed nor
    horned things;
 Neither give thy soul to women, nor thy life to Sons of
    Kings."

And those others—

"Look! the Moon, the silver roamer, from whose splen-
    dour darkness flies.
With his starry cohorts marching, like a crowned king
    through the skies.
 All the grandeur, all the glory, vanish in the Dragon's
    jaw;
 What is written on the forehead, that will be, and
    nothing more."

Here his meditations were cut short by the Tiger devouring him. And that, said Speckle-neck, is why we counselled caution.

(from *Hitopadeśa*, trans. by Sir Edward Arnold, *The Book of Good Counsels*, pp. 9-11)

CHAPTER IX

THE PHILOSOPHIC
STATEMENT OF
THE TRADITION

〰〰〰〰

During the centuries when numerous expressions of religious aspiration added to the richness of the Hindu tradition, various systems of philosophy attempted to give order and coherence to the intellectual ferment of the time. By the end of the fourth century A.D. six of these had come to be regarded as orthodox, in contrast to those that were connected with Buddhism and Jainism. Philosophy is perhaps not quite the right word for these systems, since their main function was to help men find salvation, not to discuss the kinds of problems that have interested philosophers in the West. But neither would it be correct to describe them as theologies, for although they are considered to be valid statements of truths contained in the scriptures, some of them have little concern with any questions relating to God. The basis of their orthodoxy is an acceptance of the common assumptions of the tradition—belief in karma, rebirth, and dharma—and a general agreement that the acquisition of knowledge, however defined, was the means whereby man was freed from bondage to ignorance. Because of ignorance, the Self, the permanent entity, is clouded by the passions and impurities of life, and, as a modern Indian philosopher points out, all the systems agree that "the summum bonum of life is attained when all impurities are removed and the pure nature of the Self is thoroughly and permanently apprehended and all other extraneous connections with it are absolutely dissociated." [1]

The six systems, then, were ways of dealing with ignorance, using different methods, different approaches to the problem, and different definitions of such terms as Self, knowledge, and ignorance. In the following selections three of the systems—Nyāya, Vaisheshika, and Mīmāmsā —are treated in a very cursory manner, partly because of their subject matter, but mainly because the language used in the writings of these schools was so technical that it is meaningful only with an extended commentary. The other three systems—Yoga, Sānkhya, and Vedānta—are treated more fully because not only did they all occupy an important place in the past but they also had a general influence on the development of Hindu religious thought. Two of them, Yoga and Vedānta, are still central to the tradition.

It is worthwhile pointing out that while there was general acceptance within India—even by such heretical groups as Jains and Buddhists—of the basic beliefs of karma, transmigration, and the demands of dharma, there were, nevertheless, those who rejected the whole framework of conventional assumptions. A reference to the views of one dissenting school, known as Lokāyata or Cārvāka, is probably seen in the first selection, indicating the existence of radical dissent within the Hindu tradition. On the whole, however, thoroughgoing denial of the great assumptions of the general philosophical position was rare and does not seem to have played any very creative role in Indian life.

The Basis of Logical Thinking: Nyāya

The principal aim of the Nyāya system was to clarify the means for obtaining knowledge. These means, it taught, were

[1] S. N. Dasgupta, *A History of Indian Philosophy* (Cambridge: 1922), I, 75.

perception, inference, comparison, and the verbal testimony of a reliable person or of the scriptures, and their correct use was seen as an indispensable step towards salvation. The teachings of the Nyāya school, like those of all the other schools, were preserved in the form of *sūtras*, very short, aphoristic summaries of the main points of the system. Since these sūtras were scarcely intelligible by themselves, they were commented upon by scholars, and it is these commentaries that became the foundation documents of different schools of interpretation. The selection given here shows the arguments that were used by the school to prove the existence and rebirth of the soul. While the sūtra itself may date from the first century B.C., the commentary (in brackets) is by Vātsyāyana, who probably lived in the sixth century A.D.

A sense is not soul because we can apprehend an object through both sight and touch.

("Previously I saw the jar and now I touch it:" such expressions will be meaningless if "I" is not different from eye which cannot touch and from skin which cannot see. In other words, the "I" or soul is distinct from the senses.)

This is, some say, not so because there is a fixed relation between the senses and their objects.

(Colour, for instance, is an exclusive object of the eye, sound of the ear, smell of the nose, and so on. It is the eye that, according to the objectors, apprehends colour, and there is no necessity for assuming a soul distinct from the eye for the purpose of explaining the apprehension of colour.) . . .

If the body were soul there should be release from sins as soon as the body was burnt.

(If a person has no soul beyond his body he should be freed from sins when the body is destroyed. But in reality sins pursue him in his subsequent lives. Hence the body is not soul.)

There would, says an objector, be no sin even if the body endowed with a soul were burnt for the soul is eternal.

(In the previous aphorism it was shown that the commission of sins would be impossible if we supposed the body to be the soul. In the present aphorism it is argued by an objector that we should be incapable of committing sins even on the supposition of the soul being distinct from our body, for such a soul is eternal and cannot be killed.)

In reply we say that it is not so because we are capable of killing the body which is the site of operations of the soul.

(Though the soul is indestructible we can kill the body which is the seat of its sensations. Hence we are not incapable of committing sins by killing or murder. Moreover, if we do not admit a permanent soul beyond our frail body we shall be confronted by many absurdities such as "loss of merited action" and "gain of unmerited action." A man who has committed a certain sin may not suffer its consequences in this life and unless there is a soul continuing to his next life he will not suffer them at all. This is a "loss of merited action." Again, we often find a man suffering the consequences of action which he never did in this life. This would be a "gain of unmerited action" unless we believed that his soul did the action in his previous life.) . . .

The soul is to be admitted on account of joy, fear and grief arising in a child from the memory of things previously experienced. . . .

A child's desire for milk in this life is caused by the practice of his having drunk it in the previous life.

Some deny the above by saying that a new-born child approaches the breast of his mother just as an iron approaches a loadstone (without any cause).

This is, we reply, not so because there is no approach towards any other thing.

We find that none is born without desire.

Some say that the soul is not eternal because it may be produced along with desire as other things are produced along with their qualities.

This is, we reply, not so because the desire in a new-born child is caused by the ideas left in his soul by the things he enjoyed in his previous lives.

(The desire implies that the soul existed in the previous lives or, in other words, the soul is eternal.)

(from *Nyāyā Sūtras of Gotama*, Book III, selections, in *Sacred Books of the Hindus*, VIII, pp. 63-64, 68-69)

The Atomic Nature of Reality: Vaisheshika

The Vaisheshika school was concerned with analyzing the qualities that distinguish one particular object from another, and one of its contributions was an elaborate theory of the nature of reality. It taught that the universe was composed of atoms so minute that they had no extension in space. These atoms were eternal, without beginning or end. The relevance of this theory to religious thought was that, according to the followers of the school, it made possible a true understanding of the soul and the pathway to saving knowledge. The selection given here is from commentaries on the sūtras of Kanāda, one of the early exponents of the Vaisheshika philosophy. The original sūtra is indicated by quotation marks. The dating of this material, as of most ancient Indian literary work, is quite uncertain, but the origins of the school are probably to be found somewhere between the sixth and fourth centuries B.C.

THE EFFECT IS THE MARK (OF THE EXISTENCE) OF THE ULTIMATE ATOM

According to the sūtram of Gautama: "From the evolved is the production of the evolved, on the evidence of experience by perception." Now the inter-relation of parts and wholes is perceived. If it were unlimited, there would be no difference in size or measurement between Mount Meru and a grain of mustard seed; for they would be without distinction, both being originated by infinite parts. Nor can it be said that the difference will be caused by the difference of the size of each part and of the aggregation of parts; for without a difference of number, these also would be impossible. If it be said that *pralaya*, or destruction of the creation, may be the limit of the series of parts and wholes, we reply that the final thing having no parts, *pralaya* itself would be impossible, for it is only disjunction and destruction of parts which can destroy substances. Nor is disjunction the limit, for it is impossible for it to have only one substratum. Therefore, a substance without parts must be the limit and this is the ultimate atom. A mote is not the limit; for being a visible substance, it possesses magnitude, and is composed of more substances than one; magnitude, as the cause of visual perception, presupposes, or is dependent upon, multiplicity of substance; else there would be no magnitude even, and what then would be cause? Nor are the constituent parts of the mote atoms, for we must infer that they also, as originative of a substance possessing magnitude, are composed of parts, like thread and like potsherd. Therefore, whatever substance is an effect, is composed of parts, and whatever substance is composed of parts, is an effect. So that from whichever part the nature of being an effect goes away, from it goes away also the nature of being made up of parts. This is the proof of indivisible ultimate atoms. So it has been said by Prasatadeva, "Earth is two-fold, eternal and non-eternal."

(IT IS) AN ERROR (TO SUPPOSE THAT THE ULTIMATE ATOM IS NOT ETERNAL)

It may be objected as follows: The ultimate atom is not eternal, since it is corporeal or ponderable, like a water-pot. Similarly, the possession of colour, the possession of taste, etc., may be, one by one, adduced as so many reasons. . . . Again, the non-eternality of the atom follows also from the inference which establishes transiency, the inference, that is, that all that exists is momentary. . . . To meet these objections he says: Every inference which has for its subject the non-eternality of the atom is ignorance, that is, it is of the form of error, since it springs from a fallacy. This fallacy is occasionally obstruction or opposition to the proof which comprehends the subject; always the absence of the characteristic of being pervaded (or being the mark), due to want of evidence preventive of its existence in the counter-argument; . . . sometimes unproof by itself; and others which should be learned from the kindred system (the Nyāya system).

(from *The Vaiśesika Sūtras of Kanāda*, trans. by Nandalal Sinha, in *Sacred Books of the Hindus*, VI, pp. 146-48)

Proof of the Sacred Texts: Mīmāmsā

The Mīmāmsā system was built upon the logic of the Nyāya school but gave particular emphasis to the importance of the testimony of the Vedas as a source of true knowledge. The practitioners of this school taught that the Vedas were eternal and without an author. Coupled with this uncompromising assertion of the Vedas as absolute truth went a denial of the role of a deity as creator. This rejection of theism by a religious system is an indication of how careful one must be in transferring religious terms and concepts from one tradition to another.

The selection given here is from a commentary written in the eighth century A.D. by Kumārila on the work of Jaimini, the greatest figure in the school of Mīmāmsā. Kumārila's argument would probably not convince anyone who did not accept all of his presuppositions, but this kind of reasoning played an important part in establishing the intellectual validity of Hinduism over against the teachings of the Buddhists and other heretics.

Obj:—Finding the Vedic assertions to be similar to ordinary assertions, we have a general idea of the Veda having an author; and this becomes specified by the names 'Katha,' &c., given to he different sections of the Veda. . . .

Reply:—Inasmuch as we have neither any rememberance of an author nor any need of any such,—no author is wanted for the Veda; and since the ideas of particular authorship depend upon the general notion (of such authorship), no names can point to any authors of the Veda.

Inasmuch as the names "Katha," &c., may be explained as signifying the fact of certain portions of the Veda being explained by such people,—these names cannot necessarily point to an author; specially as the affix (in the word "Katha") is also laid down as denoting the fact of being *expounded* (by Katha).

And thus *Name*, being weaker than Direct Assertion and the rest, cannot set aside the facts based upon these latter. And further, inasmuch as this (Name) is a part of the Veda, it can never possibly set aside the whole of the Veda (by pointing to the fact of its having an author).

Or these ("Katha," &c.) may be taken as conventional names, given, without any reason, to particular sections of the Veda. And the fact of these names (appearing with regard to certain sections of the Veda) being only similar in *sound*, the same words (as signifying the fact of being composed by Katha, &c.) is not to be denied on pain of any punishment (*i.e.*, there is no law which lays down that the two do not resemble in sound only).

Even though the explanation of the Veda is common to all persons (and not restricted particularly to Katha alone), yet the name may be given to certain sections of the Veda, simply on the ground of the possibility (of its being explained by Katha). . . .

The names "Katha," &c., indicating the fact of Katha, &c., being the explainers, are not such as to restrict the explicability of those sections of the Veda to those teachers alone, inasmuch as all that the name does is to show that the section of the Veda has been explained by that particular teacher *also* among others,—just as the mother of Dittha and Kapittha is called "Dittha's mother" (which does not mean that the person is not the mother of Kapittha, but that she is also the mother of Dittha, among others).

The fact that, even though the relation of the section with all teachers is the same, yet it is named after one of them only, is due to the fact that such naming is not a qualification of the agent (*i.e.*, the Teacher) and as such it is not necessary to repeat it with regard to all the Teachers); hence the naming (in accordance with Teachers) being (a qualification) for the sake of another (*i.e.* the Sections of the Veda), the mention of only one of them is necessary.

(Even if the name "Katha" were taken as implying the authorship of Katha with regard to the Veda, then too) it is only an already existing cause (in the shape of Katha) that is signified (by the name "Katha"); and it does not signify the production of something previously non-existent.

And (as for the meaning of Vedic sections according to the name of only one Teacher, it is similar to the case where) a certain sacred place, though visited by many people, is named in accordance with only one of its visitors (such as "Somatīrtha," &c.).

And if the name "Katha" be not due to human agency, then it cannot indicate non-eternality; and if it be due to human agency, then how can its truthfulness be ascertained? . . .

The Veda naturally abandons the denotation of non-eternal meanings,—inasmuch as such denotation is found to be impossible with regard to the Veda, by considering alternatives of eternality and non-eternality with regard to it. Because if the Veda be eternal its denotation cannot but be eternal; and if it be non-eternal (caused), then it can have no validity (which is not possible, as we have already proved the validity of the Veda); and as for the theory that the Veda consists of assertions of intoxicated (and senseless) people, this theory has been already rejected above—(and as such the validity and hence the eternality of the Veda cannot be doubted).

Thus up to this place, we have established by arguments, the fact of the Veda being the means of arriving at the right notion of "Dharmā."

After this (in the succeeding three *pādas*), after having divided the Veda into its three sections, we shall explain what is the meaning (and purpose) of each of these sections.

(from Kumārila, *Ślokavārtika*, Aphorisms XXVII to XXXII, trans. by G. N. Jha)

The Dualism of Matter and Spirit: Sānkhya

According to the Sānkhya system there are two eternal principles in the universe, matter (*prakriti*) and spirit (*purusha*). The Sānkhya school did not posit any creator for these entities, but simply regarded them as self-existent, without beginning or end. Matter is made up of three *gunas* or "strands," known as *sattva* (purity), *rajas* (passion), and *tamas* (darkness). It is the movement of these three strands and their combination in different proportions that create the visible universe. A preponderance of *sattva*, for example, gives things the qualities of lightness and truth, while *rajas* makes for activity and violence and *tamas* produces darkness and stupidity. The working or evolution of these strands is caused by spirit—although just how this action takes place is not clear. The result of the interaction of spirit and matter is the disturbance of the equilibrium that would exist otherwise, and out of disequilibrium comes the cosmos with all its pains and evils, the greatest of which is rebirth. Salvation consists, therefore, in withdrawing spirit from its involvement with matter and restoring the primeval balance when both principles maintained their static being. In this dualism of matter and spirit there is, it should be noted, no suggestion that matter is in any sense evil, but only that matter and spirit are intrinsically different things and, therefore, should not be confused.

Salvation for the Sānkhya system involves the use of knowledge to restore the balance of matter and spirit and to prevent the continued operation of the *gunas*. The gods are not denied, but they have no essential place within the scheme; man quite literally works out his own salvation. While Sānkhya is no longer important as a separate school its general ideas, especially the conception of *gunas*, were widely accepted by other systems. The metaphysical basis of the *Bhagavad Gītā*, for example, is very similar to the Sānkhya understanding of the world.

The selection given here is taken from a writing dated around the fourth century A.D.

Owing to man being assailed by all the kinds of misery, there arises the desire in him to know the means for the removal of such misery. Such an inquiry into the cause of the removal of misery is not rendered useless because there are known and ready remedies, for such remedies are neither invariably nor completely effective. Like those worldly remedies are those that one knows from the scriptures [namely, the performance of Vedic sacrifices to attain the joyous status of heaven]; for that scriptural remedy is impure as sacrifices involve injury [to animals], and its fruits are both perishable and liable to be excelled by other kinds of pleasure. Therefore a remedy which is the opposite of these [the seen one of the world and the heard one of the scriptures] is more beneficial; and that remedy is to be had by knowledge, the discrimination of the manifest material creation, its unmanifest cause [the object], and the presiding sentient spirit [the subject].

Primordial Matter is not an effect [modification]; the intellect, etc., seven in number, are both cause and effect; there are sixteen categories which are only effects; the spirit is neither cause nor effect.

The categories of knowledge are known from means of correct knowledge and in Sānkhya, three sources of valid knowledge are accepted: perception, inference, and valid testimony; all other means of correct knowledge are included in these three. Perception is the determination of objects by their contact with the respective senses perceiving them. Inference is of three kinds, and it results from the knowledge of a characteristic feature and of an object invariably accompanied by that feature. Valid testimony is what one hears from a reliable authority. Perception provides knowledge of sensible objects. Of things beyond the senses, knowledge is had through inference based on analogy; and those that are completely beyond the senses and cannot be established even through that process of inference are ascertained through valid testimony. A thing may not be perceived because of too great distance, of too much proximity, injury to the senses, inattention of mind, smallness or subtlety, an intervening object, suppression by another, or merging in a similar thing.

Primordial matter is not perceived because it is too subtle, not because it does not exist; for it is known from its products [the phenomenal world]. And those products are intellect, etc.; products born of primordial matter are, in their characteristics, partly like it and partly unlike it.

The effect already exists in the cause for the following reasons: what is nonexistent cannot be produced; for producing a thing, a specific material cause is resorted to; everything is not produced by everything; a specific material cause capable of producing a specific product alone produces that effect; there is such a thing as a particular cause for a particular effect.

The evolved [i.e., the product] has the following characteristics: it has been caused, it is noneternal, nonpervasive, attended by movement, manifold, resting on another, an attribute of its source in which it finally merges, endowed with parts, and depending on another for its existence. The nonevolved [i.e., the cause, primordial matter] is the opposite of all this. But the evolved and the unevolved [primordial matter] have these common properties: they are composed of three dispositions [gunas]; they are nondiscriminating and nonsentient; they are object; they are common; and their nature is to evolve. The spirit is opposed in its qualities both to one and to the other.

The three dispositions: they are of the form of pleasure, pain, and dejection; their purposes are illumination, activation, and checking; they function by prevailing over one another, resorting to one another, engendering one another, and acting in cooperation with one another. They are purity [sattva], passion [rajas], and darkness [tamas]. Purity is light, revealing and desirable; passion is stimulating and active; darkness is dense and obscuring; their harmonious functioning is directed by unity of purpose, as in the case of a lamp [in which the ingredients, fire, oil, and wick, conjointly function for the one purpose of producing light]. . . .

The properties like absence of discriminatory knowledge can be proved to exist in the evolved by reason of the latter being composed of the three dispositions and by the absence of this threefold composition of its opposite, namely the spirit. The existence of an unevolved primary cause is proved by the fact that the effect has the same properties as the cause.

The unevolved exists as the primordial cause because the diverse evolutes are all attended by limitations, because common features subsist through all of them [arguing inheritance from a common cause], because the evolved has come into being as the result of the potentiality of a cause, because the distinction of cause and effect apply to the entire world without exception.

The unevolved acts [evolves] through its three dispositions [purity, etc.] and through them conjointly, changing like water according to the difference pertaining to each of those dispositions.

As all aggregates imply one different from themselves whom they subserve, as that for whom they are intended should differ from their own nature, namely, being composed of three dispositions, etc., as such objects should have one as their presiding authority, as objects imply an enjoyer, and as there is seen through evolution a striving for liberation, there exists the spirit. The plurality of spirits is proven because of the specified nature of birth, death, and faculties in respect of each person, because of the absence of simultaneous activity on the part of all, and because of the diversity of the nature of three dispositions in different beings. By the same reason of differences from the unevolved [primordial matter] which is composed of the three dispositions, the spirit is proved to be only a spectator, distinct and unaffected, endowed with cognition but free of agency.

Hence, as a result of union with the spirit, the evolved though nonsentient, yet appears to be sentient; and on its part, the spirit, too, though the dispositions of matter alone act, appears to act but is really indifferent. It is for the sake of enlightenment of the spirit and the eventual withdrawal from primordial matter [i.e., liberation of the spirit from matter] that the two come together, even as the lame and the blind come together for mutual benefit; creation proceeds from this union.

From primordial matter proceeds intellect; from it ego; from that the group of sixteen [the five subtle elements governing sound, touch, form, taste, and smell, the five senses of knowledge, the five of action, and the mind which is the internal sense presiding over the other ten senses]; from the five [subtle elements] among those sixteen, the five gross elements [ether, air, fire, water, and earth].

The intellect is of the form of determination; its sublime [purity-dominated] forms are virtue, knowledge, dispassion, and mastery; the opposites of these [darkness-dominated vice, ignorance, passion, and powerlessness] represent its forms in delusion.

Ego is of the form of identification; from it proceed twofold creation, the group of eleven [senses] and the five subtle elements. . . .

The subtle elements are not of any specific character; from these five, the five gross elements of matter proceed and these gross elements have specified characters, peaceful, violent, and dormant [according to the relative preponderance of any of the three gunas]. These three specified forms have again a threefold manifestation [in living beings]; the subtle body, the gross body born of parents, together with the gross elements; the subtle ones endure [through transmigration], the gross ones are perishable. . . . According to the exigencies of the causes—virtue, vice, etc.—and the resultant higher or lower births, the subtle body prompted by the purpose of the spirit (viz. its liberation) makes its appearance like an actor in different

guises, thanks to the capacity of the primary cause (pra-
riti) to manifest diverse forms. . . .

By virtue one progresses toward higher forms of embodied existence; by vice, one goes down toward lower
forms; by knowledge liberation is gained and by its opposite bondage; by nonattachment to mundane objects, one
reaches the state of merging in primordial matter; from
desire impelled by passion further transmigration results;
unimpeded movement is gained through the attainment
of mastery and from its opposite, the opposite of free
movement. . . .

In this transmigratory journey, the sentient spirit experiences the misery due to old age and death till such time as
the subtle body also falls away; hence, in the very nature of
existence, everything is misery. . . .

Therefore, surely, no spirit is bound, none is released,
none transmigrates; primordial matter, taking different
forms, transmigrates, binds herself and releases herself. By
her own seven forms [virtue and vice, ignorance, detachment and attachment, mastery and the lack of it], matter
binds herself; and for the purpose of the spirit, she herself,
with one of her forms, namely knowledge, causes release.

(from Īshvarakrishna, *Sānkhya Kārikās*, I:33-69, *passim*, in
Sources of Indian Tradition, pp. 308-14)

The Way of Discipline: Yoga

The name of the fifth orthodox system of philosophy—Yoga—
is one of the most familiar of Indian religious terms, but its
fame has tended to mask the real nature of its position. In
the present context "disciplined activity" seems to give the
sense intended by its usage in the basic text of the school, the
Yogasūtra of Patanjali. The dates of this work are quite uncertain, with some scholars assigning it to the second century
B.C. and others to the fourth century A.D., but the surviving
commentaries all seem to come from a time subsequent to the
later date.

According to Patanjali, the aim of Yoga is to gain control of both physical and mental processes. The metaphysical basis of the system is very similar to that of the Sānkhya school, and the purpose of control is to end the activity of the strands or *gunas*. Unlike Sānkhya, however, the Yoga system accepts the idea of a supreme first cause as the originator of both spirit and matter. The yogic practitioner seeks through a careful process of spiritual exercises to reach a state of "isolation," of the complete separation of spirit from matter. When this is achieved the spirit is free from change and motion.

This selection describes the methods to be followed by the disciple, and while they are expressed in the telegraphic language common to the sūtra form, their meaning is relatively clear.

1. Purificatory action, study, and making God the motive of action, constitute the *yoga* of action.
2. This is for the bringing about of trance and for the purpose of attenuating afflictions.
3. The afflictions are ignorance, egoism, attachment, aversion, and love of life.
4. Ignorance is the field for the others, whether dormant, tenuous, alternated, or fully operative.
5. Ignorance is the taking of the temporal, the impure, the painful, and the not-self to be the eternal, the pure, the pleasurable, and the self.
6. Egoism is the belief that the power of seeing and the power by which one sees is a single essence.
7. Attachment is the attraction to pleasure.
8. Aversion is the repulsion from pain.
9. Flowing on by its own potency, established even in the wise, is love of life.
10. These afflictions may be overcome by their opposites.
11. Their activities are destroyed by meditation.
12. The vehicle of actions has its origin in afflictions, and is experienced in visible and invisible births.
13. It ripens into life-state, life-time, and life-experience, if the root exists.

14. They have pleasure or pain as the fruit, by reason of virtue or vice.

15. By reason of the pains of change, anxiety, and habituation, and by reason of the contrariety of the functionings of the "qualities," all indeed is pain to the discriminating.

16. But future pain is avoidable.

17. The conjunction of the knower and the knowable is the cause of avoidable pain. . . .

23. Conjunction is that which brings about the recognition of the natures of the power of owning and the capacity of being owned.

24. Ignorance is its effective cause.

25. Removal (of bondage) is the disappearance of conjunction on account of the disappearance of ignorance, and that is the absolute freedom of the knower.

26. The means of removing ignorance is through knowledge that discriminates between the soul and the objects of sense. . . .

28. On the destruction of impurity by the sustained practice of the accessories of *yoga*, the light of wisdom reaches up to discriminative knowledge.

29. Restraint, observance, posture, regulation of breath, abstraction (of the senses), concentration, meditation, and trance are the eight accessories of *yoga*.

30. Of these, the restraints are: abstinence from injury (*ahimsā*), veracity, abstinence from theft, continence, and abstinence from avariciousness.

31. They are the great vow, universal, and unlimited by origin, space, time, and circumstance.

32. The observances are cleanliness, contentment, austerity, study, and the making of the Lord the motive of all action. . . .

35. In the presence of one who has given up causing injury, all hostility is given up.

36. When one is confirmed in veracity, actions and their consequences depend upon him.

37. When one is confirmed in the habit of not stealing, all treasures come to him.
38. Continence being confirmed, vigour is obtained.
39. Non-covetousness being confirmed, knowledge of the succession of births is obtained.
40. By cleanliness is meant disgust with one's body, and cessation of contact with others.
41. And with the mind becoming pure, come purity, singleness of mind, control of the senses, and fitness for the knowledge of the self.
42. By contentment, comes the acquisition of extreme happiness.
43. By purificatory action, come the removal of impurity and the attainments of the physical body and the senses.
44. By study comes communion with the desired deity.
45. The attainment of trance comes by making God the motive of all actions.
46. Posture is steady and easy. . . .
49. Regulation of breath is the stoppage of the inhaling and exhaling movements of breath. . . .
53. Then the mind is fit for concentration (*dhāranā*).
54. Abstraction (of the senses) (*pratyāhāra*) is that by which the senses do not come into contact with their objects and follow as it were the nature of the mind.
55. Thence the senses are under the highest control.

(from Patanjali, *Yogasūtra*, Chapter II, trans. by Rama Prasad in *Sacred Books of the Hindus*, IV, revised)

Non-Dualism: The Vedānta of Shankara

The most important of all the systems of philosophy is Vedānta, which means "the end of the V*edas*." The term is properly used for the V*edānta Sūtra*, a text written some time after the fourth century B.C. that summarized the teachings of the *Upanishads* in very terse statements. Many commentaries

were written on these brief aphorisms, but by far the most famous is that of Shankara, a South Indian who lived about the
end of the eighth century. His interpretation has so dominated
Indian intellectual life, and has become so well-known in the
West, that his work has become almost synonymous with
Vedānta, although other very different interpretations were
made by scholars of great intellectual distinction. Shankara's
achievement in creating a great synthesis of knowledge has
often been compared to that of St. Thomas Aquinas, but it
is properly used for the *Vedānta Sūtra*, a text written some time
of Indian thought since his time has been much more pervasive than that of Aquinas on the West. One measure of this
influence is that it is very difficult for anyone—either Hindu or
non-Hindu—to read Indian religious texts without uncon-
sciously seeing them through the general interpretation given
by Shankara.

Shankara's main concern was the nature of the relationship
between the individual Self (*ātman*) and the Universal Self
(*brahman*). His general position was that these were completely identical, and that all appearances of plurality and difference arose from a false interpretation of the data presented
by the mind and senses. In any ultimate understanding, he insisted, the only reality was *brahman*.

In putting forward this interpretation Shankara had to meet
a number of obvious difficulties. One was the great variety of
teachings contained in the scriptures, particularly the *Upanishads*, and since Shankara was completely committed to the
truth of the sacred texts he had to meet each seeming contradiction between his teaching and the scriptures. He also had
to meet the logical arguments of his opponents, especially the
Buddhists, who met him on his own ground. And, above all,
he had to explain the commonsense perception of a plural universe, where men are in fact aware of themselves as individuals
and of different forms of matter external to themselves.

Shankara's broad answer to the objections to his system was
to posit the concept of higher and lower knowledge, and to
argue that statements were "true" depending upon the level of
experience attained by the person discussing them. The commonsense perception of plurality, for example, was perfectly
true for the man who had not reached the stage of understanding that reality was one. In the same way, the gods of popular
Hinduism were necessary for worship by those who believed

in them, but on a higher level of spiritual attainment they had no meaning. With the knowledge of the identity of *ātman* and *brahman*, or the Self and Universal Self, all the plurality of the world of lower knowledge simply vanished; plurality did not exist for the enlightened man any more than a knowledge of the unity of being existed for the man who lived in the realm of the lower knowledge. Shankara was not making any value judgment between higher and lower knowledge, suggesting that one was good and the other bad; what he was doing, he would have insisted, was describing the universe as it actually existed, and using this knowledge for the purposes of salvation.

The aim of Shankara's system, then, was the same as that of all the other great philosophical statements—the attainment of salvation, or more accurately, perhaps, of liberation. This is defined for Shankara as intuitive knowledge of the identity of *ātman* and *brahman*, not, it must be emphasized, as the reaching of unity with God. Within the great system created by Shankara, God or gods occupy an important place, but it is on the level of lower knowledge, not of higher. His Absolute Reality is not God, but must be understood as something quite different from any meaning usually given to conceptions of deity.

The selection given here is from Shankara's greatest work, his commentary on the *Vedānta Sūtra*. It illustrates his use of reason to prove that his position is a true exposition of the scriptures.

INTRODUCTION ON "SUPERIMPOSITION"

When it is well understood that "object" and "subject," comprehended as "you" and "I" and opposed in nature like darkness and light, cannot be of each other's nature, much less could the properties of the two be of each other's nature; therefore when one superimposes on the "subject" comprehended as "I" and consisting of intelligence, the "object" comprehended as "You" and its properties, and superimposes the "subject" which is the reverse thereof and its properties on the "object," this superimposition, it stands to reason to believe, is a thing to be denied.

Still, superimposing the nature and attributes of one thing on those of another and without discriminating from each other the two totally distinct things, namely, the "object" and the "subject," there is this natural usage in the world, "*I am this*" and "*This is mine*," which is due to a sublative notion and represents a confusion of the true and the false.

One may ask, what is this thing called "superimposition"? We say, it is the "appearance" in something of some other thing previously experienced and consists of a recollection. Some call it the superimposition of the attributes of one thing on another; some say that where a thing is superimposed on another, it is the illusion due to the nonperception of their difference; still others hold that where there is a superimposition, it is the fancying in a thing of a property contrary to its nature. In any case, it does not cease to have the character of one thing appearing to possess another's property. And so is our experience in the world: nacre shines like silver, and one moon, as if it had a second.

But how does the superimposition of "object" and its properties on the inner Self, which is not the "object," come about? On a thing before oneself one superimposes another thing, but you say, the inner Self, which falls outside the scope of what is comprehended as "you," is never an "object." The reply is: This inner Self is not a nonobject at all times, for it is the object of the notion "I" and there is the knowledge of the inner Self by immediate intuition. There is no such rule that a superimposition has to be made only in an object that exists in front of one; for even in an imperceivable thing like the ether, boys superimpose a surface, dirt, etc. Thus it is not contradictory to speak of superimposition on the inner Self of things which are non-Self.

The superimposition so characterized, the learned consider to be nescience, and the determination of the real nature of a thing by discriminating that which is superimposed on it, they say is knowledge. When this is so, that on which a thing is superimposed is not affected in the slightest degree by either the defect or the merit of the superimposed thing. And it is due to this superimposition over one thing of another in respect of the Self and the non-Self—which is termed nescience—that all worldly transactions, of the means of knowledge and the objects thereof, take place, and [under the same circumstance] again, do all the scriptures, with their injunctions, prohibitions, and means of liberation operate.

But how do you say that sources of valid knowledge like perception and the scriptures fall within the purview of that which is conditioned by nescience? I shall reply: One devoid of the sense of "I" and "Mine" in the body, senses, etc., cannot be a cognizer and cannot resort to a means of cognition; for without resorting to the senses, there can be no activity of perception, etc.; and without a basis [the body] the activity of the senses is not possible; and none ever acts without a body on which the sense of the Self has not been superimposed. Nor could the Self, the unattached, be a cognizer, when none of these [body, senses, etc.] exist; and without a cognizer, the means of cognition do not operate. Hence it is under what is conditioned by nescience that all means of knowledge, perception, etc., as also the scriptures, come. . . .

We said that superimposition is the seeing of a thing in something which is not that; thus, when son, wife, etc., are all right or not, one considers one's own Self as all right or not, one superimposes external attributes on the Self; even so does one superimpose on the Self the attributes of the *body* when one considers that "I am corpulent, I am lean, I am fair, I stand, I go, I jump"; similarly attributes of the *senses* when one says, "I am dumb, one-eyed, impotent, deaf, blind"; and in the same manner the properties of the *internal organs,* e.g., desire, volition, cogitation, and resolution. Even so, man superimposes the [conditioned] Self presented in the cognition of "I" on the inner Self which

is the witness of all the activities of the internal organ; and
that inner Self, the very opposite and the witness of all, on
the inner organ. . . .

It is for casting away this superimposition which is the
cause of [all] evil and for gaining the knowledge of the
oneness of the Self that all the Upanishads are begun. And
how this is the purport of all the Upanishads, we shall
show in this system of thought called the investigation
into the Self that presides over the body.

Of this system of thought [also] called the Vedānta Mīmāmsā [the enquiry into the purport of the Vedānta, i.e.,
the Upanishads], which it is my desire to explain, this is
the first aphorism:

THEN THEREFORE THE DESIRE TO KNOW THE BRAHMAN

Therefore something must be set forth [as the preceding consideration] in close succession to which the inquiry
into the Brahman is taught. I shall set it forth; the sense of
discrimination as to things permanent and evanescent,
nonattachment to objects of enjoyment here or in the
hereafter, the accumulation of accessories like quietude
and self-control, and a desire to be liberated. When these
are present, whether before an inquiry into dharma or
after it, it is possible for one to inquire into the Brahman
and know it, not when they are absent. Therefore, by the
word "then," it is taught that this desire to know the
Brahman follows immediately after the full acquisition of
the spiritual accessories set forth above. . . .

Now that Brahman may be well known or unknown; if
it is well known, there is no need to desire to know it; if on
the other hand, it is unknown, it could never be desired to
be known. The answer to this objection is as follows: The
Brahman exists, eternal, pure, enlightened, free by nature,
omniscient, and attended by all power. When the word
"Brahman" is explained etymologically, it being eternal,
pure and so on, are all understood, for these are in conformity with the meaning of the root brh [from which
Brahman is derived]. The Brahman's existence is well

known, because it is the Self of all; everyone realizes the existence of the Self, for none says, "I am not"; if the existence of the Self is not well known, the whole world of beings would have the notion "I do not exist." And the Self is the Brahman.

It may be contended that if the Brahman is well known in the world as the Self, it has already been known, and again it becomes something which need not be inquired into. It is not like that, for [while its existence in general is accepted], there are differences of opinion about its particular nature. Ordinary people and the materialists are of the view that the Self is just the body qualified by intelligence; others think that it is the intelligent sense-organs themselves that are the Self; still others, that it is the mind; some hold it as just the fleeting consciousness of the moment; some others as the void; certain others say that there is some entity, which is different from the body, etc., and which transmigrates, does and enjoys; some consider him as the enjoyer and not as the doer; some that there is, as different from the above entity, the Lord who is omniscient and omnipotent. According to still others, it is the inner Self of the enjoyer. Thus, resorting to reasonings and texts and the semblances thereof, there are many who hold divergent views. Hence one who accepts some view without examining it might be prevented from attaining the ultimate good, and might also come to grief. Therefore, by way of setting forth the inquiry into the Brahman, here is begun the discussion of the meaning of the texts of the Upanishads, aided by such ratiocination as is in conformity to Scripture and having for its fruit the Supreme Beatitude.

It has been said that the Brahman is to be inquired into; on the question as to the characteristics of that Brahman, the blessed author of the aphorisms says:

WHENCE IS THE ORIGIN . . . OF THIS

. . . Of this universe made distinct through names and forms, having many agents and enjoyers, serving as the ground of the fruits of activities attended by specific places, times, and causes, and whose nature and design cannot be conceived even in one's mind—that omniscient, omnipotent cause wherefrom the origin, maintenance, and destruction of such a universe proceeds is the Brahman; such is the full meaning to be understood. . . .

By showing the Brahman as the cause of the universe it has been suggested that the Brahman is omniscient; now to reinforce that omniscience the author of the aphorisms says:

AS IT IS THE SOURCE OF THE SCRIPTURE

Of the extensive scripture comprising the *Rig Veda*, etc., reinforced and elaborated by many branches of learning, illumining everything even as a lamp, and like unto one omniscient, the source is the Brahman. Of a scripture of this type, of the nature of the *Rig Veda* and the like, endowed with the quality of omniscience, the origin cannot be from anything other than the omniscient one. Whatever teaching has, for purposes of elaborate exposition, come forth from an eminent personage, as the science of grammar from Pānini, etc., though it is comprehensive of that branch of knowledge, it is well understood in the world that its exponent [e.g., Pānini] possesses knowledge far more than what is in his work; it therefore goes without saying that unsurpassed omniscience and omnipotence is to be found in that Supreme Being from whom, as the source, issued forth, as if in sport and without any effort, like the breathing of a person, this scripture in diverse recensions, called *Rig Veda*, etc., which is the repository of all knowledge and is responsible for the distinctions into gods, animals, humans, classes, stages of life, etc.; this is borne out by scriptural texts like: "This that is called *Rig Veda* [and so on] is the breathings out of this Great Being." . . . That Brahman, omniscient, omnipotent, and cause of the birth, existence, and dissolution of the universe *is* known from the scripture as represented by the Upanishads. How? "Because of textual harmony." In all the Upanishads the texts are in agreement in propounding, as their main purport, this idea. For example, "Dear one! this thing Existence alone was at the beginning"; "The one without a second"; "The Self, this one only, existed at first"; "This Brahman, devoid of anything before or after, inside or outside"; "This Self, the Brahman, the all-experiencing one"; "At first there was only this Brahman, the immortal one." When it is decisively known that the purport of the words in these texts is the nature of the Brahman, and when unity is seen, to imagine a different purport is improper, as thereby one will have to give up what is expressly stated and imagine something not stated. Nor could it be concluded that their purport is to set forth the nature of the agent, deity, etc.; for there are texts like "Then whom should It see and with what?," which refute action, agent, and fruit.

Because the Brahman is a thing already well established, it cannot be held to be the object of perception by senses, etc.; for the truth that the Brahman is the Self, as set forth in the text "That thou art," cannot be known without the scripture. As regards the objection that since there is nothing here to be avoided or desired, there is no use in teaching it, it is no drawback; it is from the realization that the Self is the Brahman, devoid of things to be avoided or desired, that all miseries are ended and the aspiration of man is achieved.

(from Shankara, *Brahmasūtra Bhasya*, I:1:1-4, in *Sources of Indian Tradition*, pp. 316-27)

Qualified Non-Dualism: The Vedānta of Rāmānuja

Although Shankara's interpretation of the *Upanishads* and of the scriptures in general has dominated Indian thought, other great theologians challenged his views. The most important of these was Rāmānuja, whose work dates from about 1100 A.D. Like Shankara he was a South Indian, a reminder that while the traditional home of Hinduism is in the north, many of the greatest exponents of its doctrines lived in the south.

According to Rāmānuja, the human soul and God, or Brahman, were distinct identities, and salvation for him meant a communion of the individual soul with God, not a realization of complete identity, as with Shankara. While he maintained that individual souls were ultimately dependent upon God for their existence, he insisted that they retained their separate being even after the attainment of salvation. His system is known as "qualified non-dualism," to distinguish it from Shankara's "unqualified monism," and also to indicate that it does not present a completely dualistic picture of the universe, since he admitted that the individual souls were expressions of *brahman*.

Rāmānuja's teaching played a very influential role in the history of Indian religion by providing a metaphysical basis for the devotional worship that had become common in his time (see Part Four). Thus it might be argued that while Shankara's system has appealed to philosophers, Rāmānuja's has actually served a wider segment of the Indian people.

The selection given here is Rāmānuja's comment on one of the same passages from the *Vedānta Sūtra* that Shankara had commented upon. The famous formula from the *Upanishads*, "That art thou," had been used by Shankara to sum up his monistic teachings, and Rāmānuja had to show that it could be interpreted in a non-monistic sense.

"Scripture does not teach that Release is due to the knowledge of a non-qualified Brahman.—The meaning of 'tat tvam asi.' "

Nor can we admit the assertion that Scripture teaches the cessation of avidyâ to spring only from the cognition of a Brahman devoid of all difference. Such a view is clearly negatived by passages such as the following: 'I know that great person of sun-like lustre beyond darkness; knowing him a man becomes immortal, there is no other path to go;' 'All moments sprang from lightning, the Person—none is lord over him, his name is great glory—they who know him become immortal.' For the reason that Brahman is characterised by difference all Vedic texts declare that final release results from the cognition of a qualified Brahman. And even those texts which describe Brahman by means of negations really aim at setting forth a Brahman possessing attributes.

In texts, again, such as 'Thou art that,' the co-ordination of the constituent parts is not meant to convey the idea of the absolute unity of a non-differenced substance: on the contrary, the words 'that' and 'thou' denote a Brahman distinguished by difference. The word 'that' refers to Brahman omniscient, &c., which had been introduced as the general topic of consideration in previous passages of the same section, such as 'It thought, may I be many'; the word 'thou,' which stands in co-ordination to 'that,' conveys the idea of Brahman in so far as having for its body the individual souls connected with non-intelligent matter. . . . It, moreover, is not possible (while, however, it would result from the absolute oneness of 'tat' and 'tvam') that to Brahman, whose essential nature is knowledge, which is free from all imperfections, omniscient, comprising within itself all auspicious qualities, there should belong Nescience; and that it should be the substrate of all those defects and afflictions which spring from Nescience. . . . If, on the other hand, the text is understood to refer to Brahman as having the individual souls for its body, both words ('that' and 'thou') keep their primary denotation; and, the text thus making a declaration about one substance distinguished by two aspects, the fundamental principle of 'co-ordination' is preserved. On this interpretation the text further intimates that Brahman— free from all imperfection and comprising within itself all auspicious qualities—is the internal ruler of the individual souls and possesses lordly power.

(from Rāmānuja, *Commentary on the Vedānta Sūtra*, I:1:1, in *Sacred Books of the East*, XLVIII, pp. 129-34, selections)

CHAPTER X

SACRED HISTORY

〜〜〜〜〜〜

The Hindu tradition, which is so rich in many varieties of
literature, has remarkably little historical literature of the
kind found in comparable periods either in Europe or
China, but it does possess a vast amount of writing that
deals in a special way with the past. This is the literature
known as the Purānas, a class of texts that is included in
the canon of scripture, although of a lesser degree of sanctity and authority than the Vedic writings. They are not
histories in the modern usage of the term, nor are they
even comparable to medieval chronicles, but they are sacred history, providing accounts of the origin of the universe, the deeds of the gods, and the genealogies of ancient
kings. Some of them, notably the Vishnu Purāna, contain
material that is undoubtedly factual, but their general
scope and intention is so fundamentally unhistorical that
it is virtually impossible to use them to reconstruct the
past. But their real function, the creation of a picture of
the universe in which the lives of men and gods interact, is
admirably fulfilled, and their influence over the minds and
imaginations of the people of India has been enormous. It
is through them, rather than the great Vedic texts, that
the basic ideas of Hinduism have been communicated, and

their mythological stories have been woven into the lives of the people in festivals and ceremonies of all kinds.

The Purānas are sectarian texts; they are identified with a particular god and his devotees, but the same stories, with variations, are repeated many times. Some of them may come from the early years of the Christian era, or even earlier, but in their final form they date from after 300 A.D., and many of them were added to as late as the twelfth century. According to the traditional count, there are eighteen works that are genuine Purānas, but many more have received the title, and, at least in popular estimation, not much distinction was made on the basis of age. What apparently determined a work's influence was the devotion it aroused for its particular deity. Most of the Purānas are concerned with the lives and deeds of Vishnu and Shiva, or their incarnations, and this emphasis meant that the older Vedic gods tended to become more and more subordinate. Often, for example, gods that originally had no connection with either Vishnu or Shiva were pictured as their wives and children. Thus Ganesh, the elephant-headed god, had probably been an extremely ancient deity of some primitive non-Aryan tribe, but he was brought into the Shiva cult by making him the son of Shiva and his wife Pārvati, who herself was a mother goddess imported into the pantheon from some ancient source.

The Purānas thus looked two ways and performed two functions. From one side, they brought into the main stream of Indian religious thought deities and concepts from religious traditions that had not originally been related to the Brahmanical movement. On the other hand, they gave to the local cults the prestige of the Vedic religion and linked the various sects and groups with such dominant patterns of thought as respect for Brāhmans and acceptance of the caste system. In these ways they were indispensable for the creation of a system that was able to comprehend within itself the legacy of variegated cultures and religious traditions.

A STORY OF ORIGINS:
THE CHURNING OF THE OCEAN

One of the most famous of the Puranic stories tells how the gods, when oppressed by a race of demons, called Daityas, called on Vishnu (or Hari) to save them. After agreeing to help, Vishnu told them to make a brief truce with their enemies and then to throw a variety of herbs into the ocean. Incarnating himself as a tortoise, he then helped the gods churn the ocean to obtain *amrita*, the nectar of immortality, which enabled them to defeat the demons. Among the many treasures thrown up at the same time were Lakshmī, the beautiful goddess of prosperity who became Vishnu's consort.

Being thus instructed by the god of gods, the divinities entered into alliance with the demons, and they jointly undertook the acquirement of the beverage of immortality. They collected various kinds of medicinal herbs, and cast them into the sea of milk, the waters of which were radiant as the thin and shining clouds of autumn. They then took the mountain Mandara for the staff; the serpent Vāsuki for the cord; and commenced to churn the ocean for the Amrita. The assembled gods were stationed by Krishna at the tail of the serpent; the Daityas and Dānavas at its head and neck. Scorched by the flames emitted from his inflated hood, the demons were shorn of their glory; whilst the clouds driven towards his tail by the breath of his mouth, refreshed the gods with revivifying showers. In the midst of the milky sea, Hari himself, in the form of a tortoise, served as a pivot for the mountain, as it was whirled around. The holder of the mace and discus was present in other forms amongst the gods and demons, and assisted to drag the monarch of the serpent race: and in another vast body he sat upon the summit of the mountain. With one portion of his energy, unseen by gods or demons, he sustained the serpent king; and with another, infused vigour into the gods.

From the ocean, thus churned by the gods and Dānavas, first uprose the cow Surabhi, the fountain of milk and curds, worshipped by the divinities, and beheld by them and their associates with minds disturbed, and eyes glistening with delight. The troop of Apsarases, the nymphs of heaven, were then produced, of surprising loveliness, endowed with beauty and with taste. The cool-rayed moon next rose; and then poison was engendered from the sea, of which the snake gods (Nāgas) took possession. Dhanwantari, robed in white, and bearing in his hand the cup of Amrita, next came forth. . . . Then, seated on a full-blown lotus, and holding a water-lily in her hand, the goddess Lakshmī, radiant with beauty, rose from the waves. The great sages, enraptured, hymned her with the song dedicated to her praise. . . .

The sea of milk in person presented her with a wreath of never-fading flowers; and the artist of the gods decorated her person with heavenly ornaments. Thus bathed, attired, and adorned, the goddess, in the view of the celestials, cast herself upon the breast of Hari; and there reclining, turned her eyes upon the deities, who were inspired with rapture by her gaze. . . .

The powerful and indignant Daityas then forcibly seized the Amrita-cup, that was in the hand of Dhanwantari: but Vishnu, assuming a female form, fascinated and deluded them; and recovering the Amrita from them, delivered it to the gods. The deities quaffed the ambrosia. The incensed demons, grasping their weapons, fell upon them; but the gods, into whom the ambrosial draught had infused new vigour, defeated and put their host to flight, and they fled through the regions of space, and plunged into the subterraneous realms of hell. The gods thereat greatly rejoiced, did homage to the holder of the discus and mace, and resumed their reign in heaven. The sun shone with renovated splendour, and again discharged his appointed task; and the celestial luminaries again circled, oh best of Munis, in their respective orbits. Fire once more blazed aloft, beautiful in splendour; and the minds of all beings were animated by devotion. The three worlds again were rendered happy by prosperity; and Indra, the chief of the gods, was restored to power.

(from *Vishnu Purāna*, I:9, trans. by H. H. Wilson, pp. 75-77)

THE PRICE OF DEVOTION:
THE TRIUMPH OF PRAHLĀDA

The *Purānas* have many stories of devotees who suffered for their faith. One of the most famous of these is an account of the tortures undergone by Prahlāda, a worshipper of Vishnu. His father, the demon king Hiranyakashipu, enraged that his son offered devotion to his great enemy, forbade him to continue his prayers. When the boy refused, the demon king ordered that he be put to death, but despite all kinds of ingenious tortures, he was always saved by Vishnu's intervention. In the passage given here, Prahlāda's long sufferings end with his father's death and repentance and his own assumption of the throne.

This story has had a powerful appeal for the Indian imagination and allusions are frequent to it both in literature and conversation.

Whilst with mind intent on Vishnu, Prahlāda thus pronounced his praises, the divinity, clad in yellow robes, suddenly appeared before him. Startled at the sight, with hesitating speech Prahlāda pronounced repeated salutations to Vishnu, and said, "Oh thou who removest all worldly grief, Keshava, be propitious unto me; again sanctify me, by thy sight." The deity replied, "I am pleased with the faithful attachment thou hast shewn to me: demand from me, Prahlāda, whatever thou desirest." Prahlāda replied,

"In all the thousand births through which I may be doomed to pass, may my faith in thee, never know decay; may passion, as fixed as that which the worldly-minded feel for sensual pleasures, ever animate my heart, always devoted unto thee." Vishnu answered, "Thou hast already devotion unto me, and ever shalt have it: now choose some boon, whatever is in thy wish." Prahlāda then said, "I have been hated, for that I assiduously proclaimed thy praise: do thou, oh lord, pardon in my father this sin that he hath committed. Weapons have been hurled against me; I have been thrown into the flames; I have been bitten by venomous snakes; and poison has been mixed with my food; I have been bound and cast into the sea; and heavy rocks have been heaped upon me: but all this, and whatever ill beside has been wrought against me; whatever wickedness has been done to me, because I put my faith in thee; all, through thy mercy, has been suffered by me unharmed: and do thou therefore free my father from this iniquity." To this application Vishnu replied, "All this shall be unto thee, through my favour: but I give thee another boon: demand it, son of the Asura." Prahlāda answered and said, "All my desires, oh lord, have been fulfilled by the boon that thou hast granted, that my faith in thee shall never know decay. Wealth, virtue, love, are as nothing; for even liberation is in his reach whose faith is firm in thee, root of the universal world." Vishnu said, "Since thy heart is filled immovably with trust in me, thou shalt, through my blessing, attain freedom from existence." Thus saying, Vishnu vanished from his sight; and Prahlāda repaired to his father, and bowed down before him. His father kissed him on the forehead, and embraced him, and shed tears, and said, "Dost thou live, my son?" And the great Asura repented of his former cruelty, and treated him with kindness: and Prahlāda, fulfilling his duties like any other youth, continued diligent in the service of his preceptor and his father. After his father had been put to death by Vishnu in the form of the man-lion, Prahlāda became the sovereign of the Daityas; and possessing the splendours of royalty consequent upon his piety, exercised extensive sway, and was blessed with a numerous progeny. At the expiration of an authority which was the reward of his meritorious acts, he was freed from the consequences of moral merit or demerit, and obtained, through meditation on the deity, final exemption from existence.

Such was the Daitya Prahlāda, the wise and faithful worshipper of Vishnu, of whom you wished to hear; and such was his miraculous power. Whoever listens to the history of Prahlāda is immediately cleansed from his sins: the iniquities that he commits, by night or by day, shall be expiated by once hearing, or once reading, the history of Prahlāda.

(from *Vishnu Purāna*, I:20, trans. by H. H. Wilson, pp. 144-145)

THE LINEAGE OF KINGS

An important feature of the sacred history of the Puranic literature is the tracing of the genealogy of kings back to Manu, the first man, and, through him, back to primeval deities. These genealogies gave kings divine status, but the authors of the *Purānas* were probably not primarily motivated by political considerations. They were depicting their understanding of the universe, where the supernatural was commonplace, miraculous births were ordinary, and the dividing line between the divine and human was always being blurred. Indian kings generally traced their descent either to the sun or the moon, and royalty is usually designated as belonging to the "solar race" or the "lunar race." One of the most famous of the genealogies of kings is given in the *Vishnu Purāna*. The two lines of royalty are traced back to the great deity Brahmā through Manu, whose father was the sun, but whose daughter, Ila, had a child by the son of the deity of the moon. This is obviously not history in any conventional sense, but there is an inter-weaving of the stories of the gods with the records of actual kings, such as those of the Mauryan dynasty, that gives a new dimension to both gods and men. The selection given here tells of the origin of the lunar race of kings, and the descent of the divine nymph Urvashī to live with the earthly king Purūravas, illustrating the intricate blending of earthly and heavenly scenes. Such "history" is a vital element of the Hindu tradition; the complexities of the lineages may not be known, but the stories themselves, with their sometimes gro-tesque imagery, have fed the imaginations of countless gen-erations.

Brahmā was the primeval, uncreated cause of all worlds. From the right thumb of Brahmā was born the patriarch Daksha; his daughter was Aditi, who was the mother of the sun. Manu . . . was the son of the celestial luminary. . . . Manu, being desirous of sons, offered a sacrifice for that purpose . . . but the rite being deranged through an irregularity of the ministering priest, a daughter, Ila, was produced. . . . Budha, the son of the deity of the moon, saw and espoused her, and by her a son named Purūravas.

Purūravas was a prince renowned for liberality, devotion, magnificence, and love of truth, and for personal beauty. Urvashī having incurred the imprecation of Mitra and Varuna, determined to take up her abode in the world of mortals; and descending accordingly, beheld Purūravas. As soon as she saw him she forgot all reserve, and disregarding the delights of heaven, became deeply enamoured of the prince. Beholding her infinitely superior to all other fe-males in grace, elegance, symmetry, delicacy, and beauty, Purūravas was equally fascinated by Urvashī: both were inspired by similar sentiments, and mutually feeling that each was every thing to the other, thought no more of any other object. Confiding in his merits, Purūravas addressed the nymph, and said, "Fair creature, I love you; have compassion on me, and return my affection." Urvashī, half averting her face through modesty, replied, "I will do so, if you will observe the conditions I have to propose." "What are they?" inquired the prince; "declare them." "I have two rams," said the nymph, "which I love as children; they must be kept near my bedside, and never suffered to be carried away: you must also take care never to be seen by me undressed; and clarified butter alone must be my food." To these terms the king readily gave assent.

After this, Purūravas and Urvashī dwelt together, sporting amidst the groves and lotus-crowned lakes for sixty-one thousand years. The love of Purūravas for his bride increased every day of its duration; and the affection of Urvashī augmenting equally in fervour, she never called to recollection residence amongst the immortals. Not so with the attendant spirits at the court of Indra; and nymphs, genii, and quiristers, found heaven itself but dull whilst Urvashī was away.

Knowing the agreement that Urvashī had made with the king, Vishwavasu was appointed by the Gandharbas to effect its violation; and he, coming by night to the chamber where they slept, carried off one of the rams. Urvashī was awakened by its cries, and exclaimed, "Ah me! who has stolen one of my children? Had I a husband, this would not have happened! To whom shall I apply for aid?" The Rājā overheard her lamentation, but recollecting that he was undressed, and that Urvashī might see him in that state, did not move from the couch. Then the Gandharbas came and stole the other ram; and Urvashī, hearing it bleat, cried out that a woman had no protector who was the bride of a prince so dastardly as to submit to this outrage. This incensed Purūravas highly, and trusting that the nymph would not see his person, as it was dark, he rose, and took his sword, and pursued the robbers, calling upon them to stop, and receive their punishment. At that moment the Gandharbas caused a flash of brilliant lightning to play upon the chamber, and Urvashī beheld the king undressed: the compact was violated, and the nymph immediately disappeared. The Gandharbas, abandoning the rams, departed to the region of the gods.

Having recovered the animals, the king returned delighted to his couch, but there he beheld no Urvashī; and not finding her any where, he wandered naked over the world, like one insane. At length coming to Kurukshetra, he saw Urvashī sporting with four other nymphs of heaven in a lake beautified with lotuses, and he ran to her, and called her his wife, and wildly implored her to return. "Mighty monarch," said the nymph, "refrain from this extravagance. I am now pregnant: depart at present, and come hither again at the end of a year, when I will deliver to you a son, and remain with you for one night." Purūravas, thus comforted, returned to his capital. Urvashī said to her companions, "This prince is a most excellent mortal: I lived with him long and affectionately united." "It was well done of you," they replied; "he is indeed of comely appearance, and one with whom we could live happily for ever."

When the year had expired, Urvashī and the monarch met at Kurukshetra, and she consigned to him his firstborn Āyus; and these annual interviews were repeated, until she had borne to him five sons. She then said to Purūravas, "Through regard for me, all the Gandharbas have expressed their joint purpose to bestow upon my lord their benediction: let him therefore demand a boon." The Rājā replied, "My enemies are all destroyed, my faculties are all entire; I have friends and kindred, armies and treasures: there is nothing which I may not obtain except living in the same region with my Urvashī. My only desire therefore is, to pass my life with her." When he had thus spoken, the Gandharbas brought to Purūravas a vessel with fire, and said to him, "Take this fire, and, according to the precepts of the Veda, divide it into three fires; then fixing your mind upon the idea of living with Urvashī, offer oblations, and you shall surely obtain your wishes." . . . In this way . . . Purūravas obtained a seat in the sphere of the Gandharbas and was no more separated from his beloved. (And his sons reigned in his kingdom, monarchs of the lunar line.)

(from the *Vishnu Purāna*, trans. by H. H. Wilson, pp. 348-50, 394-96)

SACRED GEOGRAPHY

One aspect of the Hindu tradition that helps to account for its great vitality through the centuries is the emphasis from very early times on India (*Bhāratavarsha*) as the holy motherland. There is hardly a river or other natural feature that has not some well-known incident of scripture connected with it. This means that there is always a sense of living in a land known intimately to the gods, of moving among scenes hallowed by deeds that were performed on earth but in which gods were the actors. The Himālayas and the Ganges (*Gangā*) are the most famous of holy places, and are part of the daily heritage of millions who have never seen them, but there are endless sites of scarcely less sanctity. In the passages given here, the holiness of India and the Ganges are especially praised, and it seems certain that this had the effect of giving the people a sense of the unity of India, even though it was divided politically. The numerous pilgrimages to sacred places must have also given the people a knowledge of the geography of the country. The great annual festivals at holy places like Prayāg (Allahabad) brought people from the far corners of India.

Bhārata is therefore the best of the divisions of the world, because it is the land of works: the others are places of enjoyment alone. It is only after many thousand births, and the aggregation of much merit, that living beings are sometimes born in Bhārata as men. The gods themselves exclaim, "Happy are those who are born, even from the condition of gods, as men in Bhārata-varsha, as that is the way to the pleasures of Paradise, or the greater blessing of final liberation. Happy are they who, consigning all the unheeded rewards of their acts to the supreme and eternal Vishnu, obtain existence in that land of works, as their path to him. We know not, when the acts that have obtained us heaven shall have been fully recompensed, where we shall renew corporeal confinement; but we know that those men are fortunate who are born with perfect faculties in Bhārata-varsha.

From the third region of the atmosphere, or seat of Vishnu, proceeds the stream that washes away all sin, the river Gangā, embrowned with the unguents of the nymphs of heaven, who have sported in her waters. Having her source in the nail of the great toe of Vishnu's left foot, Dhruva receives her, and sustains her day and night devoutly on his head; and thence the seven Rishis (Holy men) practise the exercises of austerity in her waters, wreathing their braided locks with her waves. The orb of the moon, encompassed by her accumulated current, derives augmented lustre from her contact. Falling from on high, as she issues from the moon, she alights on the summit of Meru, and thence flows to the four quarters of the earth, for its purification. . . . The offences of any man who bathes in this river are immediately expiated, and unprecedented virtue is engendered. Its waters, offered by sons to their ancestors in faith for three years, yield to the latter rarely attainable gratification. Men of the twice-born orders, who offer sacrifice in this river to the lord of sacrifice, Vishnu, obtain whatever they desire, either here or in heaven. Saints who are purified from all soil by bathing in its waters, and whose minds are intent on Vishnu, acquire thereby final liberation. This sacred stream, heard of, desired, seen, touched, bathed in, or hymned, day by day, sanctifies all beings; and those who, even at a distance of a hundred leagues, exclaim "Gangā, Gangā," atone for the sins committed during three previous lives. The place whence this river proceeds, for the purification of the three worlds, is the third division of the celestial regions, the seat of Vishnu.

(from *Vishnu Purāna*, II:3 and 8, trans. by H. H. Wilson, pp. 178, 228-29)

THE NATURE OF HISTORY

While it is impossible to speak of a "Hindu view of history," since this phrase implies a way of looking at the world that was foreign to Indian thought, there is, however, an understanding of the nature of the historical process that is of fundamental importance for the Hindu tradition. The principal feature of this understanding, which is given an elaborate analysis in the *Purānas*, is that human existence must be seen against a background of an almost unimaginable duration of time. In contrast to other civilizations which have been content to see man's history in terms of thousands of years, Indians—Buddhists and Jains as well as Hindus—spoke of billions of years. But even these figures, which are nearly meaningless in their magnitude, are dwarfed by the concept of cycles of aeons, endlessly renewing themselves, without beginning or end. Time and the historical process are parts of a vast cyclical movement, but not, as in some cyclical versions of history, a simple cycle of birth, growth, death and then rebirth with a repetition of the past. The Hindu model is of concentric circles, moving within each other in a complex series of retrogressive movements. The vastest cycle was "a year of Brahmā," which by some reckonings was 311,040,000 million years long, with Brahmā's life lasting for one hundred of these cycles. This was followed by dissolution of all the worlds—those of men and gods—and then creation once more took place.

Within these cycles there were other cycles which were of more imaginable dimensions, and it is these which are of primary significance for human history. A *kalpa*, or day of Brahmā, was 4,320 million years long, and within this were the smallest cycles, the four *yugas*. The *Krita Yuga*, the golden age, lasted for 1,728,000 years; the *Tretā*, for 1,296,000 years; the *Dvā-para* for 864,000 years; and the *Kali* for 432,000 years. The four ages are calculated as a descending arithmetical progression, marked by progressive physical and spiritual deterioration. Present history is taking place within the *Kali Yuga*, which explains the violence and evil of human history. When this age comes to an end, a new cycle will begin—one of the thousand cycles of *yugas* that make up a day of Brahmā.

Man cannot save the social process from the decay and dissolution that is an inherent part of its structure, but he can save himself from within the process. The point is made, indeed, that one mark of the wickedness of the *Kali Yuga* is that salvation has been made much easier than in the former ages, since men of this age could not be expected to fulfill the rigorous requirements of a better time.

The selection gives a graphic picture of the Kali Age as a time when the bonds of society are broken and virtue perishes from the earth. It is probably partly to be understood as a warning of things to come if men do not follow the teachings of religion, but it can also be read as a description of how the world seemed to a pious man living at a time when India was invaded by foreigners or *Mleccha*, "barbarians," as the Hindus referred to those outside the boundaries of India. Possibly this is a reference to an invasion by the Huns in fifth century or to the raids by the Turks in the tenth century. In any case, the times were so evil that, as the passage indicates, men looked for the coming of Vishnu in a new incarnation to restore the social order. With the coming of Vishnu as Kalki the Kali Age will end, and Krita, the golden age, will begin once more.

MAITREYA.—You have narrated to me, illustrious sage, the creation of the world, the genealogies of the patriarchs, the duration of the great cycles, and the dynasties of princes, in detail. I am now desirous to hear from you an account of the dissolution of the world, the season of total destruction, and that which occurs at the expiration of a Kalpa.

PARĀSHARA.—Hear from me, Maitreya, exactly the circumstances of the end of all things, and the dissolution that occurs either at the expiration of a Kalpa, or that which takes place at the close of the life of Brahmā. A month of mortals is a day and night of the progenitors: a year of mortals is a day and night of the gods. Twice a thousand aggregates of the four ages is a day and night of Brahmā. The four ages are the Krita, Treta, Dwāpara, and Kali; comprehending together twelve thousand years of the gods. There are infinite successions of these four ages, of a similar description, the first of which is always called the Krita, and the last the Kali. In the first, the Krita, is that age which is created by Brahmā; in the last, which is the Kali age, a dissolution of the world occurs. . . .

At that time there will be monarchs, reigning over the earth; kings of churlish spirit, violent temper, and ever addicted to falsehood and wickedness. They will inflict death on women, children, and cows; they will seize upon the property of their subjects; they will be of limited power, and will for the most part rapidly rise and fall; their lives will be short, their desires insatiable, and they will display but little piety. The people of the various countries intermingling with them will follow their example, and the barbarians being powerful in the patronage of the princes, whilst purer tribes are neglected, the people will perish. Wealth and piety will decrease day by day, until the world will be wholly depraved. Then property alone will confer rank; wealth will be the only source of devotion; passion will be the sole bond of union between the sexes; falsehood will be the only means of success in litigation; and women will be objects merely of sensual gratification. Earth will be venerated but for its mineral treasures; the Brahmanical thread will constitute a Brāhman; external types (as the staff and red garb) will be the only distinctions of the several orders of life; dishonesty will be the universal means of subsistence; weakness will be the cause of dependence; menace and presumption will be substituted for learning; liberality will be devotion; simple ablution will be purification; mutual assent will be marriage; fine clothes will be dignity; and water afar off will be esteemed a holy spring. Amidst all castes he who is the strongest will reign over a principality thus vitiated by many faults. The people, unable to bear the heavy burdens imposed upon them by their avaricious sovereigns, will take refuge amongst the valleys of the mountains, and will be glad to feed upon wild honey, herbs, roots, fruits, flowers, and leaves: their only covering will be the bark of trees, and they will be exposed to the cold, and wind, and sun, and rain. No man's life will exceed three and twenty years. Thus in the Kali age shall decay constantly proceed, until the human race approaches its annihilation.

When the practices taught by the Vedas and the institutes of law shall nearly have ceased, and the close of the Kali age shall be nigh, a portion of that divine being who exists of his own spiritual nature in the character of Brahmā, and who is the beginning and the end, and who comprehends all things, shall descend upon earth: he will be born as Kalki in the family of an eminent Brāhman of Sambhala village, endowed with the eight superhuman faculties. By his irresistible might he will destroy all the Mlechchhas and thieves, and all whose minds are devoted to iniquity. He will then reestablish righteousness upon earth; and the minds of those who live at the end of the Kali age shall be awakened, and shall be as pellucid as crystal. The men who are thus changed by virtue of that peculiar time shall be as the seeds of human beings, and shall give birth to a race who shall follow the laws of the Krita age, or age of purity. As it is said; "When the sun and moon, and the lunar asterism Tishya, and the planet Jupiter, are in one mansion, the Krita age shall return."

(from *Vishnu Purāna*, VI:1 and IV:24, selections, in H. H. Wilson, pp. 621 and 482-84)

PART FOUR

THE TRADITION AND THE PEOPLE'S FAITH

INTRODUCTION

For lack of a better term, the belief and practices of the great bulk of the people of India are often referred to as "Popular Hinduism," and very frequently the implication in this usage is that the religion of the masses is debased and corrupt, in contrast with the religion of the great scriptural texts. This suggestion is heightened by the use of "higher Hinduism" and "lower Hinduism" to distinguish what seem to be obvious enough differences between the faith of the ordinary people and that of the seers and saints. But while it is true that in Hinduism, as in every tradition, the realization of the ethical and spiritual ideals is often at variance with the intention of the texts, nevertheless, the divergence between the "high" culture and the "low" is not as great as it appears from the outside. The rarefied intellectual abstractions of the Vedānta philosophy of Shankara, for example, may seem to have nothing in common with the faith of the peasant as he worships his crudely-formed idol beneath a tree, but, as has been suggested in the discussion of Vedānta, it is possible to bring both beliefs under one systematic statement.

It is a part of the genius of the Hindu tradition that the external dissimilarities between the levels of faith and practice have been transcended. One way in which this was accomplished was through the recognition of inherent differences in spiritual and moral capabilities—an acceptance that found institutional form in the caste system as well as in the ideal structures of the four classes, the four stages of life, and the four ends of man. Then the great assumptions of the tradition, a belief in *karma* and the obligations of *dharma*, further enforced the acceptance of differing standards of behavior and different levels of spiritual attainment. But perhaps most important of all influences working for a unity that bound together various levels of cultural and religious experience were the songs of the poet-saints who expressed the values of the great tradition in the language of the common people. Thus it is that while the practice of the peasant may differ very radically from that of the learned man, and while he may not be able to formulate his religious belief, nevertheless, the hymns and songs that have been the source of nourishment for his spiritual life have brought him into contact with the fundamentals of the "high" religion.

The classical Sanskrit in which the literary and philosophical works of the Hindu tradition were written was the *lingua franca* of the learned and upper classes of India, but it was almost certainly never the language of the people. In North India, the people spoke a variety of Indo-Aryan languages related to it, known as *Prākrits*, meaning "natural" or "unrefined," and out of these developed the great languages of modern India, such as Bengali, Marathi, and Hindi. In South India, the people spoke Dravidian languages, which were very different from the Indo-Aryan tongues of North India. The most important of these were Tamil and Telugu, and while Sanskrit became the language of religion in the South, these indigenous languages remained the medium of communication for all ordinary purposes. To meet the needs of the people who did not know Sanskrit, it was necessary that there be hymns and songs written in the ordinary languages, and this need was amply fulfilled by a great number of religious poets in both North and South.

This new class of literature first made its appearance in South India, partly perhaps because the need was greater, since languages like Tamil were so alien to the Sanskrit, but also partly because there seems to have been a quite well-developed literary tradition among the Tamil-speaking people. The poetry that was written in the common languages gave particular expression to the devotional theism, *bhakti,* which had a long history of development. The ideas expressed in the *bhakti* hymns were not new, but they made more appeal to the hearts of the people than other forms of religion.

It was not only the devotion of *bhakti* religion, however, that found expression in the vernacular hymns. The great stories of the tradition, the mythological background, the exhortations to virtuous conduct, all these were given a place in the songs of the poets, who as agents of the high culture helped to create the pervasive unity of Hinduism.

The movement for expressing religious truth in the language of the people began in the South by at least the seventh century A.D. The time and place are both significant, for they make clear that the impetus towards devotional religion came from within the tradition itself, not, as has sometimes been suggested, from contact with Islam in the twelfth century. The devotional literature in Tamil, as in most of the Indian languages, was centered on either Shiva or Vishnu, with the hymns to Shiva being the earliest and most abundant. Along the western coast, a great succession of poets awakened love for Vishnu among the Marathi-speaking peoples from the thirteenth century on, and by the fifteenth century poets were praising him in the Hindi dialects of North India. In eastern India, both Shiva and Vishnu were the objects of a great literary movement by Bengali poets.

During the centuries when the poet-saints were winning the hearts of the people of India for Vishnu and Shiva, Hindu civilization was threatened by incursions by Islamic peoples from the north-west, the historic route taken by invaders of the country. The first invasions by Muslims date from the eighth century when Arab forces established themselves along the lower reaches of the Indus River, in what is now Pakistan, but this conquest had little effect on the rest of India, as the area was so remote from the main centers of life. The real threat to Hindu culture came from a Turkish people who had accepted Islam and had settled in Afghanistan. Beginning at the end of the tenth century they raided North India, plundering the great temples and carrying away people as slaves, but not attempting to set up kingdoms. At the end of the twelfth century, however, one of the ablest of the Turkish rulers defeated Prithvi Rāj, the last important northern Hindu king, at a great battle in 1192 at Tarain, north of Delhi.

Muhammad Ghori's victory did not mean that India, or even all of North India, came under Muslim rule, for many Hindu rulers survived. Their effective leadership, however, had disappeared. In succeeding centuries various Muslim dynasties ruled from Delhi, which had become the chief city of North India after the defeat of Prithvi Rāj, and eventually they expanded their power throughout the country. In the extreme South, Hindu kingdoms survived up to the sixteenth century, when the last one, Vijayanagar, was finally destroyed. Meanwhile, elsewhere in India, a large number of Muslim generals and military adventurers had carved out kingdoms for themselves whenever the ruler at Delhi had been unable to exert his authority.

In the sixteenth century new Muslim invaders, the people from Central Asia known as the Mughals, captured Delhi, and under four great rulers, Akbar (1556-1605), Jahāngīr (1605-1627), Shāh Jahān (1627-1658), and Aurangzīb (1658-1707), created an imposing empire. At the death of Aurangzīb most of India was under the control of the dynasty, but in fact the Muslim hegemony was nearing its end. Within fifty years western powers were struggling for supremacy, and by the end of the eighteenth century the British had firmly entrenched themselves in Bengal. Thus political power was to pass, not to the followers of the ancient tradition, but to another group, like the Muslims, alien in religion, race, and language.

The effects of Islamic conquest on India were great—the most striking evidence of this is the existence of at least one hundred and thirty million Muslims in the area at the present time—but the long centuries of alien domination had not destroyed either Hindu religion or culture. In all of history, no other civilization has ever been subjected to such a strain and managed to endure so unchanged in fundamentals as did the Hindu. There are many reasons for this, such as the vast Hindu population in comparison with the small number of invaders, the strength of the Hindu class system, and the attitudes of the Muslim rulers themselves, but much credit must be given to the poet-saints who made the immemorial tradition a living reality for the people of India. The songs of Hinduism were the products of a passionate faith that enabled men to live by old standards and old values by giving them relevance in a world that must have seemed hostile and menacing.

CHAPTER XI

IN PRAISE OF SHIVA

~~~~~~~~~~

Although Shiva was known throughout India in ancient times—what appears to be his image was found in the ruins of the Indus Valley civilization—his worship was most widespread in the South. While little is known with certainty of religious developments there, the Brahmanical religion from North India, with its great literature and ritual, had gained a strong position by the early centuries of the Christian era. In addition, both Buddhism and Jainism had many adherents, especially, as the many artistic remains suggest, among kings and wealthy merchants. Around the seventh century A.D., however, there appears to have been a great revival of emphasis on the worship of Shiva and an assertion of the claims of Hinduism against Buddhism and Jainism. As a result, the two unorthodox faiths lost their standing in the South, as they did elsewhere.

The instruments of this awakening or renewal of Shiva worship were a series of poet-saints who between the seventh and eleventh centuries produced a literature that is remarkable for both literary beauty and devotional passion. According to tradition there were sixty-three of these nāyanārs, or singers of the praises of Shiva, but four of them have left most of the legacy of poetry and song to the Tamil-speaking people of India. Of these, Appar (also known as Tirunāvukkarashu) and Sambandar (or Jñānasambandha) lived in the seventh century, Mānik-kavāchakar, who lived in the eighth century, and Sundara-mūrthi, who lived in the ninth century. Their poems contain many references to the legends of Shiva, suggesting that the stories themselves were well-known, and needed only an allusion on the part of the poet to bring them to the mind of the people.

Paralleling the worship of Shiva, and frequently coalescing with it, was the worship of shakti, which literally means "power," the personification of the dynamic, active forces of the universe. Sometimes Shiva himself was thought of as these powers—as, for example, when he is pictured as Lord of the Dance,—but more often shakti is identified with the consort of Shiva, under the name of Kālī or Durgā. The worship of shakti as a goddess under these or some other names is widespread not only in the South but also in Bengal, and probably can be traced back to very ancient fertility cults. This form of worship, which is a very vital element in Hinduism, was expounded in eso-teric works known as Tantras. One of the many methods for gaining salvation advocated by the Tantras is the ritual use of forbidden, or normally unlawful, acts, such as the eating of meat, the drinking of liquor, or promiscuous sexual intercourse, as a religious rite. One explanation of the introduction of these elements into worship of Shiva and his consort is that through them the worshipper asserts the oneness of all life, even those aspects usually considered unclean. Another possible explanation is that poison is used to drive out poison. By deliberately engaging in repulsive acts the devotee makes clear that he is not depending upon external goodness for his salvation. He does demonstrates his willingness to break with all conventional life. It points out, in any case, the recognition by Hinduism of the possibility of every facet of life being used for the great

end of salvation, and it speaks "to many fears and passions
that are deep in the human soul and seem to be part of the
secret of the universe." ¹

A DESCRIPTION OF SHIVA

Descriptions of Shiva's physical appearance, and references to
his special attributes, occupy an important place in the devotional literature. Associated with him, on the one hand, are
all the dark and terrifying products of the human imagination
—skulls, graveyards, demons, blood sacrifices; on the other
hand, there are many songs in praise of his matchless beauty.
Furthermore, he is the deity who has claimed the minds and
hearts of many of India's greatest intellectual figures, notably
Shankara (see Chapter IX). The explanation, as the following
passage from the *Mahābhārata* suggests, is that Shiva comprehends in his purpose all forms of being. For the philosopher,
Shiva stands as a symbol for the Absolute; for the simple devotee, he is present in the form of an image. Shiva's most common symbolic form, the *lingam*, or phallus, can be understood,
as the passage shows, as an indication that all living beings are
marked with a sign that proclaims Shiva's omnipresence. The
speaker here is a great saint, Upamanyu, whose mother had
told him of having had the glory of Shiva revealed to her. This
passage provides a useful background for the poet-saints who
wrote in praise of Shiva.

My mother said,—Mahādeva is exceedingly difficult to be
known by persons of uncleansed souls. These men are incapable of bearing him in their hearts or comprehending
him at all. They cannot retain him in their minds. They
cannot seize him, nor can they obtain a sight of him. Men
of wisdom aver that his forms are many. Many, again, are

¹ Nicol Macnicol, *Indian Theism* (London: 1915), p. 185.

the places in which he resides. Many are the forms of his Grace. . . .

Shiva assumes the forms of Brahmā and Vishnu and the chief of the celestials; of the Rudras, the Ādityas, and the Ashwins; and of those deities that are called Vishwedevas. He assumes the forms also of men and women, of ghosts and spirits and of all aquatic animals. . . . He assumes the forms of tortoises and fishes and conchs. He it is that assumes the forms of those coral sprouts that are used as ornaments by men. Indeed, the illustrious god assumes the forms of all creatures too that live in holes. He assumes the forms of tigers and lions and deer, of wolves and bears and birds, of owls and of jackals as well. He it is that assumes the forms of swans and crows and peacocks, of chameleons and lizards and storks. . . . He it is that assumes the form of Shesha (the snake), who sustains the world on his head. He has snakes for his belt, and his ears are adorned with ear-rings made of snakes. Snakes form also the sacred thread he wears. An elephant skin forms his upper garment. He sometimes laughs and sometimes sings and sometimes dances most beautifully. Surrounded by innumerable spirits and ghosts, he sometimes plays on musical instruments. Diverse again are the instruments upon which he plays, and sweet the sounds they yield. He sometimes wanders (over crematoria), sometimes yawns, sometimes cries, and sometimes causes others to cry. He sometimes assumes the guise of one that is mad, and sometimes of one that is intoxicated, and he sometimes utters words that are exceedingly sweet. He sometimes performs penances and sometimes becomes the deity for whose adoration those penances are undergone. He sometimes makes gifts and sometimes receives those gifts; sometimes disposes himself in Yoga and sometimes becomes the object of the Yoga contemplation of others. He may be seen on the sacrificial platform or in the sacrificial stake; in the midst of the cowpen or in the fire. He may not again be seen there. He may be seen as a boy or as an old man.

He sports with the daughters and the spouses of the Rishis. His hair is long and stands erect. He is perfectly naked, for he has the horizon for his garments. He is endued with terrible eyes. He is fair, he is darkish, he is dark, he is pale, he is of the color of smoke, and he is red. He is possessed of eyes that are large and terrible. He has empty space for his covering and he it is that covers all things.

He is the cause of the continuance and the creation (of the universe). He is the cause of the universe and the cause also of its destruction. He is the Past, the Present, and the Future. He is the parent of all things. Verily, he is the cause of every thing. He is that which is mutable, he is the unmanifest, he is Knowledge; he is Ignorance; he is every act; he is every omission; he is righteousness; and he is unrighteousness. Him, Behold, O Indra, in the image of Mahādeva the indications of both the sexes. That god of gods, Shiva, that cause of both creation and destruction, displays in his form the indications of both the sexes as the one cause of the creation of the universe.

If Maheshwara be not accepted, tell me, if thou hast ever heard of it, who else is there whose sign has been worshipped or is being worshipped by all the deities? He whose sign is always worshipped by Brahman, by Vishnu, by thee, O Indra, with all the other deities, is verily the foremost of all adorable deities. Brahman has for his sign the lotus. Vishnu has for his the discus. Indra has for his the thunder-bolt. But the creatures of the world do not bear any of the signs that distinguish these deities. On the other hand, all creatures bear the signs that mark Mahādeva and his spouse, Umā. Hence, all creatures must be regarded as belonging to Maheshwara. All creatures of the feminine sex, have sprung from Umā's nature as their cause, and hence it is they bear the mark of femeninity that distinguishes Umā; while all creatures that are masculine, having sprung from Shiva, bear the masculine mark that distinguishes Shiva. That person who says that there is, in the three worlds with their mobile and immobile creatures, any other cause than the Supreme Lord, and

that which is not marked with the mark of either Mahādeva or his spouse, should be regarded as very wretched.

(from *Mahābhārata*, Anushāsana Parva in P. C. Roy, XII, pp.
62-65, 72-73)

APPAR

According to tradition, Appar (seventh century) was born into
a Hindu family but became a Jain monk. He was reconverted
to Hinduism, however, when having contracted an incurable
disease, he was saved through the prayers of his sister to Shiva.
Because of this, he devoted the rest of his life to singing songs
in praise of Shiva and to preaching about him to the people.
His most illustrious convert is said to have been the king of the
Pallava country, the territory on the south-east coast of India.
This tradition probably indicates the return of the people, notably the kings, from allegiance to Buddhism and Jainism, to
the orthodox tradition.

In the first poem, the worshipper dedicates himself to Shiva,
naming over the parts of the body. The fourth verse is often
recited by the dying or to them. The second poem speaks of
the true freedom that comes to one who serves Shiva as a
servant. The reference in the first poem to Shiva drinking "the
dark sea's bane" recalls the churning of the ocean by Vishnu
(see Chapter X), when among the things churned up was a
poison. To save mankind from being harmed by it, Shiva drank
it. This is understood by his devotees to be a measure of his
love for mankind.

Consecration to Shiva

Head of mine, bow to Him,
  True Head, skull garlanded,
A skull was His strange begging-bowl,
  Bow low to Him, my head.

Eyes of mine, gaze on Him
   Who drank the dark sea's bane.
Eight arms He brandishes in dance,
   At Him agaze remain.

Ears of mine, hear His praise,
   Shiva, our flaming king.
Flaming as coral red His form:
   Ears, hear men praises sing.

What kinsmen in that hour
   When life departs, have we?
Who but Kuttālam's dancing lord
   Can then our kinsman be?

How proud shall I be there,
   One of His heavenly host,
At His fair feet who holds the deer,
   How proud will be my boast!

I sought Him and I found.
   Brahmā sought in vain on high.
Vishnu delved vainly underground.
   Him in my soul found I.

Triumph Through Shiva

We are not subject to any; we are not afraid of death;
   We will not suffer in hell; we live in no illusion;
We feel elated; we know no ills; we bend to none;
   It is all one happiness for us; there is no sorrow,
For we have become servants, once for all,
      Of the independent Lord,
And have become one at the beautiful flower-strewn feet
      Of that Lord.

(from Appar, in F. Kingsbury and G. E. Phillips, *Hymns of the Tamil Śaivite Saints*, pp. 53-55, and *Sources of Indian Tradition*, p. 353)

SAMBANDAR

Sambandar (seventh century) is reputed to have composed ten thousand hymns before he died at the age of sixteen. His marvellous songs are credited with having helped in the reconversion of many Jains and Buddhists to Hinduism. The first hymn given here was supposed to have been written when he was three years old. The second one makes the claim that Shiva is so all-encompassing in his power that he is the source of both good and evil.

Shiva's Glory

The serpent is his ear-stud, he rides the bull, he is
   crowned with the pure white crescent;
He is smeared with the ashes of destroyed forests;
He is decked with a garland of full-blossoming flowers;
When of old his devotees called him, he came to glittering
   Piramapuram,
He bestowed his grace upon all;
He is indeed the thief who has stolen my soul away.

The Lord Is Everything

   Thou art error, thou art merit, O Lord of Kūdal Ālavāi!
   Thou art kith and kin, Thou art master!
Thou art the light which shines without a break.
Thou art the inner meaning of all the sacred texts.
Material gain, the joys of love, all that man seeks, Thou
   art.
What can I utter in praise before Thee?

(from Sambandar, in R. C. Majumdar, *The Classical Age*, p. 330, and *Sources of Indian Tradition*, p. 354)

MĀNIKKAVĀCHAKAR

Mānikkavāchakar is said to have been the Prime Minister of the King of the Pāndya Kingdom (the southern tip of India) in the eighth century. Becoming a devotee of Shiva, he renounced the world and spent his life seeking to win followers for him.

In many temples the images of the gods are put to bed at night, and then awakened in the morning. This poem is a song sung to awaken Shiva, and admirably expresses the attitude of the pious worshipper towards the image itself. Modern interpreters frequently argue that the idol is only an aid to worship, but this is almost certainly a rationalization of what the devotee genuinely feels as he bows in reverence: for him, the idol is in a very real sense the dwelling place of God. G. U. Pope, whose translation is used here, suggested that for the poet there was an identity between the god imagined in his mind and the visible image to which he offered his devotion, and this seems to be the mood of the poem. "If it is remembered," Pope wrote, "that some of these images have been actually worshipped . . . for a thousand years . . . that each generation has done them service and lavished gifts upon them; that they are connected by association with the long line of saints and sages, and that it is earnestly believed that (Shiva's) method of gracious manifestation is by, through, and in, these,—or what we should call sacraments of his perpetual presence—we shall understand with what profound awe and enthusiastic affection even images . . . can be beheld by multitudes of good and excellent people."

A Song to Awaken Shiva

Hail! Being, Source to me of all life's joys! 'Tis dawn;
   upon Thy flower-like feet twin wreaths of blooms we lay,
And worship, 'neath the beauteous smile of grace benign
   that from Thy sacred face beams on us. Shiva-Lord,
Who dwell'st in Perun-turrai girt with cool rice-fields,

where 'mid the fertile soil th' expanding lotus blooms!
Thou on Whose lifted banner is the Bull! Master!
    Our mighty Lord! FROM OFF THY COUCH IN GRACE ARISE!

The sun has neared the eastern bound; darkness departs;
    dawn broadens out; and, like that sun, the tenderness
Of Thy blest face's flower uprising shines; and so,
    while bourgeons forth the fragrant flower of Thine eyes'
    beam,
Round the King's dwelling fair hum myriad swarms of bees.
    See, Shiva-Lord, in Perun-turrai's hallowed shrine Who
    dwell'st!
Mountains of bliss, treasures of grace Who com'st to yield!
    O surging Sea! FROM OFF THY COUCH IN GRACE ARISE!

The tender Koel's note is heard; the cocks have crowed;
    the little birds sing out; sound loud the tuneful shells;
Starlights have paled; day's lights upon the eastern hill
    are mustering. In favouring love O show to us
Thy twin feet, anklet-decked, divinely bright;—
    Shiva-Lord, in Perun-turrai's hallowed shrine Who
    dwell'st!
Thee all find hard to know; easy to us Thine own!
    Our mighty Lord! FROM OFF THY COUCH IN GRACE ARISE!

There stand the players on the sweet-voiced lute and lyre;
    there those that utter praises with the Vēdic chaunt;
There those whose hands bear wreaths of flowers entwined;
    there those that bend, that weep, in ecstasy that faint;
There those that clasp above their heads adoring hands;—
    Shiva-Lord, in Perun-turrai's hallowed shrine Who
    dwell'st!
Me too make Thou Thine own, on me sweet grace bestow!
    Our mighty Lord! FROM OFF THY COUCH IN GRACE ARISE!

(from Mānikkavāchakar, in G. U. Pope, *The Tiruvācagam*, pp. 207-09)

SUNDARAMŪRTHI

Known as the "Friend of God," Sundaramūrthi (ninth century) is credited with the performance of many miracles. The great significance attached to particular places associated with Shiva is brought out in these verses from some of his best-known hymns. Another noteworthy feature is the striking metaphor that compares Shiva to a madman; this indicates the ecstatic passion that fills the songs of many of the mystic poets.

Shiva's Dwelling Places

Ah sinful, I have left the path of love and service
    pure!
    Now know I well the meaning of my sickness
      and my pain.
    I will go worship. Fool! how long can I so far
      remain
From Him, my pearl, my diamond rare, the king
    of great Ārūr.

.   .   .   .   .   .

O madman with the moon-crowned hair,
    Thou lord of men, thou fount of grace,
How to forget Thee could I bear?
    My soul hath aye for Thee a place.
Venney-nallūr, in "Grace's shrine"
    South of the stream of Pennai, there
My father, I became all thine;
    How could I now myself forswear?

I roamed, a cur, for many days
    Without a single thought of Thee,
Roamed and grew weary, then such grace
    As none could win Thou gavest me.
Venney-nallūr, in "Grace's shrine"
    Where bamboos fringe the Pennai, there

My Shepherd, I became all thine;
   How could I now myself forswear?

Henceforth for me no birth, no death,
   No creeping age, bull-rider mine.
Sinful and full of lying breath
   Am I, but do Thou mark me Thine.
Venney-nallūr, in "Grace's shrine"
   South of the wooded Pennai, there
My Master, I became all thine;
   How could I now myself forswear?

   .   .   .   .   .   .

Linked to naught else in life, my mind thinks only
   of Thy holy feet.
   I'm born anew, from this time forth I pass the
      way of birth no more.
In Kodumudi, lord austere, where wise men Thee
   with praises greet,
      Should I forget Thee, my own tongue 'Hail,
      Śiva'! crying, would adore.

When will the end draw nigh, sense fade, life
   close, and I the bier ascend?
      This, naught but this, is all my thought. But,
      lord of speech, Thou light on high,
Where the bright streams of Kāviri to Kodumudi
   coolness lend,
      Should I forget Thee, my own tongue to Thee
      would loud 'Hail, Śiva' cry.

(from Sundaramūrthi, in F. Kingsbury and G. E. Phillips, pp. 75-9)

RĀMAPRASĀD

Rāmaprasād's dates—1718 to 1775—are a reminder that the great tradition of *bhakti* literature in praise of Shiva had an unbroken tradition of over a thousand years. One of the greatest of the many poets of Bengal, Rāmaprasād sang hymns in honor of a number of gods, but those he wrote for Kālī, the mother goddess, consort of Shiva and embodiment of *shakti*, or power, have a special importance. That Kālī is usually portrayed as dark and fearsome did not deter the poet from speaking of her in tones of great affection.

Shiva's Consort, Kālī

When you lie down,
Think you are doing obeisance to Her;
When you sleep, meditate on the Mother.
When you eat,
Think you are offering oblations to the Mother;
Whatever you hear with the ear is Her sacred incantation;
Each one the fifty letters of the alphabet represents Her
   alone.
Rāmaprasād declares in joy:
The Mother pervades everything;
When you move about in the city, you are walking around
   the Mother.

(from Rāmaprasād, in *Sources of Indian Tradition*, pp. 364-365)

LALLĀ

Kashmir was a center of Shiva worship, and, according to some traditions, it was from there that devotional Shaivism passed to the rest of India. Of the many mystics and poets of Kashmir who sang Shiva's praises, the most famous was a woman, Lallā, who lived in the fourteenth century. One of her poems is given here. Like many of the *bhakti* poets, she emphasized the need of inward experience, and the uselessness of formal worship that did not express true devotion. At the same time, Lallā makes use of the same metaphysical and theological structure of thought that one finds in the great intellectual statements, such as that of Shankara. Her hymns, which are still very popular in Kashmir, illustrate the way in which the teachings of the high tradition were passed on to the ordinary people.

The Indwelling Lord

I, Lallā, went far in search of Shiva,
    The Omnipresent Lord;
After wandering, I found Him within my own self,
    Abiding in His own Home.
The temples and images that you have fashioned
    Are no better than stone;
The Lord is immeasurable and consists of intelligence;
What is needed to realize him is unified concentration
    Of breath and mind.
Let them blame me or praise me or adore me with flowers;
I will become neither joyous nor sad,
For I rest in myself and am drunk with the nectar
    Of the Pure Lord.
With the help of the gardeners called Mind and Love,
Plucking the flower called Steady Contemplation,
Offering the water of the flood of the Self's own Bliss,
Worship the Lord with the sacred formula of silence!

(from Lallā, in *Sources of Indian Tradition*, p. 360, revised)

CHAPTER XII

IN PRAISE OF VISHNU
AS KRISHNA AND RĀMA

〰〰〰〰

Although the worship of Vishnu as supreme deity was very ancient, the great flowering of the cult dedicated to him took place after the eleventh century. Like the worship of Shiva, the cult found its first wide acceptance in the South. The poets who sang Vishnu's praise are known as the Ālvārs, and, along with the Shaivite nāyanārs, they have provided a rich religious literature. The intellectual framework for the Vishnu cult was provided by the great theologian Rāmānuja, whose philosophical position has already been noted (Chapter IX). Building on his interpretation of the Bhagavad Gītā as a work that exalts Vishnu as God, he argued that the weight of the Vedic tradition supported the worship of a personal deity, not the abstract Absolute of the followers of Shankara.

Unlike Shiva, Vishnu was usually worshipped under the form of one of his incarnations, not in his own person. The best known of these incarnations were Krishna and Rāma, with Krishna undoubtedly representing an older strain of religion, since he is the central figure of the Bhagavad Gītā which predates the first Christian century. When Krishna appears in the Purānas his character, or at least the legends associated with him, has undergone a considerable change from its portrayal in the Gītā, with the emphasis on his activities as a lover of the milkmaids and as the performer of mighty deeds. The stories of his many loves, but especially his love for Radha, are among the most familiar themes of Indian art, and when his praises were sung by the poets in the languages of the people the image frequently used is that of a passionate woman longing for the embrace of her lover. Thus the union of man and woman becomes the great symbol for the devotees of Krishna for the union of the soul with God.

The first of the Ālvārs lived some time between the sixth century and the ninth, but beyond that their dates cannot be ascertained with any certainty. There were twelve of them in all, and they have left four thousand hymns that are still the basis of devotion for the followers of Vishnu in the Tamil-speaking areas. In the fifteenth century a spiritual descendant of the Ālvārs, Vallabhāchārya (c. 1479-1531), went to North India and gave new life to the Krishna cult in Mathura, the ancient homeland of Lord Krishna. His influence was seen in Sūrdās (sixteenth century), in Mīrābāī, a Rajput Princess, and above all in Chaitanya (c. 1485-1533), who was said to have been his son-in-law. Chaitanya's teaching that the passionate longing that filled Radha's soul for union with Krishna should be reduplicated in the soul of each devotee as he sought for God placed a great emphasis on emotional experience. Like many of the mystics, he repudiated caste restrictions, and welcomed outcastes and Muslims into his movement. This attitude never became, however, a full-fledged social protest, and as his followers were absorbed into the complex web of Hindu society their particular religious emphasis proved attractive to many but they did not in any way threaten the main structure of religious beliefs and practices.

Even before the Krishna movement had spread to the Hindi and Bengali areas, it had firmly established itself along the western coast and among the hills in the Marāthi-speaking areas. The pioneer in the use of the

Marāthi language for learned purposes was Jnānadeva (c. 1275-1296), but the most famous of the Marātha saints was Tukārām (1598-1649). The particular deity which he and the Marāthas worshipped was called Vitobhā, and whether or not he was originally identified with Krishna, by Tukārām's time the Krishna legends and stories had been transferred to him.

Many of the devotees of Vishnu as Supreme God at times would praise Krishna and at times his other great incarnation, Rāma, but most of the poets tended to focus their worship rather exclusively on one or the other. Rāma, the Prince and King of Ayodhya, had, like all great kings in the Indian epics, a semi-divine quality, but in Valmiki's poem (see Chapter VII) he was not the deity he had become by the eleventh or twelfth century. Probably his deification was a long process and owed much to the faith of ordinary people in North India, but it was a South Indian, Rāmānanda, who, early in the fifteenth century, settled at Benares, the holiest of Hindu cities, and formed the nucleus of a cult devoted to the spreading of his worship. From this center radiated influences that have profoundly affected the religious life of India ever since.

Two different streams of devotional piety can be traced to Rāmānanda's circle. One of these drew for inspiration from Muslim sources as well as Hindu, and, indeed, there is good reason for supposing that the greatest figure of this blended movement, Kabīr (c. 1440-1518), came from a Muslim home. His poetry and that of some of his followers will be noted in the following chapter. The other stream of bhakti religion coming from Rāmānanda is purely Hindu in its inspiration. The greatest ornament of this movement is Tulasīdās (c. 1532-1623), and it would be difficult to overestimate his significance for the religious and moral life of North India.

The claim made by Sir George Grierson, a great nineteenth century student of Indian literary history, that no figure except Buddha so profoundly influenced as many Indians as did Tulasīdās, seems well-founded. Through

his poem, Rāmācharitamanas, *"The Lake of the Deeds of
Rāma," the story of Rāma and Sītā has become as familiar to the people of North India as the daily events of their
own lives. Through his poem, rather than through the
great Sanskrit scriptures, the ideas and concepts of Hinduism have permeated the lives of the people. Westerners
used to say that Tulasīdās' work was the Bible of India,
but that comparison is inadequate now, for Tulasīdās' book
is probably better known today in North India than the
Bible is in any country in the West. A selection from this
work is given to suggest something of its nature, but even
more than the other works, its attraction is not translata-
ble. As is the case with all devotional poetry, the believing
hearer or reader brings to it an attitude of reverence, and a
desire to be brought nearer to the deity it exalts, that neither sympathy nor interest alone can really duplicate.*

PURANDARADĀSA

Purandaradāsa (1480-1564) was the leading figure in a sect of
Krishna devotees in Karnataka (the modern Mysore). Like
most of the followers of Vishnu, he emphasized that what was
needed for salvation was inward devotion of the heart, not outward ritual observances, nor, as the following poem argues,
mortification of the body and fasting. The translation of the
original title, "Stomach Austerity," indicates the poet's contempt for those whose piety was ostentatious but devoid of
true devotion.

Stomach Austerity

This austerity is really for the sake of the stomach:
This austerity devoid of devotion to the Lord—
This rising at early dawn, this telling, with shivering frame,
  Of having bathed in the river,

While all the time the mind is filled with jealousy and
    anger;
This display of large numbers of images, like a bronze shop
    in the bazaar,

This conducting of worship with bright lights, to impress
    others. . . .
All these acts done without the abandonment of the sense
    of "I,"
Without communion with holy souls,
Without belief that everything depends only upon the
    Lord,
Without the vision in silence of the Lord,
All these are austerities practiced merely for livelihood.

(from Purandaradāsa, in *Sources of Indian Tradition*, p. 358)

JNĀNADEVA

Jnānadeva (1275-1296) is said to have written his great work,
Jnāneśvari, a commentary on the *Bhagavad Gītā* in Marāthi,
at the age of nineteen. There are a number of legends illustrating his saintliness, such as the famous story of how he
caused a water-buffalo to recite the *Vedas* to show a Brāhman
that the rote memorization of the scriptures was a sign neither
of intelligence nor piety.

A Prayer for Grace

Let the Lord of the Universe be pleased with this sacred
literary activity of mine, and being pleased, let him bestow
on me this grace:
May the wicked leave their crookedness,
May they cultivate increasing love for the good;
Let universal friendship reign among all beings,

Let the darkness of evil disappear.
Let the sun of true religion rise in the world,
Let all beings obtain their desires.
May all beings be endowed with happiness,
May they offer ceaseless devotion to the Primeval Being. . . .

(from *Jnānesvari*, in *Sources of Indian Tradition*, p. 358)

TUKĀRĀM

The songs of Tukārām (1598-1649) are the common property of the Marāthi speaking people of western India, and his influence on their lives has been very great. In most Indian devotional literature it is difficult to see much awareness of social conditions, or to trace any connection of religious movements with political events. The Marāthi saints are an exception to this general rule, for in their poetry one senses a strong note of dissatisfaction with the prevailing social arrangements, and in the seventeenth and eighteenth century their poetry helped bind the Marāthas together in their great struggle against the Mughals. Like many of the leaders of the *bhakti* movement, Tukārām came from a low caste, and this perhaps explains his strong egalitarian emphasis and his insistence that righteous living is the only criterion of worth. His writings are characterized by a passionate plea for moral living and a sense that life imposes almost intolerable burdens on man. Perhaps in no other author of the Indian tradition is there such an overwhelming feeling of the horror of the human condition because of man's accumulation of sin through endless rebirths. Escape from this is found through faith in the grace of Nārāyana, or Vishnu, who bears men's burden without consideration of their merit.

The Burden of the Past

I have been harassed by the world.
I have dwelt in my mother's womb and I must enter the
  gate of the womb eight million times.
I was born a needy beggar and my life is passed under a
  stranger's power.
I am bound fast in the meshes of my past and its fated
  influence continues with me,
It puts forth its power and whirls me along.
My stomach is empty and I am never at rest.
I have no fixed course or home or village.
I have no power, O God, to end my wanderings;
My soul dances about like rice in a frying pan.
Ages have passed in this way and I do not know how many
  more await me.
I cannot end my course, for it begins again;
Only the ending of the world can set me free.
Who will finish this suffering of mine?
Who will take my burden on himself?
Thy name will carry me over the sea of this world,
Thou dost run to help the distressed.
Now run to me, Nārāyaṇa, to me, poor and wretched as I
  am.
Consider neither my merits nor my faults.
Tukārām implores thy mercy.

(from Tukārām in J. N. Fraser and K. B. Marathe, *The Poems
of Tukārām*, pp. 114-15, revised)

MĪRĀBĀĪ

Many stories are told of how the devotion of Mīrābāī (c. 1500-
1550) for Krishna led her to abandon her husband, who was
the ruler of the ancient Rajput state of Mewār, and to pass her

life in complete dedication to the praise of her God. Once, for example, her husband, hearing her talking in a closed room to a man, rushed in with drawn sword to kill her for her unfaithfulness. But it was Krishna with her, and he transformed her into a multitude of forms so that the king could not tell which one was really his wife. In response to her continual pleading for a demonstration of his love for her, Krishna finally revealed himself in his glory and absorbed her soul into his. Her hauntingly lovely songs are still popular in western India and Rajasthan. In this poem, Giridhar Gopāl is a name of Krishna.

Krishna's Bride

My only Lord is Giridhar Gopāl,
None else, none else, in this false world;
I have forsaken my family and friends,
I sit among saintly souls,
I have lost regard for wordly fame and honor.
My heart swells at the sight of the godly,
It shrinks at the sight of the worldly.
I have watered the creeper of God's love with my own tears.
Churning the curds of life, I have taken out the butter, and thrown away the rest.
The King, my husband, sent me a cup of poison:
I drank it with pleasure.
The news is now public, everyone knows now
That Mīrābāī has fallen in love with God!
It does not matter now: what was fated to happen, has happened.

(from Mīrābāī, in *Sources of Indian Tradition*, p. 359, revised)

SŪRDĀS

Sūrdās (c. 1485-1563) was a follower of Vallabācharya, the theologian who provided a systematic basis for the Krishna cult. Sūrdās himself, however, cared little for systematic statements of theology, and his poetry is an intense outpouring of his love for Krishna. All that mattered was to lose oneself in an emotion that in some way duplicated the experience of Krishna. As he put it in a remarkable verse, "Whether through passion, anger, love or friendship, if a man thinks of God constantly, he becomes God." In the following poem, which uses the metaphor of the abandoned dancing of the professional dancing-girl, the poet conveys his sense of the futility of life apart from God. Gopāl is a name that recalls Krishna's life as cowherd; Nanda is the name of his foster father.

I have danced my full now, O Gopāl!
With passion and fury for my petticoat,
With lust for physical pleasure as my necklace,
With delusion jingling as my anklets,
With words of abuse as poetry,
With my mind full of false ideas as the big drum,
With my movement in the company of the sinful as the
    steps,
With avarice as the earthen pitcher making sound inside,
Beating time in various ways,
I have danced enough.
I have worn illusion as my girdle,
I have put on material craving as the mark on my fore-
    head;
I have endlessly demonstrated my wants, without regard to
    time or place;
O Son of Nanda, put an end to all this nonsense!

(from Sūrdās, as in *Sources of Indian Tradition*, p. 362-63, revised)

CHAITANYA

Chaitanya (c. 1485-1533) was one of the vital forces in the shaping of Bengali religion and literature. Unlike the other mystic poets and preachers, however, he did not leave a large legacy of songs, but only the memory of his extraordinary sense of the presence of the deity with him. He is credited with a number of important statements on the teaching of his sect, and one of them is given here. As a catechism of the Vaishnavite faith, it sums up the teachings of many of the groups. It is cast in the form of a dialogue between Chaitanya and a high official of the Kingdom of Orissa.

Question	Which knowledge is the highest of all?
Answer	There is no knowledge but devotion to Krishna.
Ques.	What is the highest glory in all types of glory?
Ans.	Being reputed to be Krishna's devotee.
Ques.	What is counted wealth among human possessions?
Ans.	He is immensely wealthy who has love for Rādhā-Krishna.
Ques.	What is the heaviest of all sorrows?
Ans.	There is no sorrow except separation from Krishna.
Ques.	Who is considered liberated among those who are liberated?
Ans.	He is the foremost of the liberated who practices devotion to Krishna.
Ques.	Among songs what song is natural to creatures?
Ans.	It is the song whose heart is the love-sports of Rādhā-Krishna.
Ques.	What is the highest good of all creatures?
Ans.	There is none except the society of those who are devoted to Krishna.
Ques.	Whom do creatures incessantly remember?

Ans.   The chief things to be remembered are Krishna's name, qualities and sports.

Ques.   Among objects of meditation which should creatures meditate on?

Ans.   The supreme meditation is on the lotus-feet of Rādhā-Krishna.

Ques.   Where should creatures live leaving all behind?

Ans.   It is the glorious land of Brindāban, where the rās-līlā is eternal.

Ques.   What is the best of things to be heard by creatures?

Ans.   The Rādhā-Krishna love sports are a delight to the ear.

Ques.   What is chief among the objects of worship?

Ans.   The name of the most adorable couple, Rādhā-Krishna.

(from *Chaitanya Charitamrita*, II:8, in M. T. Kennedy, *The Chaitanya Movement*, pp. 115-16)

TULASĪDĀS

Tulasīdās retold the familiar story of Rāma's exile in the forest with his wife Sītā and his brother Lakshman and of Sītā's capture by Rāvan, the demon king of Ceylon, but the epic tale was transformed to exalt Rāma as Supreme Lord. The author fulfilled his intention of awakening devotion to Rāma as creator of the Universe and Lord of all life by writing a work that combined to a perhaps unique degree the most lofty religious themes with a story calculated to appeal to the imagination of an unsophisticated audience. This does not mean that Tulasīdās' work appeals only to the uneducated, since it is in fact beloved by all classes, but only that it can speak directly to men and women on all levels of cultural and spiritual attainment.

As an example of the blending of ethical and religious teaching with narrative excitement the famous passage describing the attempt of the Vulture King, Jatāvu, to prevent the abduction of Sītā by Rāvan, the demon king of Ceylon, is given here. In the original story, Rāma had been lured away from the hermitage by a trick, but in Tulasīdās' version, as Supreme God he knows perfectly well that the deer he is hunting is a mirage called up by the demon Rāvan. But the poet's concern is to inspire his hearers with faith in Rāma's grace, not to tell a convincing story.

Rāvan angrily seized Sītā and seated her in his chariot. As he took his way through the air, he was so agitated with fear that he could scarcely drive. . . . Manifold were the lamentations that Sītā uttered. "My affectionate and loving lord is far away; who will tell him of my calamity; that an ass is devouring the oblation intended for the gods!" At the sound of Sītā's woeful lament every created being, whether animate or inanimate, was made sad. The vulture-king, too, heard her piteous cry and recognized the wife of the glory of Raghu's line, whom the vile demon was carrying away, as it were the famous dun cow that had fallen into the hands of some savage. "Fear not, Sītā my daughter, I will annihilate this monster." The bird darted forth in its fury, like a thunderbolt launched against a mountain. "Stop, you villain, how dare you go on thus and take no heed of me." . . . The vulture rushed on in a fury, crying: "Hearken Rāvan, to my advice; surrender Sītā and go home in peace; if not, despite your many arms, it will turn out thus; Rāma's wrath is like a fierce flame, and your whole house will be consumed in it like a moth." The warrior demon gave no answer. Then the vulture rushed wildly on and clutched him by the hair and dragged him from his chariot so that he fell to the ground. Again, having sheltered Sītā, the vulture turned and with his beak tore and rent his body. For nearly half an hour the demon was in a swoon, then gnashed his teeth with rage and drew his monstrous sword and cut off Jaṭāyu's wings. The bird fell to the ground, calling upon Rāma, and doing marvellous feats of courage. Then Rāvan again seated Sītā in the chariot and drove off in haste. Sītā was borne through the air lamenting, like a frightened fawn in the power of a huntsman.

Though he tried every kind of threat and blandishment, the monster could not make her yield to him, and at last after exhausting all his devices he left her under the Asoka tree. With Rāma's beauteous form impressed upon her heart, as he appeared when pursuing the mimic deer, Sītā was incessantly invoking his name, 'O Hari, Hari!' . . . When Rāma found the hermitage bereft of Sītā, he was as agitated as any common man. "Alas! Jānaki, my precious Sītā, so beautiful and amiable, so divinely pious and devoted! . . . How can I endure this cruelty at your hands; why do you not at once disclose yourself, my beloved?" In this manner the Lord searched and lamented, like a fond lover distressed by separation. Rāma, who has no wish unsatisfied, the perfection of bliss, the uncreated and the everlasting, acted the part of a man. Further on he saw the vulture-king lying, with his thoughts fixed on the prints of Rāma's feet.

The compassionate Raghubīr laid his lotus hands upon his head. At the sight of Rāma's lovely face all his pain was forgotten, and the vulture recovered himself and spoke as follows: "Hearken Rāma, remover of life's troubles. My lord, this is Rāvan's doing; he is the wretch, who has carried off Janak's daughter. He took her away, sire, to the south, crying as piteously as an osprey. I have kept alive, my lord, only to see you; now, O most merciful, I would depart." Said Rāma: "Remain alive, father." He smiled and answered: "He, by the repetition of whose name at the hour of death the vilest sinner, as the scriptures declare, attains salvation, has come in bodily form before my eyes; what need is there, sire, for me to live any longer?" Raghu-rāi's eyes filled with tears as he replied: "Father, it is your own good deeds that have saved you. There is nothing in the world beyond the reach of those who devote their soul to the good of others. When you pass out of the body, father, ascend to my sphere in heaven. What more can I give you? your every wish is gratified." Dropping the form of a vulture, he appeared in all the beauty of Hari, bedecked with jewels and in gorgeous yellow attire, with dark-hued body and four mighty arms, and with his eyes full of tears he chanted this hymn of praise:

"Glory to Rāma of incomparable beauty; the bodiless, the embodied; the veritable source of every bodily element; who with his mighty arrows has broken the might of the arm of the ten-headed demon; the ornament of the earth. With his body dark as a rain-cloud, with his lotus face and his eyes large as the lotus flower, I unceasingly worship Rāma the merciful, the mighty-armed, the dispeller of all life's terrors; of immeasurable strength; without beginning and unborn; the indivisible; the one; beyond the reach of all the senses; the incarnate Govinda; the annihilator of duality; the profound in wisdom; the supporter of the earth; an everlasting delight to the soul of the saints, who practise the spell of Rāma's name. I unceasingly worship Rāma, the friend of the unsensual, the destroyer of lust and every other wickedness. He, whom the scriptures hymn under the name of the passionless Brahm, the all-pervading, the supreme spirit, the unbegotten; to whom the saints attain after infinite study and contemplation, penance and abstraction; he the all-merciful, the all-radiant, the unapproachable, has now become manifest for the delight of the world. He who is at once inaccessible and accessible, like and unlike, the essentially pure, the unfailing comforter, whom ascetics behold only when they have laboriously subdued their mind and senses; even Rāma, the spouse of Lakshmi, who is ever at the command of his servants, though the lord of the three spheres, may he abide in my heart, the terminator of transmigration, whose praises make pure."

After asking the boon of perfect faith, the vulture departed for Hari's sphere. Rāma with his own hands performed his funeral rites with all due ceremony.

The tender-hearted and compassionate Raghunāth, who shows mercy even on the undeserving, bestowed upon a vulture, an unclean flesh-eating bird, such a place in heaven as the greatest ascetics desire. Hearken, then: the most miserable of men are they who abandon Hari and become attached to objects of sense.

(from Tulasīdās, *Rāmacaritamānasa*, III, selections in F. S. Growse, *The Rāmāyana of Tulsīdās*, pp. 345-56)

CHAPTER XIII

THE MEETING OF HINDU
AND MUSLIM DEVOTION

〜〜〜〜〜〜〜〜

As noted in the last chapter, of the two main groups of poets and religious singers affected by the influence of Rāmānanda, one, represented by Tulasīdās, remained wholly within the framework of traditional Hindu orthodoxy; the other, represented by Kabīr, was influenced by Islam and had a tendency to either move outside orthodoxy or at least to be related to it very loosely.

Although in general the spirit and temper of Islam was not congenial to any kind of meeting with Hinduism, there was one aspect of the invaders' faith that provided a common meeting ground. This was the religious experience of the Sūfīs, the Islamic mystics, who like the followers of Hindu bhakti religion sought salvation through an ardent and passionate love for God. Often suspect within Islamic orthodoxy because they spoke of a union with the Divine that seemed at variance with the insistence on the majesty and oneness of God, the Sūfīs found India a congenial home for their teachings. Many of the converts made to Islam in India were attracted by the message of these mystics and were not, as is sometimes thought, impelled by force or fear. And even when conversion did not take place, the Sūfī emphasis on experience as over against *doctrine made it possible for them to influence, and be influenced by, the poet-saints of Hinduism.*

Three great figures stand out in the religious history of India for their attempt to blend into a living faith concepts and values drawn from both Islam and Hinduism. Kabīr (1440-1518) was the earliest of the three and his influence was probably the most widespread. Nānak (1469-1538), the founder of the Sikh religion, owed much to Kabīr but he had also read the works of the Sūfīs. The third, Dādū (1544-1603), was also influenced by Kabīr, but his teachings had a stamp of originality. All of them would have denied that they were innovators, claiming that they were restoring the true religion which had become corrupted and superstitious, but in fact they introduced very real changes into the religious life of the peoples of North India, where they all had their homes. The surest evidence for this is that they were attacked by the guardians of the orthodox traditions, both Hindu and Muslim, as perverters of the true faith. But while they were innovators, it is also true that they contributed to the strengthening of Hinduism in North India—even Nānak, whose sect was markedly different from Hinduism. If one sought an analogy for their lives in Western religion one would find it not in the Protestant reformers of the fifteenth and sixteenth centuries of Europe, but rather in saints and mystics of the Middle Ages, who brought about internal change in the Church without altering its structure. Like all the great leaders of the bhakti movement, they were "mad after God," and although they might denounce caste and class and all the external things of Hinduism, such as fasts and pilgrimages, their real concern was with singing the praises of God, and getting men to experience his grace and love.

These poets—Kabīr, Nānak and Dādū—differed from the other bhakti singers in one important way: they tended to define God in somewhat abstract terms, and did not call upon him under the form of any of the incarnations of Shiva or Vishnu. This emphasis is probably an indica-

tion of Muslim influence, although there is precedent for it within Hinduism itself.

KABĪR

Kabīr (c. 1440-1518) was the first great spokesman for a faith that drew upon both Islamic and Hindu sources, and it is indicative of the esteem in which he was held by the common people, if not by the orthodox, that both religions claimed him as their own. As a child, he was apparently brought up as a Muslim, but he came under the influence of Rāmānanda, the mystic and theologian, and most of his ideas can be accounted for from within the Hindu tradition. His strict monotheism, however, as well as his rejection of caste and his contempt for idol worship, show Muslim influence. It is true that he addresses God as "Rāma" but this is not an incarnation, as is the Rāma of ordinary Hindu thought; it is, rather, a word for God, used, very likely, for lack of a better one, and also because at this time Rāma was assuming many characteristics of a Supreme God.

He wrote many poems in a dialect of Hindi and these have helped to give the language a literary form. Many of his sayings were expressed in brief form, and have the appearance of proverbs or folk wisdom, rather than deliberate compositions —many of them have actually passed into the common language. The first translations given here are by Rabīndranāth Tagore, the most famous of modern Indian poets. They express the warm humanity and deep sense of God's presence that have made Kabīr one of the most beloved of India's many singers of religious songs. Since Tagore's translations are rather more elegant than the originals, a few familiar verses are given in a more literal translation.

Open your eyes of love, and see Him who pervades this
   world! consider it well, and know that this is your own
   country.

When you meet the true Guru, He will awaken your
  heart;
He will tell you the secret of love and detachment, and
  then you will know indeed that He transcends this universe.

This world is the City of Truth, its maze of paths enchants
  the heart:
We can reach the goal without crossing the road, such is
  the sport unending.
Where the ring of manifold joys ever dances about Him,
  there is the sport of Eternal Bliss.
When we know this, then all our receiving and renouncing is over;
Thenceforth the heat of having shall never scorch us more.

He is the Ultimate Rest unbounded:
He has spread His form of love throughout all the world.
From that Ray which is Truth, streams of new forms are
  perpetually springing: and He pervades those forms.
All the gardens and groves and bowers are abounding
  with blossom; and the air breaks forth into ripples of
  joy. . . .
There the Eternal Fountain is playing its endless life-
  streams of birth and death.
They call Him Emptiness who is the Truth of Truths, in
  Whom all truths are stored!
There is an endless world, O my Brother! and there is the
  Nameless Being, of whom naught can be said.
Only he knows it who has reached that region: it is other
  than all that is heard and said.
No form, no body, no length, no breadth is seen there:
  how can I tell you that which it is?
He comes to the Path of the Infinite on whom the grace of
  the Lord descends: he is freed from births and deaths
  who attains to Him.
Kabīr says: "It cannot be told by the words of the mouth,
  it cannot be written on paper:

It is like a dumb person who tastes a sweet thing—how shall it be explained?"

(from Kabīr, in Rabīndranāth Tagore, *Songs of Kabīr*, pp. 118-21)

O Saints, the world has gone mad; if I tell the truth it comes down upon me to kill me, but believes a lie. I have seen the devout and the pious who regularly bathe in the mornings. They forsake God and worship stones; in them there is no wisdom. . . . They have commenced to worship brass and stones and are proud of their pilgrimages. They wear garlands, caps and frontal marks and signs on their arms, and engage in singing the praises of their gods; they have forsaken God.

The beads are of wood, the gods of stone, the Ganges and the Jumna are water. Rāma and Krishna are dead. The four Vedas are fictitious stories.

If by worshipping stones one can find God, I shall worship a mountain: better than these stones (idols) are the stones of the flour mill with which men grind their corn.

Although I entreat much, even falling at their feet, with tears in my eyes, the Hindus do not forsake idol-worship and the Muhammadans are too stiff-necked to hear any thing.

Kabīr says, I am completely at a loss; Is the holy place great or the servant of God?

(from Kabīr, in G. H. Westcott, *Kabīr and the Kabīr Panth*, pp. 58-59)

NĀNAK

Nānak (1469-1538) has an important place in the history of India as the founder of Sikhism, one of the most remarkable religious movements of modern times. However, his actual teachings do not have a direct causal connection with the later growth of this militant sect, which should be understood largely in terms of the historical events of the seventeenth and eighteenth centuries, when the chances of history made the Sikhs bitter enemies of the Muslim rulers. At that time the distinguishing marks of the faith were adopted—the uncut hair, the turban, the iron bracelet and dagger—and the followers of Nānak were welded into a fighting community.

The transformation of the Sikhs into a group hostile to Islam is one of the ironies of history, for Nānak's message aimed at the reconciliation of Hindus and Muslims through a common faith. This message was not by any means an artificial syncretism of what he considered the best features of both religions, but the influences that came to him from both can be discerned. His emphasis on monotheism, on the oneness and uniqueness of the Creator God, on the necessity of worshipping One who is the source of one's own existence, is Islamic in its inspiration. Also Islamic is his insistence on obedience to God. But his underlying metaphysical structure is Hindu: the belief in *karma* and rebirth, a feeling that ultimately Reality is undifferentiated, that there is no barrier between the human soul and the Absolute. These concepts keep Nānak and Sikhism firmly within the Hindu tradition.

The passage given here is from the *japjī*, the morning prayer, which is said by Sikhs every morning. In the convention of Indian poetry, Nānak included his name in each of the main verses.

Morning Prayer

There is but one God whose name is true, the Creator, devoid of fear and enmity, immortal, unborn, self-existent. The True one was in the beginning; the True One was in the primal age.
The True One is now also, O Nanak; the True One also shall be.

By thinking I cannot obtain a conception *of Him*, even though I think hundreds of thousands of times.

Even though I be silent and keep my attention firmly fixed on Him, I cannot preserve silence.

The hunger of the hungry *for God* subsideth not though they obtain the load of the worlds.

If man should have thousands and hundreds of thousands of devices, even one would not assist him in obtaining God.

How shall *man* become true before God? How shall the veil of falsehood be rent?

By walking, O Nanak, according to the will of the Commander as preordained.

True is the Lord, true is His name; it is uttered with endless love.

People pray and beg, 'Give us, give us'; the Giver giveth His gifts;

Then what can we offer Him whereby His court may be seen?

What words shall we utter with our lips, on hearing which He may love us?

At the ambrosial hour of *morning* meditate on the true Name and *God's* greatness.

The Kind One will give us a robe of honour, and by His favour we shall reach the gate of salvation.

Nanak, we shall thus know that God is altogether true.

If I knew Him, should I not describe Him? He cannot be described by words.

My Guru hath explained one thing to me—

That there is *but* one Bestower on all living beings; may I not forget Him!

(from Nānak, in M. A. Macauliffe, *The Sikh Religion*, I, pp. 195-96)

DĀDŪ

Dādū (1544-1603) was the third of the important teachers in whose verses and songs can be seen the influence of Islamic doctrines on traditional Hindu thought. Born to a family whose members were probably recent converts to Islam from Hinduism, Dādū broke with Islam as the result of a religious experience. While the inspiration of this experience may have been Hindu, Dādū did not find his spiritual home within Hindu orthodoxy but in the *bhakti* movements that were reinvigorating the religious life of North India at that time. Nor did he make any conscious attempt, as did Nānak, to bridge the gap between the two faiths; rather, he appears to have been repelled by what he saw in both. Turning from both, he urged men to find truth through devotion to the Living God who is known only in the heart. But despite his attacks on Islam and Hinduism, Dādū had been influenced, as was Nānak, by the ethical monotheism of Islam, and, even more than Nānak, his general religious outlook was thoroughly Hindu.

His teachings are contained in a collection of poems known as *Bāni*, or inspired speech. This is revered as scripture by many sects of modern India; one of the most curious of these was a group of warrior ascetics who, in the nineteenth century, served as border guards for Jaipur State.

In many bonds is this wretched soul bound.
Of its own strength it cannot escape. The Beloved is the
    Deliverer.
Dadu is the prisoner, Thou the Master who sets him free.
Keep me no longer in bondage, O gracious Lord.
The heart is soiled within: it is full of clamant desires.
Reveal and take them wholly away: this is Dadu's cry.
All things possess me, O Rama: nothing departs.
What should I hide from Thee? Behold all that is within.

When a mighty thorn is lodged in the mind, how can one
 forget Rama?

How am I to endure this pain? Help me, O Lord.

Keep Thou, O Keeper, keep this heart of mine.

There is no other but Thou: the saints bear witness.

Let my mind flee from illusion and the distractions of
 sense;

Make it such, O Lord, that it may delight in Thee.

Give me those eyes by which the self beholds the Self.

Grant me, O my Master, this boon, that Dadu may behold
 Thee.

Give me each day new devotion, each day a new Name by
 which to call Thee;

Give me each day new love. I offer myself in sacrifice.

Lord, give me true contentment, love, devotion, trust;

Give me uprightness, patience, truth: this does Thy servant Dadu beg.

Lord, take away my misgivings, destroy my doubts,

Dispel the error, the suspense, the awful pain. Make me
 truly one with Thee. . . .

Dadu stands at the Master's door and cries night and day:

Be gracious, O my Lord: O Master, grant me the vision.

Dadu is athrist for love: O Lord Rama, give me to drink;

Fill the cup before mine eyes, and give life to the dead.

O Allah, Lord of Light, ever fill the cup and give me to
 drink;

Make me to drink of Thy love: intoxicate me with it.

Many hast Thou such as I; I have no other such as Thou.

Cast not Dadu away: remain Thou before mine eyes. . . .

What was pleasing to myself have I done, not what Thou
 didst please.

Dadu is a sinner: I have beheld my mind within.

Do with me as Thou wilt: I surrender myself to Thee.

If it please Thee, pardon Thy servant; if it please Thee, lay
 hold of him and slay him.

Says Dadu: If the Lord should call me to account, then
 would he behead and impale me.

If, of His goodness and compassion, He forgives, then do I
   live indeed.

(from Dādū, *Bāni*, in W. G. Orr, *A Sixteenth Century Indian
Mystic*, pp. 89-91)

PART FIVE

THE TRADITION AND
THE MODERN WORLD

INTRODUCTION

After reaching its maturity, Hindu civilization had to withstand the shock of two alien intrusions. The first of these, already briefly noted in the last section, was the series of invasions by Islamic peoples from Central Asia that ended in the establishment of political control over almost all of India. The second shock was the coming of the European peoples as a part of the great wave of expansion that had begun late in the fifteenth century and, as far as India was concerned, reached its height in the nineteenth century. Of the two, the Islamic period of domination was longer than the European, and left a legacy of a large Islamic population, but the ultimate effects of the Western intrusion have probably been greater. Not only have the political and economic structures of Indian society been far more profoundly modified by the Western impact than they were by the Islamic, but the cultural and religious life of the people has been challenged by the pervasive forces of Western modernity. In this final section, the selections are focused on the nature of these modifications that have taken place in the great tradition and on the ways in which the challenges to the ancient faith were met by its defenders.

The age of European expansion into India began with

the arrival of the Portuguese expedition under Vasco da Gama in 1498. The ultimate result of this first voyage was that the Portuguese gained control of the trade between Asia and Europe, which for centuries had been in the hands of Muslim traders. The fundamental feature of the Portuguese maritime empire was the possession of strategically located bases around the rim of the Indian Ocean: she did not have the resources to expand her power into the interior. From the great city of Goa, which she built on the western Indian coast, Portugal ruled her mercantile empire for over a century until she was challenged by the arrival in the Eastern seas of other European powers, notably the Dutch and English.

Throughout the seventeenth century the European trading companies competed with each other for the trade between the East and Europe, and for concessions from the Mughal Emperor, but none of them made important territorial gains in India. The traders were not representatives of national states, even though their companies had trading monopolies from their different governments, and their impact on the life of India was minimal until the end of the first half of the eighteenth century. Then, with the breakdown of the Mughal Empire after the death of Aurangzīb in 1707, change took place. A many-sided contest for power ensued, with the Europeans, particularly the French and English, fighting each other and also fighting the rulers of Indian states which had been created from the wreckage of the Mughal Empire. The English emerged victorious among the European powers, while the Marāthas, whose great religious revival was noted in Chapter XII, were the chief Indian contenders for control of the subcontinent. It was not until 1818 that the English administered a final defeat to the Marāthas, and even then they remained one of the groups most hostile to British rule. This was evidenced to some extent by the support given to the rebels in the Mutiny of 1857 by a few Marātha princes, but even more at the end of the century by the vigorous opposition to British rule that arose in the Marāthī-speaking regions of western India.

Up until the beginning of the nineteenth century there is very little indication of the reaction of Indians to the ideas and values of the West, even though there was opportunity at least from the beginning of the fifteenth century for cultural interchange. It was widely believed in the nineteenth century that the *bhakti* movement, with its many very striking resemblances to Christianity, had been influenced through contact with the ancient Christian Church of South India, but few scholars would now feel that this interpretation of the evidence was justified. It seems reasonably clear that the great movements that took place within Hinduism in earlier ages arose from forces long latent within the tradition itself. This is not the case, however, with the changes that took place in the nineteenth century; here the results of Western influence are plain. But while emphasizing this, it is important to avoid the impression that the cultural and religious movements of nineteenth and twentieth century India lack roots in the Hindu tradition. All the essential ideas and values of Hinduism remained, and, while challenged, were not destroyed. Instead, the educated, urban middle-classes—in a sense, a product of westernization, but, in most cases, drawn from the Brāhman class—drew freely upon the West for social and political concepts to meet the problems of the new day. Almost always, however, in their personal style of living and in the intimacy of family life they maintained the traditional values and customs.

The variety of responses made by Indians to the impact of the West can be roughly classified under four headings. One reaction was indifference, and this was not purely negative in its results, for it meant that religious and social movements that had their roots in the Hindu tradition continued to flourish, and the nineteenth century saw a remarkable proliferation of cults and sects of all kinds with Hinduism. But even though these movements seem completely indigenous in their inspiration, it is quite possible that they were reflecting a general malaise and unrest caused by the intrusion of the West. Of the numerous saints and mystics that had local fame, one achieved a wider reputation. This was Srī Rāmakrishna, who stands in direct spiritual succession to the great mystics of an earlier period. Another, and very different response, was the rejection of the old tradition and the acceptance of everything Western, including Christianity. This attitude was not very common, but it contributed something to the general process of growth and change that characterized the time. More common, and of much greater significance, was the reaction to the West that was both critical and selective. Aware of weaknesses within traditional Hindu society, many sought to reform it by using features of Western culture, particularly its political arrangements or its science and technology. This classification covers a very wide spectrum of opinion, including individuals of the most antithetical views, such as Rāmmohan Roy, K. C. Sen, the Tagore family, Vivekānanda, Aurobindo Ghose, Gokhale, Rānade, and Gāndhi.

The fourth reaction was outright and hostile rejection of the values and ideas of the Western world. This response must have been fairly widespread, and even though it did not receive literary form until late in the nineteenth century, it was an important element in the Mutiny of 1857. Dayānanda Saraswatī and B. G. Tilak are the most famous names among those who adopted this general attitude, but here again the range of opinion, and degree of rejection, varied greatly.

Out of the mingling of these reactions came the intellectual ferment of the nineteenth and twentieth centuries in India. Perhaps nowhere else in the history of the world can one see a meeting of cultures and traditions comparable to that which took place in India as Western civilization, confident of its own greatness and proud of its achievements, met the Hindu tradition. Although for a time uncertain and confused, Hinduism rallied to assert an equal pride and confidence in its greatness. Something of the fruitfulness—and the losses—of the confrontation of the two cultures is seen in the following selections. More important, they indicate the enduring richness and variety of the Hindu tradition.

As will be seen from the readings, one of the most important features of the period was the reinterpretation that took place of the meaning of many of the values and ideals of the tradition. This was a characteristic both of those who, like Rāmmohan Roy, enthusiastically welcomed the ideas of the West, and of those like Dayānanda who rejected them. The general aim of those who were involved in this process was to show that the ancient scriptures were relevant to the needs of the time, and that they need not be rejected because of the new forces of the West that were at work in Indian life. Like most religious reformers, they were anxious to show they were calling for a return to the pure springs of doctrine and not advocating anything new, but there can be little doubt that in many ways they departed from the original meanings of the texts. Another important aspect of this work of reinterpretation was the claim that the ancient scriptures of India contained all the ideas that were being held up as new and Western. This was partly a necessary defence against the charges of the orthodox that the new forces were utterly alien and should be rejected, but probably more often it sprang from the desire to prove that Indian culture was not inferior to that of the West. But whatever the motivation, this task of reinterpretation was necessary for the renaissance of Hinduism to meet the conditions of the modern world.

CHAPTER XIV

ACCEPTANCE
AND REFORM

∞∞∞∞∞

One of the most fruitful responses to the impact of the West came from a small group of Hindus who throughout the nineteenth and on into the twentieth century sought, through a blending of the most valuable elements of the Western with the Hindu tradition, to create a purified Hinduism and a reformed social order. As interpreters of the West, they endeavored to convince their fellow countrymen that change did not mean destruction of the old order but rather that it pointed to its renewal. Deeply rooted in their own tradition, they were convinced that the future of Hinduism—and of India—lay in an acceptance of the modern world.

The first figure in this movement is Rāmmohan Roy (1772-1833), one of the most interesting minds produced in modern India. The son of orthodox Hindu parents, he had a brief but successful career as a revenue official in the services of the East India Company, into whose hands the control of Bengal had passed in the last half of the eighteenth century.

From his youth he had been convinced that Hinduism was infected by evils which must be removed, and after his retirement from the Company's service in 1815 he devoted his energy to religious and social reform. The sources of his reforming zeal are not altogether clear, but they appear to have been partly Indian in origin—an acquaintance with the Muslim as well as the Hindu tradition—and partly a knowledge of the main currents of European thought, especially the criticism of orthodox religion associated with Deism. Both these influences are reflected in his criticism of the idol-worship and polytheism that seemed to him to disfigure and corrupt Hinduism. Another of his main concerns, the removal of social disabilities from Indian women, appears to have had its origin in his sensitive reaction to the custom, then common in Bengal, of women burning themselves on their husband's funeral pyres. The method of reform that he adopted was generally adopted by later reformers. Hinduism had been corrupted, he argued, because the people had forgotten the ancient scriptures: if these were appealed to, it would be discovered that the customs and beliefs that disfigured society had no sanctions in the sacred texts. In pursuit of this goal, he translated the Upanishads into English and Bengali, and in his commentaries on them he argued that they spoke of belief in one God, showing no signs of such later developments as idol-worship and caste.

At the same time that he was urging reform on his fellow Hindus, Rāmmohan felt it necessary to defend Hinduism against the attacks that were made on it by a number of Europeans, especially the missionaries who had begun to come to Bengal in increasing numbers. Believing that their denunciations of Hinduism were unfair in that they identified it completely with its worst features, he countered by charging that Christianity in its current forms was as much marred by superstition as was Hinduism. He was fighting, then, on two fronts: against the orthodox Hindus who accused him of injecting Christian ideas into the Upanishads, and against orthodox Christians who thought his interpretation of the Bible had been colored by Hinduism.

Rāmmohan's ideas found institutional expression in the Brāhmo Samāj, an organization he founded in 1828. Like

*many other religious reformers, he claimed that he was not
starting a new sect, but only purifying the old religion.
There were elements in Rāmmohan's thought, however,
that made it virtually certain that the Brāhmo Samāj
would separate itself from the main stream of Hinduism.
His rejection of the use of idols in worship, his attachment
to eighteenth century rationalism, his disbelief in transmigration, all ran counter to traditional Hinduism. But although the Brāhmo Samāj moved away from Hinduism, it
rendered the parent religion great services. Negatively, the
Samāj's criticism of existing customs and beliefs forced orthodoxy to examine its own position. More positively,
through the leadership taken by 15 members in social reform movements, it helped Hindu society adjust itself to
the challenges of the modern world. It also provided its
members, many of whom were men of great ability, with
an opportunity to discuss the important issues of the time.
The Samāj's strength was confined to Bengal, but it was
from there that the new currents of thought were radiating
in the first half of the nineteenth century.*

*The leadership of the Brāhmo Samāj passed to Deben-
dranāth Tagore (1817-1905), the son of one of Rāmmohan's closest associates. A man of deep religious feeling, he
emphasized, as Rāmmohan had not, the mystical elements
of faith. He turned to the Upanishads for his inspiration,
finding the ancient texts a record of mystical experience
that echoed the teachings of the great European mystics.*

*The third great leader of the Brāhmo Samāj was Keshub
Chunder Sen (1838-1884). A far more ardent advocate of
social reform than were his predecessors, he vehemently
denounced caste distinctions and child marriage. He was
also more influenced by evangelical Christianity than they
had been, and he made much use of Christian terminology. Yet, despite frequent avowals of his acceptance of the
divinity of Christ, he remained a Hindu. He was, indeed,
within the great tradition of bhakti religion, and his use of
Christian terms is as much an indication of the similarities
of bhakti to Christianity as it is of actual influence.*

The three figures mentioned above were all from Bengal, but western India also felt the stirring of new patterns of thought and action at this time. Among the Marāthi-speaking peoples particularly, the stimulus provided by the growth of Bombay as a great commercial center led to an attempt to bring the old religion into the modern world. A number of Marātha Brāhmans of great energy and intellectual brilliance argued for the acceptance of the challenge posed by the impact of the West through an abandonment of customs that hindered social progress. The whole complex of social customs that buttressed the Hindu family system—the seclusion of women, the institution of child marriage, the prohibition of widow remarriage—was attacked. In addition they argued that Indians, as a preliminary step towards national reform, should seek more active participation in the new structure of government created by the British.

The representative of this western Indian group chosen for inclusion here is Mahadev Govind Rānade (1842-1901). He was one of the many gifted Indians who found a career in the courts of law established by the British in the nineteenth century. A member of the Prārthana Samāj, or Prayer Society, a religious organization closely modeled on the Brāhmo Samāj, Rānade was the most forceful spokesman for social reform in western India. Rānade argued that reform meant the revitalization of Hinduism, not its abandonment, and he and his friends remained more definitely a part of Hindu society than was the case with some of their counterparts in Bengal. Conceivably this was because a tradition of social and religious protest was indigenous to the Marāthi-speaking peoples, and therefore the reformers did not feel constrained to move outside the bounds of the old society. But, all of the men, whether from Bombay or Bengal, who accepted the experience of the West as valuable for India and sought in its light to reform Hindu society, helped to create the temper and mood of modern India.

RĀMMOHAN ROY:
RATIONALIST PROPHET

One of the ways in which Rāmmohan sought to convince his
fellow Hindus of the corruption of contemporary religion was
by translating the *Upanishads* into Bengali and English, so
that all might understand the grandeur of the ancient faith.
The first selection is from the preface to the translation of the
Isha Upanishad, published in 1816. In it he emphasizes his
conviction that original Hinduism did not worship idols but
acknowledged one supreme God. The second selection shows
another important aspect of his teaching—a defence of Hinduism against the attacks of Christian polemicists. Rāmmohan wanted to make clear that although Hinduism was corrupted, its basis was a pure rationalism. In this article Rāmmohan wrote under a pseudonym, speaking of himself in the
third person, a device which he frequently adopted.

Original Hinduism

Sorrow and remorse can scarcely fail sooner or later to be
the portion of him, who is conscious of having neglected
opportunities of rendering benefit to his fellow creatures.
From considerations like these, it has been that I, (although born a *Brahmin*, and instructed in my youth in all
the principles of that sect,) being thoroughly convinced of
the lamentable errors of my countrymen, have been stimu-
lated to employ every means in my power to improve their
minds, and lead them to the knowledge of a purer system
of morality. Living constantly amongst *Hindoos* of different sects and professions, I have had ample opportunity of
observing the superstitious puerilities into which they have
been thrown by their self-interested guides; who, in defiance of the law as well as of common sense, have succeeded but too well in conducting them to the temple of
Idolatry; and while they hid from their view the true sub-

stance of morality, have infused into their simple hearts a weak attachment for its mere shadow.

For the chief part of the theory and practice of *Hindooism,* I am sorry to say, is made to consist in the adoption of a peculiar mode of diet; the least aberration from which, (even though the conduct of the offender may in other respects be pure and blameless) is not only visited with the severest censure, but actually punished by exclusion from the society of his family and friends. In a word, he is doomed to undergo what is commonly called loss of cast.

On the contrary the rigid observance of this grand article of *Hindoo* faith is considered in so high a light, as to compensate for every moral defect. Even the most atrocious crimes weigh little or nothing in the balance against the supposed guilt of its violation.

Murder, theft, or perjury, though brought home to the party by a judicial sentence, so far from inducing loss of cast, is visited in their society with no peculiar mark of infamy or disgrace.

A trifling present to the *Brahmin,* commonly called *Prāyaschit,* with the performance of a few idle ceremonies, are held as a sufficient atonement for all those crimes; and the delinquent is at once freed from all temporal inconvenience, as well as all dread of future retribution.

My reflections upon these solemn truths have been most painful for many years. I have never ceased to contemplate with the strongest feelings of regret, the obstinate adherence of my countrymen to their fatal system of idolatry, inducing, for the sake of propitiating their supposed Deities, the violation of every humane and social feeling. And this in various instances; but more especially in the dreadful acts of self-destruction and the immolation of the nearest relations, under the delusion of conforming to sacred religious rites. I have never ceased, I repeat, to contemplate these practices with the strongest feelings of regret, and to view in them the moral debasement of a race who, I cannot help thinking, are capable of better things;—whose susceptibility, patience and mildness of character render them worthy of a better destiny. Under these impressions, therefore, I have been impelled to lay before them genuine translations of parts of their scripture, which inculcates not only the enlightened worship of one God, but the purest principles of morality, accompanied with such notices as I deemed requisite to oppose the arguments employed by the *Brahmins*, in defiance of their beloved system. Most earnestly do I pray, that the whole may sooner or later prove efficient in producing on the minds of *Hindoos* in general, a conviction of the rationality of believing in and adoring the Supreme Being only; together with a complete perception and practice of that grand and comprehensive moral principle—*Do unto others as ye would be done by.*

(from Rāmmohan Roy, *Translations of the Isa Upanishad*, pp. ii-v)

A Defence of Hinduism

A few queries written in the Bengali language, having again issued from the Mission Press, Sreerampore, directed against the Vedanta system of religion, and a missionary gentleman having brought these queries to the notice of our friend, Rammohun Roy, I naturally expected that the latter would publish a reply.

Disappointed in my expectation, and much hurt at the stigma thrown upon the religion which I profess, following the divine guidance of the Vedas and the dictates of pure reason, I deem it incumbent upon me to defend what I believe to be true, against so unprovoked an aggression.

In his prefatory lines, the author says, that from reading the translation of the Vedanta by Rammohun Roy, he understands that the Vedas declare a knowledge of God to be unattainable by man, and therefore he begs that Rammohun Roy will cease to impart their doctrines until he shall acquire a knowledge of the Deity from some other religious source.

This author, in common with a great number of his fellow-believers, not resting contented with the perversion and misrepresentation of the purport of his own Bible, has been zealously endeavouring to misquote the writings, revered by others as sacred authority, for the purpose of exposing them to ridicule. To prove this assertion I quote here the very first passage of the translation of the abridgement of the Vedanta by Rammohun Roy, to which the querist refers in his prefatory lines.—viz.

"The illustrious Vyasa, in his celebrated work, the Ve-
"danta, insinuates in the first text, that it is absolutely
"necessary for mankind to acquire knowledge respecting
"the Supreme Being; but he found from the following pas-
"sages of the Vedas that this inquiry is *limited to very*
"*narrow bounds.*—Vyasa also, from the result of various
"arguments coinciding with the Veda, found that an
"*accurate* and *positive* knowledge of the Supreme Being,
"is not within the boundary of comprehension, *i.e., what*
"and *how* the Supreme Being is, cannot be *definitely* ascer-
"tained. He has, therefore, in the second text, *explained*
"the Supreme Being by his *effects* and *works*, without
"attempting to *define* his *essence.*"

Now my readers will plainly perceive in the above quotation, that a perfect knowledge respecting the nature and essence of the Deity is, declared in the Vedanta "to be unattainable:" while a knowledge of his existence through "his effects and works" is duly revealed by the Veda and consequently is zealously studied and imparted by us. We find in the Christian Scriptures declarations to the same purport. Psalm CXLV. "Great is the Lord and greatly to be praised; and his greatness is *unsearchable.*" Job XXVI. 26. God is great and we *know him not: neither* can the number of his years *be searched out.*" Will the author of these queries justify any one in following his example, by suggesting to the missionary gentlemen not to inculcate Christian doctrines; on the ground that the Scriptures declare a knowledge of God and the number of the years of his existence *unsearchable?* I think he will not listen to such a suggestion, and will perhaps say in defence of the missionaries, that since the real nature of God is said in Scripture to be unsearchable, they have never attempted to preach the divine nature and essence. If such be their defence, how could prejudice completely shut the eyes of this interrogator against the plain declaration found in the translation of the Vedanta both in Bengalee and English, which he says he has read: *viz.*, "He (Vyasa) has, there- "fore, in the second text, explained the Supreme Being by "his *effects* and *works* without attempting to define his es- "sence."

In answer to his first query, *i.e.*, "Did one God create "the world or not?" I refer him to the next passage and to a subsequent passage of the same translation of the Ve- danta, *viz.*, "He, by whom the birth, existence, and anni- "hilation of the world is regulated, is the Supreme Being." "All the Vedas prove nothing but the *unity* of the Su- preme Being." "God is indeed one and has *no second*." These passages will, I hope, be sufficient to convince the querist, that the doctrine of the *unity* of God is an essen- tial principle of the Vedanta system, however unwelcome it may be to him, as opposing his favorite notion of three Gods, or three Persons equally powerful under an *abstract idea of Godhead*.

Now, unbiassed readers will judge, which of these two opinions is the more consistent with reason and divine rev- elation, to wit, the denying of properties to God according to the human notion of qualities in objects, as done by the Vedanta; or the equalising of the number of Gods, or per- sons under a Godhead, with the number of the supposed principal qualities belonging to the Deity (namely Crea- tion, Redemption, and Sanctification) as practised by the querist and his fellow-believers, who have provided them- selves with a God the Father, for the work of creation, a God the Son, for redemption and a God the Holy Ghost, for sanctification.

I do not wonder, that our religious principles are com- pared with those of atheists, by one, whose ideas of the divine nature are so gross, that he can consider God, as having been born and circumcised, as having grown and been subject to parental authority, as eating and drinking, and even as dying and as having been totally annihilated (though for three days only, the period intervening from the crucifixion of Christ to his resurrection); nor can it give me any concern, if a person, labouring under such extravagant fancies, should, at the same time, insinuate atheism against us, since he must thereby only expose himself to the derision of the discerning public.

As to his sixth and seventh queries, viz. "Do not wicked "actions proceed in this world from the depravity of man-"kind?" 7th. "By what penance can that guilt be expiated, "which men contract by the practice of wickedness?" I beg to observe, that a desire of indulging the appetites and of gratifying the passions is, by nature, common to man with the other animals. But the Vedas, coinciding with the nat-ural desire of social intercourse implanted in the human constitution, as the original cause of sympathy with others, require of men to moderate those appetites and regulate those passions, in a manner calculated to preserve the peace and comfort of society, and secure their future hap-piness; so that mankind may maintain their superiority over the rest of the animal creation, and benefit by one another. For each person to indulge without restraint all the appetites and passions, would be destructive of the harmony of society, which mankind is naturally desirous to preserve. These sentiments are contained in the following passages of the same translation of the Vedanta, viz., "A "command over our passions and over the external senses "of the body, and good acts, are declared by the Veda to "be indispensable in the mind's approximation to God. "They should, therefore, be strictly taken care of, and at-"tended to both previously and subsequently to such ap-"proximation to the Supreme Being."

In the constant internal struggles between this desire of indulgence, always working powerfully upon the mind, and the social inclination, displayed in various modes, ac-cording to the difference of circumstances, of habits, and

of education, some yield often to the passions. In that case
the only means of attaining an ultimate victory over them
is sincere repentance and solemn meditation, which occasion mental disquiet and anxiety forming the punishment
of sin; and which are calculated to prevent future surren-
ders to the passions on similar occasions. The sin which
mankind contracts against God, by the practice of wickedness, is believed by us to be expiated by these penances,
and not, as supposed by the querist, by the blood of a son
of man or son of God, who never participated in our
transgressions.

(from Rāmmohan Roy, *The English Works of Raja Rammohan Roy*, pp. 181-87)

DEBENDRANĀTH TAGORE:
MYSTICISM AND REFORM

Although Debendranāth Tagore's personal religious experience
reflected the language and thought of the *Upanishads*, he was
critical of all existing texts as a possible basis of the purified
religion that he sought to establish in the Brāhmo Samāj. In
a remarkable passage in his autobiography, he tells how he
selected those parts of the *Upanishads* which were congenial
to his thought and rejected those that he found distasteful. He
tells how, to his surprise, he discovered that there were not
eleven *Upanishads*, but one hundred and forty seven.

These Upanishads could not meet all our needs; could not
fill our hearts. Then what was to be done now? What
hope was there for us? Where should we seek a refuge for
Brahmaism? It could not be founded on the Vedas, it
could not be founded on the Upanishads. Where was its
foundation to be laid?
I came to see that the pure heart, filled with the light of
intuitive knowledge,—this was its basis. Brahma reigned in

the pure heart alone. The pure, unsophisticated heart was the seat of Brahmaism. We could accept those texts only of the Upanishads which accorded with that heart. Those sayings which disagreed with the heart we could not accept. These were the relations which were now established between ourselves and the Upanishads, the highest of all *shastras*. In the Upanishad itself we read that God is revealed through worship to the heart illumined by an intellect free from all doubt. To the soul of the righteous is revealed the wisdom of God. The Rishi of old who by means of contemplation and the grace of wisdom had seen the Perfect Brahma in his own pure heart, records his experience in these words: "The pure in spirit, enlightened by wisdom, sees the holy God by means of worship and meditation."

These words accorded with experience of my own heart, hence I accepted them.

Again I read in the Upanishads that those who remain in their own villages and perform sacrifices and other prescribed rites, after death attain the region of smoke. From smoke they pass into night, from night to the dark fortnight, from the dark fortnight to the months of the summer solstice, from those months to the region of the fathers, from that region to the sky, from the sky to the region of the moon; and having enjoyed the fruit of their good actions in that region, they, in order to be born again into this world, fall from the region of the moon into the sky, from the sky they pass on to the air, from air they become smoke, from smoke they turn into vapour, from vapour to cloud, from the clouds they are rained down and spring up here as wheat, barley, food-plants, trees, sesame, and pulse. Of those men and women who eat that wheat, barley, and other food-stuffs they are born here as living creatures. These appeared to me to be unworthy vain imaginings. I could not respond to them. They were not the transcription of the prompting of my heart.

But my heart assented fully to the following noble saying of the Upanishad:

After having studied the Vedas in your preceptor's home, and having duly served your spiritual guide, return to your home; and after marriage read the Vedas in some holy spot, instruct your pupils and pious sons in the way of wisdom, and after having brought the senses under perfect control, support your life by wealth justly earned without giving pain to any living creature. He who lives thus for the whole term of his life upon this earth enters Brahma-loka after death, and never returns to this world again; no, never again.

He who purifies his soul in this world by the doing of virtuous deeds in obedience to God's commandments, attains to sacred regions upon leaving this earth; and casting off his animal nature receives a body divine. In that sacred sphere he obtains a brighter vision of the glory of God, and having reached higher stages of wisdom, love, and virtue he is translated to higher regions. Thus rising higher and higher he progresses from holy to holier spheres, from innumerable heavens to other heavens, and returns not to earth again. In heaven there is no animality, no hunger, no thirst; there is no desire of women or wealth, neither lust, nor anger, nor greed. There is eternal life, eternal youth. Thus from one heaven to another, the tides of wisdom, love, virtue, and goodness carry that divine soul onward towards everlasting progress, and from his heart the fount of joy perennially springs. . . . By the grace of God the soul is infinitely progressive. Overcoming sin and sorrow this progressive soul must and will progress onwards and upwards; it will not decline again upon earth. Sin never reigns triumphant in God's holy kingdom. The soul is first born in the human body. After death it will assume appropriate forms, and pass from sphere to sphere in order to work out the fruits of its merit and demerit, and will not again return here.

Again, when I saw in the Upanishads that the worship of Brahma leads to Nirvâna, my soul was dismayed at the idea:

Deeds, together with the sentient soul, all become one in Brahma.

If this means that the sentient soul loses its separate consciousness, then this is not the sign of salvation but of terrible extinction. What a vast difference between the eternal progress of the soul according to the Brahma Dharma on the one hand, and this salvation by annihilation on the other! This Nirvâna-salvation of the Upanishads did not find a place in my heart. This soul instinct with consciousness—whether it dwells in high heaven or upon this lowly earth—when all its worldly desires become extinct, and when the only desire that burns night and day within it is that of attaining the Supreme indwelling Soul; when it is free from desire and desirous of the Spirit, and when in that state it performs all the good works commanded by Him, serving Him with all humility and patience; then it is free from its mortal coil, and crossing to this world's farther shore finds refuge in the bosom of the Eternal Brahma, which is beyond the pale of darkness, radiant with wisdom, and anointed with love! There, filled with new life, and purified by His grace, it remains eternally united in wisdom, love, and joy with that Infinite Wisdom, Love, and Joy, even as shadow unto light. That moment lasts for ever. "This Kingdom of Brahma eternally shines."

This is its final goal, this is its uttermost gain, this is its highest heaven, this is its supreme bliss.

At these sublime words of the Vedas, the mind is satisfied, the soul finds peace, and the heart, filled to the brim with joy, says perpetually: "O how great is the freedom from fear which is attained by the realisation of Brahma!"

O Perfect Wisdom,
When will thy truth, ever new and full of light,
Shine in the sky of my heart?
Through the long night I wait
And watch the eastern horizon,
With face upturned and folded hands,

In hope of new happiness, new life, and a new dawn of
  day.
What shall I see, what shall I know?
I know not what that joy shall be.
New light within my inmost heart;
By that light, full of great joy I will go singing towards my
  home—
Who would desire to linger in dreary exile?

Now this blessing of His has descended upon my heart:
"May your way to Brahma-loka be safe and clear on the
farther side of this world of darkness!" Having received
this blessing I can feel the eternal Brahma-loka from this
world.

(from D. Tagore, *Autobiography*, pp. 160-66)

KESHUB CHUNDER SEN:
CHRIST AND INDIA

K. C. Sen's emphasis on Christ as the center of his worship
antagonized many members of the Brāhmo Samāj. But while
it seemed as if he had moved very close to an acceptance of a
Christian position, actually he remained within the Hindu
tradition, even in his most extravagant praise of "the Asiatic
Christ." He declared that Christ was the unique Son of God,
but his interpretation of the phrase was not that of orthodox
Christianity, for he was equally insistent that all religions are
one, although using different symbols to speak of the same
truth. Here he was moving on a level of understanding that
was congenial to many strands of the Hindu tradition, and
although there are not many Hindus today who would accept
K. C. Sen's position fully, his general emphasis would probably
be approved by a wide range of opinion.

You will find on reflection that the doctrine of divine humanity is essentially a Hindu doctrine, and the picture of

Christ's life and character I have drawn is altogether a picture of ideal Hindu life. Surely, the idea of absorption and immersion in the Deity is one of those ideas of Vedantic Hinduism which prevail extensively in India. From the highest sage to the humblest peasant, millions of men in this land believe in the pantheistic doctrine of man's identity with the Godhead. The most illiterate man is heard to say he and the Lord are one! The doctrine of absorption in the Deity is India's creed, and through this idea, I believe, India will reach Christ. Will he not fulfil the Indian scripture? I am reminded of the passage in the Gospel in which he says,—"I am not come to destroy but to fulfil." The Mosaic dispensation only? Perhaps the Hindu dispensation also. In India he will fulfil the Hindu dispensation. The earliest scriptures of our nation are full of pantheism, and though there are errors therein, the truths of pantheism will be fulfilled and perfected in Christ. The religion of our ancestors was pantheism from the beginning to the end. But what is Hindu pantheism? Essentially, it is nothing but the identification of all things with God. I do not mean that you should adopt pantheism as it exists in Hindu books. Far from it. Oh! there are mischievous errors and absurd ideas mixed up with it, which you must eschew. Christ's pantheism is a pantheism of a loftier and more perfect type. It is the conscious union of the human with the Divine Spirit in truth, love and joy. The Hindu sage realizes this union only during meditation, and he seeks unconscious absorption in his God, with all his faults and short-comings about him. His will is not at one with the will of God. But Christ's communion is active and righteous; it combines purity of character with devotion. Hindu pantheism in its worst form is proud, being based upon the belief that man is God; it is quietism and trance. Christ's pantheism is the active self-surrender of the will. It is the union of the obedient, humble and loving son with the Father. In the midst of activity, Christ was absorbed in God. . . . In Christ you see true pantheism. And as the basis of early Hinduism is pantheism, you, my countrymen, cannot help accepting Christ in the spirit of your national scriptures. You have already seen how in his outward form and appearance, with his flowing garment, he is acceptable to you. Now, you find that even the spirit of Christ draws you through your national instincts. You have a national affinity to the invisible as well as to the visible Christ. Can you deny it?

Behold Christ cometh to us as an Asiatic in race, as a Hindu in faith, as a kinsman and a brother, and he demands your heart's affection. Will you not give him your affection? He comes to fulfil and perfect that religion of communion for which India has been panting, as the hart panteth after the waterbrooks. Yes, after long centuries shall this communion be perfected through Christ. For Christ is a true Yogi, and he will surely help us to realize our national ideal of a Yogi. India must, therefore, honor him. You have learnt to give the homage of your hearts to dear Chaitanya, the prophet of Nuddea, and you have also learnt to give honor unto Guru Nanuk, the prophet of the Punjab. These are your national prophets, and you do well to love and revere them. And if you look upon Asia as your home, you cannot but regard Christ, too, as one of your Eastern prophets, entitled to your loyalty and attachment. He comes to you after all as a Yogi, full of Hindu devotion and communion. . . . He gave his Father not only his soul but also his will. In accepting him, therefore, you accept the spirit of a devout Yogi, and a loving Bhakta,—the fulfilment of your national scriptures and prophets. . . . Young men of India, who are so jealous in the cause of reformation and enlightenment, turn your attention to this point. Believe and remember what Christ has said, and be ready to receive him. He is coming, and in the fulness of time he will come to you. He will come to you as self-surrender, as asceticism, as Yoga, as the life of God in man, as obedient and humble sonship. For Christ is nothing else. The bridegroom cometh. Do not, like the foolish virgins, fall asleep. But trim your lamps, put on your best apparel, and go forth with the enthusiasm and joy which all oriental nations display upon such occasions, to receive the bridegroom. Oh! the bridegroom is coming; there is no knowing when he cometh. Let India, beloved India, be decked in all her jewellery,—those "sparkling orient gems," for which this land is famous, so that at the time of the wedding we may find her a really happy and glorious bride. The bridegroom is coming. Let India be ready in due season.

(Keshub Chunder Sen, *Lectures in India*, pp. 257-61)

M. G. RĀNADE: THE NEED
FOR SOCIAL REFORM

Few Hindus have written so critically, yet with such insight, about their tradition as has Rānade. He watched the rise of the revivalist movements, described in the next chapter, with great disquietude. He was convinced that the appeal to the past was based on a false understanding both of the nature of India's tradition and of the modern world. A patriot and a religious man, he believed that if India was to gain its freedom from British domination it would first have to see a radical transformation in the cultural values that determined social life.

It is not the outward form but the inward form, the thought and the idea which determines the outward form, that has to be changed, if real reformation is desired. Now what have been the inward forms or ideas which have been hastening our decline during the past three thousand years? These ideas may be briefly set forth as isolation, submission to outward force or power more than to the voice of the inward conscience, perception of factitious difference between men and men, due to heredity and birth, a passive acquiescence in evil or wrong-doing, and a general indifference to secular well-being, almost bordering upon fatalism. These have been the root ideas of our social system. They have, as their natural result, led to the existing family arrangements, where the woman is entirely subordinated to the man, and the lower castes to the higher castes, to the length of depriving men of their natural respect for humanity. All the evils we seek to combat flow from the prevalence of these ideas. They are mere corollaries to these axiomatic assumptions. They prevent our people from realising that they really are in all conscience neither better nor worse than their fellows, and that the average man, whatever garb he may put on, is the worse for his assuming dignities and powers which do not, in fact, belong to him. As long as these ideas remain operative on our mind we may change our outward forms and institutions, and be none the better for the change. These ideas have produced their results, and we must judge of their good or bad qualities, as St. Paul says, by their fruits. Now that these results have been disastrous nobody disputes or doubts, and the lesson to be drawn for our guidance in the future from this fact is that the current of these ideas must be changed, and in the place of the old worship, we must accustom ourselves and others to worship and reverence new ideals. In place of isolation we must have fraternity, or rather elastic expansiveness. At present it is everybody's ambition to pride himself upon being a member of the smallest community that can be conceived, and the smaller the number of those with whom you can dine or marry or associate, the higher your purity and perfection. The purest person is he who cooks his own food, and does not allow the shadow of his nearest friend to fall upon his cooked food. Every caste and every sect has thus a tendency to split itself into smaller castes and smaller sects in practical life. Even in philosophy, it is a received maxim that knowledge and salvation are only possible for the esoteric few, with whom only is true wisdom and power, and for the rest of mankind, they must be left to grovel in superstition and vice, with only a colouring of so-called religion to make them respectable. Now all this must be changed. The new mould of thought must be cast, as stated above, in fraternity, or all-attracting expansiveness, and cohesion in society. Increase your circle of friends and associates, slowly and cautiously if you will, but the tendency must be to turn our face towards a general recognition of the essential equality between man and man. That will beget sympathy and power. It will strengthen your own hands by the sense that you have numbers with you, and not against you, or, as you foolishly imagine, below you. The next idea which lies at the root of our helplessness is that we were always intended to remain children, to be subject to outside control, and never to rise to the dignity of self-control by making our conscience and our reason the sole guides to our conduct. All our past history has been a terrible witness to the havoc committed by this misconception. We are children, no doubt, but the children of God, and not of man, and the voice of God in us is the only voice to which we are bound to listen. Of course, all of us cannot listen to that voice when we desire it, because from long neglect we have benumbed the faculty of conscience in us. With too many of us, a thing is true or false, righteous or sinful, simply because somebody else has said that it is so. Duties and obligations are duties and obligations, not because we feel them to be so, but because somebody, reputed to be wise, has laid it down to be so. Of course, in small matters of manners and courtesies, this outward dictation is not without its use. But when we abandon ourselves entirely to this helplessness, and depend on others' wills, it is no wonder that we become as helpless as children. Now, the new idea which should take its place is not the idea of rebellious independence and overthrow of all authority, but that of freedom responsible to God alone. Great and wise men in the past or in the present, have a claim on our regards. But they must not come between us and our God—the Divine principle seated within everyone of us, high or low. It is this sense of self-respect, or rather of respect to the God in us, which has to be cultivated, and it is a tender plant which takes years and years to cultivate. But we have the capacity, and we owe it as a duty to ourselves to undertake the task. Reverence all human authority, pay your respects to all prophets and revelations, but subordinate that reverence to the Divine command in us.

(M. G. Rānade, *Religious and Social Reform*, pp. 170-75)

CHAPTER XV

REJECTION
AND REVIVAL

~~~~~~~~

In the last half of the nineteenth century the intellectual movement associated with Rāmmohan Roy and his successors, which was characterized by a general tendency to adapt the Hindu tradition to Western values, met strong opposition. The criticism of Hindu institutions and beliefs which had been engendered by the first contacts with modern Western thought was replaced by a mood of resurgent self-confidence. Instead of an attempt to show that pure Hinduism was basically similar to the highest reaches of Western thought, there was a proud assertion that the Hindu tradition needed no support from the finding of identities, real or fancied, with Christianity. The leaders of this new movement, to which the title "Hindu Renaissance" is sometimes given, did not speak with one voice since they differed widely on the correct interpretation of the traditional values, but the cumulative effect of their teaching was to give Hinduism a self-awareness and a pride in its greatness that had long been lacking.

Three quite distinct groups can be identified within this general movement of rejection of Western values and revival of the Hindu tradition. There were, first of all, those who agreed that Hinduism needed reform, but who believed that this could be achieved through the revival of *virtues of Hinduism itself, not through those of the West. Dayānanda Saraswatī (1824-1883), one of the most influential figures in modern Indian history, was one of these. He found no satisfaction in the religious orthodoxy of his family, and, following the classic Indian model, set out as a young man to wander through India seeking truth. After years of travel to the sacred places he became convinced that the contemporary leaders of Hinduism were corrupt and ignorant. The root cause of this condition, he believed, was that the great original scriptures, particularly the Rig Veda, had been abandoned, and that their place had been taken by later religious texts, such as the Purānas. For Dayānanda, the Vedas were not only true, but they contained all truth, including the ideas of modern science. Above all, they taught a rigorous monotheism, giving no sanction to either the polytheism or idol-worship of later Hinduism. From these two basic principles—the inerrancy of the Vedas and monotheism—he mounted a wide-ranging criticism of all aspects of contemporary Hinduism. Along with this went a fierce polemic against other religious groups, particularly Islam and Christianity, as false alien religions that sought to destroy the Hindu faith. This was an unfortunate emphasis in the eyes of those who regarded religious toleration as a primary virtue, but it was undoubtedly of great importance in giving Hindus a sense of their own value and significance.*

Unlike most Indian religious leaders, Dayānanda was not content with inspiring a personal loyalty in a group of followers, but sought to create institutions that would embody his ideas. This led to the formation of the Ārya Samāj, or the society of true Aryan believers. Motivated by a missionary enthusiasm that paralleled, and was no doubt to a degree copied from, that of Christian missionaries, the Ārya Samāj moved into the villages and created a network of schools and colleges. The movement enjoyed its greatest success in the Panjāb, where the revival of a strong Hindu self-consciousness was to later play an important role in the nationalist struggle.

Similar to Dayānanda in general temperament and outlook, but differing in that he was primarily a political leader, was Bāl Gangādhar Tilak (1856-1920). At a time when the other leaders of the Indian National Congress, which had been founded in 1885, were committed to a program of social reform on Western lines, Tilak made a bold demand for a nationalism rooted in Indian religious and social values. More than any other individual, he changed the mood of Indian political life from one of cooperation with the British rulers, coupled with an appeal to British good intentions, to one of outright defiance. Central to this achievement was his interpretation of Hinduism as a dynamic social religion, concerned with action in this world. He rejected as a perversion of the truth the widely held view that the scriptures enjoined a life of meditation and world-negation, arguing that in the days of its glory Hinduism had inspired men to deeds of heroic valor in war. The text to which he turned for support for this interpretation was the Bhagavad Gītā, which he read as a rallying call to a life of action. Krishna's advice to the hesitant Arjuna to fight in battle was taken to be a message to the young men of India to fight the British, by violence if necessary, in order to regain political supremacy.

The second religious group that gave Hindus a renewed confidence in their own tradition was associated with Srī Rāmakrishna (1834-1886), the most famous of nineteenth century Indian saints. Rāmakrishna was of a totally different temperament from either Dayānanda or Tilak; he had no concern with either social or political reform, living a life wholly dedicated to religious experience. His influence, nevertheless, was felt throughout the social life of Bengal where he passed his life in continuation of the bhakti tradition so deeply-rooted in that region. He stands, not as a defender of the Hindu way, but as one who accepted the tradition in all its richness and contradictions, and his great achievement was to show to his generation that sainthood, as understood within the Hindu tradition, had a unique value for India's life in the modern world.

Rāmakrishna was, as he himself once said, "mad for God." The central object of his devotion was the goddess *Kālī*, but his passionate longing to experience God in every conceivable way led him to seek communion with all the deities of Hinduism as well as with Buddha, Christ and Allah. Through enormous spiritual struggles he attained his goals, and thousands flocked to see him, drawn by the tales of his sanctity.

The heart of his message, insofar as it can be separated from the appeal of his personality, was the claim that in his own personal religious experience he had discovered that all the deities, *Kālī*, Christ, or Allah, were identical in the communion of the mystic. All experience, religious or otherwise, was seen by him as part of a total unity. This led *Rāmakrishna* to perform acts which must, to modern Western man, seem bizarre and aberrant, as when he went about dressed as a woman to enter more fully into the passion enjoyed by *Rādha* in her communion with *Krishna*. Coupled with this emphasis on the need for complete absorption in life of the deity being worshipped, went an acceptance of all aspects of the tradition, even those that to reformers seemed most in need of alteration, including the worship of *Kālī* herself.

Among the crowds that went to see *Rāmakrishna* were Keshub Chunder Sen (see Chapter XIV), then at the height of his fame as an orator and preacher, and a young college student, Narendra Nāth Datta (1863-1902). Sen found in the saint's presence evidence of the universality of religious experience, but young Datta found a master. He became *Rāmakrishna's* favorite disciple, and took the name of *Vivekānanda*. Although he had been brought up in the atmosphere of the *Brāhmo Samāj*, he abandoned the westernized Calcutta life he had known, and became a *sannyāsī*, or hermit. In 1892 he aroused interest in India by his remarkable personal presence and his oratory, and the following year he went to Chicago to attend the Parliament of Religions. He made an enormous impression, and for the next three years toured the United States and

England. On his return to India he organized the Rāma-krishna Mission, whose members are devoted to social service and the spread of Rāmakrishna's message.

The ideas that Vivekānanda enunciated are simple enough, but he expressed them in such a way that they caught the imagination of both Indians and Westerners. To the familiar argument that all religions were true, being but different pathways to the same goal, Vivekānanda tended to add the suggestion that Hinduism was the only one of the great religions profound enough to recognize this fact. The insight of Hinduism meant that India had a spiritual secret that sharpened the contrast between her and the materialistic nations of the West. It was true that India could learn from the technology of the West, but, he argued, the West must learn to drink from the fountain of Indian spirituality. This idea became one of the most common clichés on India in relation to the West, and whatever its validity, it played an important part in giving Indians a sense of the worth and value of their Hindu tradition.

A third group that must be distinguished in the general category of those that helped restore Hindu self-confidence were not Indian in origin, but found their home there. The Theosophical Society was founded in New York in 1875, but its significance both as a world and Indian movement came when Mrs. Annie Besant went to India as its leader. With her appearance, Indians for the first time heard Hinduism exalted by a Westerner as superior to Christianity in its ethics and institutional life, including the caste system, so long denounced by both Indians and Westerners as the most malevolent feature of Indian life. This emphasis provided a link with the revivalism of Tilak and Dayānanda as well as with the emotional fervor of Vivekānanda, while the rationalistic formulations of the Theosophical creed made an appeal to a number of intellectuals.

The influences of these three groups flowed together to strengthen the Hindu tradition at the very moment when it seemed most likely to have been overwhelmed by the assault of the West. In addition to giving Hindus a new awareness of the greatness of their faith, they emphasized the spoken languages of the people rather than the foreign medium, English, which was used by the reformers. Another result was a growth of interest in the Indian past, and great rulers, notably Ashoka and Sivaji, were made to serve as symbols of a unity that India had once enjoyed and might know again. There was a revival of interest, too, in the study of Sanskrit and of the ancient religious texts. After ages of neglect the great art forms of the past were studied with enthusiasm, and the wealth of sculpture, music and dance forms became known to the common people as well as to scholars.

In every area of life the defence of the Hindu tradition led to a revitalization of a way of life that a hundred years before had seemed moribund and marked for destruction. The result is that Hinduism is almost certainly stronger and more vigorous today than it was at the beginning of the nineteenth century. In the process of revival many changes took place, and in many instances what was revived was not the same as the ancient forms that were imitated—this is true both in art and religion—but the line of continuity is clear between the great ages of Hinduism and the present.

DAYĀNANDA SARASWATĪ:
AGGRESSIVE REFORMER

The selections chosen from Dayānanda's writings illustrate two important aspects of his influence. The first passage is a summary of his teaching that the *Vedas* teach a pure monotheism. The others are examples of his polemical writings directed against the great missionary faiths, Islam and

Christianity, which had won many converts from Hinduism. However illiberal this phase of the Hindu revival may appear, it was a vital element in the emergence of modern India. Christians and Muslims have often charged Hindus with being superstitious; in these passages Dayānanda returns the indictment with interest. One of the unforeseen consequences of this new polemic was to harden the lines of division between Hindus and Muslims, thus making possible the demand in the twentieth century by Muslims for a separate homeland.

God and the Veda

They are atheists and of weak intellect, and continually remain sunk in the depths of misery and pain who do not believe in, know, and commune with Him who is Resplendent, All-glorious, All-Holy, All-knowledge, sustainer of the sun, the earth and other planets, Who pervades all like ether, is the Lord of all and is above all *devatās*. It is by the knowledge and contemplation of God alone that all men attain true happiness.

Q.—There are more gods than one mentioned in the Vedas. Do you believe this or not?

A.—No, we do not; as nowhere in all the four Vedas there is written anything that could go to show that there are more gods·than one. On the other hand, it is clearly said in many places that there is only one God.

Q.—What is meant by the mention of various *devatās* in the Vedas then?

A.—Whatsoever or whosoever possesses useful and brilliant qualities is called a *devatā*, as the earth for instance; but it is nowhere said that it is God or is the object of our adoration. Even in the above *mantra* it is said that He, who is the sustainer of all *devatās*, is the adorable God, and is worthy of being sought after. They are greatly mistaken who take the word *devatā* to mean God. He is called *devatā of devatās*—greatest of all *devatās*,—because He alone is the author of Creation, Sustenance and Dissolution of the Universe, the Great Judge and Lord of all. . . .

Q.—Does God incarnate or not?

A.—No; because it is said in the *Yajur Veda.* "He is un-born" again "He overspreads all. He is pure, is never born, never takes on a human form." It is clear from these quotations that God is never born.

Q.—But *Krishna* says in the *Gita.* "Whenever there is decay of virtue I take on a human form." What is your answer to this?

A.—Being opposed to the *Veda* it can not be held to be an authority. Though it is possible that *Krishna,* being very virtuous and being extremely anxious to further the cause of righteousness, might have wished that he would like to be born again and again at different times to protect the good and punish the wicked. If such was the case, there is no harm in it; because 'whatever the good and the great possess—their wealth, their bodies, aye even their hearts—is at the service of humanity.' In spite of all this *Krishna* could never be God.

Q.—If this be the case, why do people then believe in the twenty-four incarnations of God?

A.—From want of knowledge of the *Vedas,* from being led astray by the sectarians and being themselves unedu-cated, people are involved in ignorance and, therefore, no wonder, believe in and say such false things. . . . Whoso-ever ponders over the great things that God has done in this universe, can not but come to the conclusion that "There is no one like Him, nor shall ever be." Nor can the incarnation of God be demonstrated by reason, just as the saying of a man, that space entered a womb or was put in a closed hand, can never be true, for space being Infinite and omnipresent can neither go in, nor come out; similarly, God, being Infinite and All-pervading, it can never be predicated of him that He can go in or come out.

Q.—Does God forgive the sins of His devotees or not?

A.—No; for, were He to forgive their sins, His Law of Justice would be destroyed, and all men would become most sinful. Knowing that their sins will be forgiven, they will become fearless and will be greatly encouraged to commit sins. . . . Therefore it is God's duty to give souls the just fruits of their deeds and not to forgive their sins.

(Dayānanda Saraswatī, *Satyārtha Prākāsh*, pp. 230-231, 249-251)

Against Christianity

The Christians go about preaching "Come, embrace our religion, get your sins forgiven and he saved." All this is untrue, since had Christ possessed the power of having sins remitted, instil faith in others and purifying them, why would he have not freed his disciples from sin, made them faithful and pure. When he could not make those who went about with him pure, faithful and sinless, how could he now that no one knows where he is purify any one? Now disciples of Christ were destitute of as much faith as a grain of mustard seed and it is they that wrote the Bible, how could then such a book be held as an authority. Those who seek happiness should not believe in the works of the faithless, the impure (at heart) and the unrighteous. . . . All such things as one's being possessed of devils, or casting them out, curing of disease without proper medicine and diet are impossible as they are opposed to the dictum of knowledge and contrary to the laws of nature. Only the ignorant people can believe in them. . . .

Are these things any better than the tricks of a wonder-worker or of a juggler of to-day? Where did all these loaves come from (to feed the multitude)? Had Christ possessed such miraculous powers, why would he have hankered after the fruit of a fig tree when he was hungry? Why did he not turn stones, earth and water into loaves and delicious sweets? These things look more like children's play. Many a *Vairagee* and other mendicants defraud guileless, ignorant men of their money by such tricks (as these). . . .

—If the conversion of a man by the offering of his will be the cause of his entering into heaven and his not doing so the cause of his going to hell, it is clear then that no one can take upon himself the sins or virtues of another. And the use of the expression "except ye . . . become as little children," etc., shows that most of the teaching of Christ were opposed to the dictum of knowledge and contrary to the laws of nature, and he also wished that the people should accept them like children without questioning their validity, in other words, accept them with their eyes closed. Plenty of Christians have blind faith like children, otherwise why should they believe in such things as are opposed to reason and science. It is also clear that had not Christ himself been as destitute of knowledge and understanding as a child, he would not have taught others to become as children, since a man always wants to make others like himself.

(Dayānanda Saraswatī, *Satyārtha Prākāsh*, pp. 708-711)

Against Islam

(In the following attack on Islam, Dayānanda used the method of selecting verses from the Koran that seemed to be contrary to common sense and morality.)

"The true religion with God is Islam." Quran, III:17.
—Is God the Lord of the Muslims alone? Did not Divine religion exist at all thirteen hundred years back? It shows that the Quran is not the word of God, but of some bigot. . . .
"And fight for the cause of God against those who fight against you. And kill them wherever ye shall find them; and eject them from whatever place they have ejected you! for civil discord is worse than courage. Fight therefore against them until there be no more civil discord."
(Quran, II:186, 187, 189.)

—Had not such teachings existed in the Quran, the Muslims would not have been so cruel to the non-Muslims. They have greatly sinned by slaughtering the innocent. They hold that one who does not believe in the Muslim religion is an infidel, and that it is better to put the infidels to sword. They have always lived up to their professions in this respect. They have lost their political supremacy while "fighting" for the cause of their God. This religion does indeed teach cruelty toward the non-Muslims. . . . Such things can never be taught by God nor by one of His enlightened votaries, nor could they be found in His Word. They can only be the utterances of an ignorant and selfish man.

Is it not sheer prejudice to call those, who do not profess Islam, infidels? That Being can not be God who teaches that the Muslims should not associate even with good people of other faiths, while they may take even the wicked Muslims for their friends. One is therefore fully justified in inferring that this Quran, its God and the Muslims are embodiments of bigotry and ignorance. Now reader mark! How clever Mohammad is! He makes his God say in this verse that God will love those who follow Mohammad and even their sins will be forgiven. This shows that the heart of Mohammad was not pure. It appears that Mohammad (made or) had the Quran made in order to serve his selfish interests.

(Dayānanda Sarasvatī, *Satyārtha Prakāsh,* pp. 754, 758, 759)

B. G. TILAK:

THE CALL TO ACTION

The leaders of the Hindu Renaissance attached great importance to the interpretation of the great scriptural texts. The application of the methods of modern scholarship to the texts was first made by European and American scholars, and while Indians were quick to adopt the techniques, many objected to the interpretations given by the Western scholars. B. G. Tilak found particularly objectionable the assumption made by Western scholars that the scriptures provided no basis for social action. If this were so, then inspiration would have to come from the West, and, more specifically, from Christianity. In the *Bhagavad Gītā* Tilak found a gospel of life-affirmation and a call to action that was admirably suited to the needs of that time. That this interpretation is, in fact, true to the *Gītā* would be denied by many scholars, including many Indians, but Tilak's vigorous argument was welcomed by those who wanted to engage in social action without having to acknowledge a debt to Western idealism.

Let me begin by telling you what induced me to take up the study of *Bhagavad Gita*. When I was quite a boy, I was often told by my elders that strictly religious and really philosophic life was incompatible with the hum-drum life of every day. If one was ambitious enough to try to attain Moksha, the highest goal a person could attain, then he must divest himself of all earthly desires and renounce this world. One could not serve two masters, the world and God. I understood this to mean that if one would lead a life which was the life worth living, according to the religion in which I was born, then the sooner the world was given up the better. This set me thinking. The question that I formulated for myself to be solved was: Does my religion want me to give up this world and renounce it before I attempt to, or in order to be able to, attain the perfection of manhood? In my boy-hood I was also told that *Bhagavad Gita* was universally acknowledged to be a book containing all the principles and philosophy of the Hindu religion, and I thought if this be so I should find an answer in this book to my query; and thus began my study of the *Bhagavad Gita*. I approached the book with a mind prepossessed by no previous ideas about any philosophy, and had no theory of my own for which I sought any support in the *Gita*. A person whose mind is prepossessed by certain ideas reads the book with a prejudiced mind, for instance, when a Christian reads it he does not want to know what the *Gita* says but wants to find out if there are any principles in the *Gita* which he has already met within Bible, and if so the conclusion he rushes to is that the *Gita* was copied from the Bible. It have dealt with this topic in my book *Gita Rahasya* and I need hardly say much about it here, but what I want to emphasise is this, that when you want to read and understand a book, especially a great work like the *Gita*—you must approach it with an unprejudiced and unprepossessed mind. To do this, I know is one of the most difficult things. Those who profess to do it may have a lurking thought or prejudice in their minds which vitiates the reading of the book to some extent. However I am describing to you the frame of mind one must get into if one wants to get at the truth and however difficult it be, it has to be done. The next thing one has to do is to take into consideration the time and the circumstances in which the book was written and the purpose for which the book was written. In short the book must not be read devoid of its context. This is especially true about a book like *Bhagavad Gita*. Various commentators have put as many interpretations on the book, and surely the writer or composer could not have written or composed the book for so many interpretations being put on it. He must have but one meaning and one purpose running through the book, and that I have tried to find out. I believe I have succeeded in it, because having no theory of mine for which I sought any support from the book so universally respected, I had no reason to twist the text to suit my theory. There has not been a commentator of the *Gita* who did not advocate a pet theory of his own and has not tried to support the same by showing that the *Bhagavad Gita* lent him support. The conclusion I have come to is that the *Gita* advocates the performance of action in this world even after the actor has achieved the highest union with the supreme Deity by Gnana (knowledge) or Bhakti

(Devotion). This action must be done to keep the world going by the right path of evolution which the Creator has destined the world to follow. In order that the action may not bind the actor it must be done with the aim of helping his purpose, and without any attachment to the coming result. This I hold is the lesson of the *Gita*. Gnanayoga there is, yes. Bhaktiyoga there is, yes. Who says not? But they are both subservient to the Karmayoga preached in the *Gita*. If the *Gita* was preached to desponding Arjuna to make him ready for the fight—for the action—how can it be said that the ultimate lesson of the great book is Bhakti or Gnana alone? In fact there is blending of all these Yogas in the *Gita* and as the air is not Oxygen or Hydrogen or any other gas alone but a composition of all these in a certain proportion so in the *Gita* all these Yogas blended into one.

I differ from almost all commentators when I say that the *Gita* enjoins action even after the perfection in Gnana and Bhakti is attained and the Deity is reached through these mediums. Now there is a fundamental unity underlying the Logos (Ishvara), man, and world. The world is in existence because the Logos has willed it so. It is His Will that holds it together. Man strives to gain union with God; and when this union is achieved the individual Will merges in the mighty Universal Will. When this is achieved will the individual say; "I shall do no action, and I shall not help the world"—the world which is because the Will with which he has sought union has willed it to be so? It does not stand to reason. It is not I who say so; the *Gita* says so. Shri Krishna himself says that there is nothing in all the three worlds that He need acquire, and *still* he acts. He acts because if He did not, the world will be ruined. If man seeks unity with the Deity, he must necessarily seek unity with the interests of the world also, and work for it. If he does not, then the unity is not perfect, because there is union between two elements out of the 3 (man and Deity) and the third (the world) is left out. I have thus solved the question for myself and I hold that serving the world, and thus serving His Will, is the surest way of Salvation, and this way can be followed by remaining *in* the world and not going away from it.

(B. G. Tilak, *His Writings and Speeches*, pp. 258-63)

SRĪ RĀMAKRISHNA: SAINTHOOD
AND THE MODERN WORLD

Rāmakrishna's teachings, such as the presence of God in all human experience, are deeply rooted in the Hindu tradition. His great achievement, which was not the product of conscious intention but of his own personality, was to make the life of an Indian saint relevant to the people of nineteenth and twentieth century India. His sayings, in the form of dialogues with his disciples and visitors, were preserved by his followers, and this selection is taken from the collection made by one of them. The brief descriptive passage indicates the effect the saint had on many of his visitors.

(*i*)

The disciple asked: "Bhagavân, one may believe that God is with form, but surely He is not in the earthen images that are worshipped?" Srî Râmakrishna replied: "My dear sir, why do you say earthen images? The image of the Divine Being is made of the spirit." The disciple could not understand the meaning of this, but answered: "Yet should it not be one's duty to make clear to those who worship images that God is not the same as the images and that at the time of worship they should think of God Himself and not of the image made of clay?" The Bhagavân said: "The Lord of the universe teaches mankind. He who has made the sun and moon, men and brutes; He who has created things for them to live upon, parents to tend and rear them; He who has done so many things will surely do something to bring them to the light. The Lord dwells in the temple of the human body. He knows our innermost thoughts. If there is anything wrong in image worship, does He not know that all worship is meant for Him? He will be pleased to accept it knowing that it is for Him. Why should you worry yourself about things which are beyond your reach? Try to realize God and love Him. This is your first duty.

"You speak of images made of clay. Well, there often comes a necessity for worshipping such images and symbols. In Vedânta it is said, the absolute Existence-Intelligence-Bliss pervades the universe and manifests itself through all forms. What harm is done by worshipping the Absolute through images and symbols? We see little girls with their dolls. How long do they play with them? So long as they are not married. After marriage they put away those dolls. Similarly, one needs images and symbols so long as God is not realized in His true form. It is God Himself who has provided these various forms of worship. The Master of the universe has done all this to suit different men in different stages of spiritual growth and knowledge. The mother so arranges the food for her children that each one gets what is best for him. Suppose a mother has five children with one fish to cook for all. She will make different dishes of it that she may give to each just what suits him,—the rich *pilau* for one, soup for another, fried fish for a third, fish with sour tamarind for a fourth, and so on, exactly according to the power of digestion of each. Do you now understand?"

The disciple replied: "Yes, Bhagavân, now I do. But, Revered Sir, how can one fix one's mind on God?"

Srî Râmakrishna: To that end one must always sing forth the Holy Name of God and talk without ceasing of His glory and attributes. Then one must seek the company of holy men. One must from time to time visit the Lord's devotees or those who have given up attachment to the things of the world for the sake of the Lord. It is, however, difficult to fix one's mind upon God in the midst of worldly cares and anxieties; hence the necessity of going into solitude now and again with a view to meditating on Him.

The disciple asked: "Bhagavân, is it possible to see God?"

Srî Râmakrishna: Certainly. The following are some of the means of seeing God: Going from time to time into solitude; singing forth His name and His attributes; discrimination.

The disciple: Bhagavân, what state of mind leads to God-vision?

Srî Râmakrishna: Cry to God with a yearning heart and then you will see Him. People will shed a jugful of tears for the sake of their wife or children; they will be carried away by a stream of their own tears for the sake of money; but who sheds a tear for God? Cry for Him, not for show, but with a longing and yearning heart. The rosy light of the dawn comes before the rising sun; likewise a longing and yearning heart is the sign of God-vision that comes after.

Extreme longing is the surest way to God-vision. Through extreme longing the mind remains fixed on the Supreme Being. One should have faith like that of an innocent child and such longing as a child has when it wants to see its mother.

(*ii*)

SOME INCIDENTS IN THE LIFE OF SRÎ RÂMA-
KRISHNA (AS TOLD BY HIMSELF)

I practised austerities for a long time. I cared very little for the body. My longing for the Divine Mother was so great that I would not eat or sleep. I would lie on the bare ground, placing my head on a lump of earth, and cry out loudly: "Mother, Mother, why dost Thou not come to me?" I did not know how the days and nights passed away. I used to have ecstasy all the time. I saw my disciples as my own people, like children and relations, long before they came to me. I used to cry before my Mother, saying: "O Mother! I am dying for my beloved ones (Bhaktas); do Thou bring them to me as quickly as possible."

When I reached the state of continuous ecstasy, I gave up all external forms of worship; I could no longer perform them. Then I prayed to my Divine Mother: "Mother, who will now take care of me? I have no power to take care of myself. I like to hear Thy name and feed Thy Bhaktas and help the poor. Who will make it possible for me to do these things? Send me someone who will be able to do these for me." As the answer to this prayer came Mathura Bâbu, who served me so long and with such intense devotion and faith! . . .

(iii)

In referring to the time of joyous illumination which immediately followed His enlightenment, He exclaimed:

What a state it was! The slightest cause aroused in me the thought of the Divine Ideal. One day I went to the Zoological Garden in Calcutta. I desired especially to see the lion, but when I beheld him, I lost all sense-consciousness and went into Samâdhi. Those who were with me wished to show me the other animals, but I replied: "I saw everything when I saw the king of beasts. Take me home." The strength of the lion had aroused in me the consciousness of the omnipotence of God and had lifted me above the world of phenomena. . . .

(iv)

Bhagavân Srî Râmakrishna, again losing all sense-consciousness, entered into God-consciousness and remained motionless like a carven image. Seeing this wonderful sight, some of the devotees shed tears of joy and happiness while others kneeled and began to pray to the Bhagavân. Each one fixed his eyes upon Srî Râmakrishna and, according to the innermost feeling of his heart, realized his Ideal in Him. Some saw in Him the Ideal Devotee, while others recognized the Divine Incarnation in a human form. Mahima, with tears of joy in his eyes chanted: "Behold, behold, the embodiment of Divine Love!" And after a few minutes, as if catching a glimpse of the Absolute Brahman in Râmakrishna, he exclaimed: "Infinite Existence, Intelligence and Love, beyond Unity and Diversity!"

After remaining in this state for a long time, Bhagavân Râmakrishna came down once more on the human plane and said: God incarnates Himself in a human form. It is true that He dwells everywhere, in all living creatures, but the desires of the human soul cannot be fulfilled except by an *Avatâra* or Divine Incarnation. The human being longs to see Him, touch Him, be with Him and enjoy His Divine company. In order to fulfill such desires, the Incarnation of God is necessary.

(*The Gospel of Râmakrishna*, pp. 62-65, 70-71, 206-09, 408-409)

VIVEKĀNANDA: HINDU PROPHET
TO THE WESTERN WORLD

The following selection differs from others in this book in that it is addressed to those who stand outside the Hindu tradition, not to those who accept in some form its presuppositions. This in itself indicates the magnitude of the change that was at work in India at the end of the nineteenth century. Hinduism had reached a stage of self-awareness that made it possible for Vivekānanda to declare to America and Europe that India had spiritual resources to cure the maladies of the West. As the editor of Vivekānanda's papers remarked, when this speech was given at the Parliament of Religions in 1893, "Hinduism had been created." The image of Hinduism that Vivekānanda presented to the world—a religion tolerant of all faiths, profoundly spiritual, yet utterly simple in its creed—was widely accepted. It became, in effect, the stereotype that vied with the earlier image of Hinduism as corrupt and superstitious.

. . . . The Hindu believes that he is a spirit. Him the sword cannot pierce—him the fire cannot burn—him the water cannot melt—him the air cannot dry. The Hindu believes that every soul is a circle whose circumference is nowhere, but whose centre is located in the body, and that death means the change of this centre from body to body. Nor is the soul bound by the conditions of matter. In its very essence, it is free, unbounded, holy, pure and perfect. But somehow or other it finds itself tied down to matter, and thinks of itself as matter.

Why should the free, perfect and pure being be thus under the thraldom of matter, is the next question. How can the perfect soul be deluded into the belief that it is imperfect? . . . . The Hindu is sincere. He does not want to take shelter under sophistry. He is brave enough to face the question in a manly fashion; and his answer is, "I do not know. I do not know how the perfect being, the soul, came to think of itself as imperfect, as joined to and conditioned by matter." . . .

The human soul is eternal and immortal, perfect and infinite, and death means only a change of centre from one body to another. The present is determined by our past actions, and the future by the present. The soul will go on evolving up or reverting back from birth to birth and death to death. But here is another question: is man a tiny boat in a tempest, raised one moment on the foamy crest of a billow and dashed down into a yawning chasm the next, rolling to and fro at the mercy of good and bad actions—a powerless, helpless wreck in an ever-raging, ever-rushing, uncompromising current of cause and effect; a little moth placed under the wheel of causation, which rolls on crushing everything in its way, and waits not for the widow's tears or the orphan's cry? The heart sinks at the idea, yet this is the law of Nature. Is there no hope? Is there no escape?—was the cry that went up from the bottom of the heart of despair. It reached the throne of mercy, and words of hope and consolation came down and inspired a Vedic sage, and he stood up before the world and in trumpet voice proclaimed the glad tidings: "Hear, ye children of immortal bliss! even ye that reside in higher spheres! I have found the Ancient One, who is beyond all darkness, all delusion: knowing Him alone you shall be saved from death over again." . . .

Thus it is that the Vedas proclaim not a dreadful combination of unforgiving laws, not an endless prison of cause and effect, but that at the head of all these laws, in and through every particle of matter and force, stands One, "By whose command the wind blows, the fire burns, the clouds rain, and death stalks upon the earth." . . .

The Vedas teach that the soul is divine, only held in the bondage of matter; perfection will be reached when this bond will burst, and the word they use for it is therefore *mukti*—freedom, freedom from the bonds of imperfection, freedom from death and misery. So the best proof a Hindu sage gives about the soul, about God, is "I have seen the soul; I have seen God." And that is the only condition of perfection. The Hindu religion does not consist in struggles and attempts to believe a certain doctrine or dogma, but in realizing—not in believing, but in being and becoming.

Thus the whole object of their system is by constant struggle to become perfect, to become divine, to reach God and see God, and this reaching God, seeing God, becoming perfect even as the Father in Heaven is perfect, constitutes the religion of the Hindus.

And what becomes of a man when he attains perfection? He lives a life of bliss infinite. He enjoys infinite and perfect bliss, having obtained the only thing in which man ought to have pleasure, namely God, and enjoys the bliss with God.

So far all the Hindus are agreed. This is the common religion of all the sects of India; but then perfection is absolute, and the absolute cannot be two or three. It cannot have any qualities. It cannot be an individual. . . .

Therefore, to gain this infinite universal individuality, this miserable little prison-individuality must go. Then alone can death cease when I am one with life, then alone can misery cease when I am one with happiness itself; then alone can all errors cease when I am one with knowledge itself; and this is the necessary scientific conclusion. Science has proved to me that physical individuality is a delusion, that really my body is one little continuously changing body in an unbroken ocean of matter and *Advaitam* (unity) is the necessary conclusion with my other counterpart. Soul. . . .

Descend we now from the aspirations of philosophy to the religion of the ignorant. At the very outset, I may tell you that there is no *polytheism* in India. In every temple, if one stands by and listens, one will find the worshippers applying all the attributes of God, including omnipresence, to the images. . . .

As we find that somehow or other, by the laws of our mental constitution, we have to associate our ideas of infinity with the image of the blue sky, or of the sea, so we naturally connect our idea of holiness with the image of a church, a mosque or a cross. The Hindus have associated the ideas of holiness, purity, truth, omnipresence, and such other ideas with different images and forms. But with this difference that while some people devote their whole lives to their idol of a church and never rise higher, because with them religion means an intellectual assent to certain doctrines and doing good to their fellows, the whole religion of the Hindu is centred in realization. Man is to become divine by realizing the divine; idols or temples or churches or books are only the supports, the helps, of his spiritual childhood: but on and on he must progress. . . .

If a man can realize his divine nature with the help of

an image, would it be right to call that a sin? Nor even when he has passed that stage, should he call it an error. To the Hindu, man is not travelling from error to truth, but from truth to truth, from lower to higher truth. To him all the religions, from the lowest fetichism to the highest absolutism, mean so many attempts of the human soul to grasp and realize the Infinite, each determined by the conditions of its birth and association, and each of these marks a stage of progress; and every soul is a young eagle soaring higher and higher, gathering more and more strength till it reaches the Glorious Sun. . . .

To the Hindu, then, the whole world of religions is only a travelling, a coming up, of different men and women, through various conditions and circumstances, to the same goal. Every religion is only an evolving a God out of the material man, and the same God is the inspirer of all of them. Why, then, are there so many contradictions? They are only apparent, says the Hindu. The contradictions come from the same truth adapting itself to the varying circumstances of different natures. . . .

This, brethren, is a short sketch of the religious ideas of the Hindus. The Hindu may have failed to carry out all his plans, but if there is ever to be a universal religion, it must be one which will have no location in place or time; which will be infinite, like the God it will preach, and whose sun will shine upon the followers of Krishna and of Christ, on saints and sinners alike; which will not be Brahmanic or Buddhistic, Christian or Mahommedan, but the sum-total of all these, and still have infinite space for development; which in its catholicity will embrace in its infinite arms, and find a place for, every human being, from the lowest grovelling savage not far removed from the brute, to the highest man towering by the virtues of his head and heart almost above humanity, making society stand in awe of him and doubt his human nature. It will be a religion which will have no place for persecution or intolerance in its polity, which will recognize divinity in every man and

woman, and whose whole scope, whose whole force, will
be centred in aiding humanity to realize its own true, divine nature.

(Vivekānanda, *Complete Works*, I, pp. 4-17)

MRS. ANNIE BESANT:
THEOSOPHY'S INTERPRETATION
OF HINDUISM

Mrs. Annie Besant is remembered in India for two contributions: her services to the cause of Indian independence as a
member of the Indian National Congress Party, and her defence of the values and institutions of Hinduism. An example
of her method of handling the tradition is shown in her
interpretation of the famous story of Lord Krishna's theft of
the clothes of the milkmaids while they were bathing. For
critics of Hinduism, such stories had long been used to illustrate the licentious character of the religion and of its devotees. Many Hindus had come to share this embarrassment,
and reformers like Dayānanda had denounced the Krishna
legends as perversions of the true faith. Mrs. Besant argued
that such stories were really instructive morality dramas, and
she transformed them through an allegorical treatment.

Let me take one instance which ignorant lips have used
most in order to insult, to try to defame the majesty that
they do not understand. But let me say this: that I believe
that in most cases where these bitter insults are uttered,
they are uttered by people who have never really read the
story, and who have heard only bits of it and have supplied
the rest out of their own imaginations. I therefore take a
particular incident which I have heard most spoken of
with bitterness as a proof of the frightful immorality of
Shrî Krishna.

While the child of six was one day wandering along, as He would, a number of the Gopîs were bathing nude in the river, having cast aside their cloths—as they should not have done, that being against the law and showing carelessness of woman modesty. Leaving their garments on the bank they had plunged into the river. The child of six saw this with the eye of insight, and He gathered up their cloths and climbed up a tree near by, carrying them with Him, and threw them round His own shoulders and waited to see what would chance. The water was bitterly cold and the Gopîs were shivering; but they did not like to come out of it before the clear steady eyes of the child. And He called them to come and get the garments they had thrown off; and as they hesitated, the baby lips told them that they had sinned against God by immodestly casting aside the garments that should have been worn, and must therefore expiate their sin by coming and taking from His hands that which they had cast aside. They came and worshipped, and He gave them back their robes. An immoral story, with a child of six as the central figure! It is spoken of as though he were a full grown man, insulting the modesty of women. The Gopîs were Rishis, and the Lord, the Supreme, as a babe is teaching them a lesson. But there is more than that; there is a profound occult lesson below the story—a story repeated over and over again in different forms—and it is this: that when the soul is approaching the supreme Lord at one great stage of initiation, it has to pass through a great ordeal; stripped of everything on which it has hitherto relied, stripped of everything that is not of its inner Self, deprived of all external aid, of all external protection, of all external covering, the soul itself, in its own inherent life, must stand naked and alone with nothing to rely on, save the life of the Self within it. If it flinches before the ordeal, if it clings to anything to which hitherto it has looked for help, if in that supreme hour it cries out for friend or helper, nay even for the Guru himself, the soul fails in that ordeal. Naked and alone it must go forth, with absolutely none to aid it save the divinity within itself. And it is that nakedness of the soul as it approaches the supreme goal, that is told of in that story of Shrî Krishna, the child, and the Gopîs, the nakedness of life before the One who gave it. You find many another similar allegory. When the Lord comes in the Kalki, the tenth, Avatâra, He fights on the battlefield and is overcome. He uses all His weapons; every weapon fails Him; and it is not till He casts every weapon aside and fights with His naked hands, that He conquers. Exactly the same idea. Intellect, everything, fails the naked soul before God.

If I have taken up this story specially, out of hundreds of stories, to dwell upon, it is because it is one of the points of attack, and because you who are Hindus by birth ought to know enough of the inner truths of your own religion not to stand silent and ashamed when attacks are made, but should speak with knowledge and thus prevent such blasphemies.

(Annie Besant, *Avatāras*, pp. 100-04)

CHAPTER XVI

FOUR TWENTIETH
CENTURY STATEMENTS

〰〰〰

It is curious that while the Hindu tradition in the nineteenth and twentieth centuries produced saints and social
reformers it has produced few theologians or philosophers
whose works have won acclaim from their peers in the
West, or, indeed, in India itself. The reason for this may
be bound up with the cultural and political conditions of
the last hundred years: intellectual energy has gone into
the reforming of the old society and the building up of a
new political structure. Or it may be that fundamentally
the Hindu tradition is interested in the verification of religious and philosophical truth through personal experience,
and current intellectual movements in the West are perhaps not congenial to the Hindu pragmatism that exam-
ines statements in terms of their usefulness to man's
search for salvation. There have, however, been many attempts made in India on the part of Hindu thinkers to
express the values of the tradition in statements that will
be relevant to the needs of those who have accepted the
methods and presuppositions of Western science and hu-
manistic learning. Four of the most famous of these have
been chosen to suggest the problems that have presented
themselves to their minds, and the ways that they dealt
with them. All of them had first-hand experience of the

West but were deeply committed to Hinduism, and all of them, with the exception of Rabīndranāth Tagore, were involved in political life. Two of them, Tagore and Sarve-palli Rādhakrishnan, conform to familiar patterns of Western intellectual achievement, while the other two, Mohandās Gāndhi and Aurobindo Ghose, lived lives that at points contradicted normal patterns of both Indian and Western experience.

Rabīndranāth Tagore (1861-1941) was the son of Debendranāth Tagore, who had revitalized the Brāhmo Samāj in the middle of the nineteenth century, and, although not very closely identified with the Samāj as an organization, his relationship to its particular intellectual milieu is clear. In many ways he is the spiritual legatee of the movement that attempted to bring new life into India by simultaneously returning to the sources of the Hindu tradition and turning to the West. From a very early age he was familiar with the poetry of the humble people of Bengal, especially of the Bāuls, a sect noted for their devotional songs and the unconventionality of their lives. The contrast between the scion of one of the wealthiest and most intellectual families of Bengal and the wandering, il-literate Bāuls is great, but they shared a passion for spirit-ual freedom and a desire to express in poetry the pain and glory of man's search after God.

But Tagore was more than a poet; he was also one of the most famous Indians of his generation. The award of the Nobel Prize in 1913 for his poetry made him a world figure and gave him enormous prestige in India. This meant that, whatever his own inclinations might be, he had to relate himself to the nationalist movement then gaining momen-tum. Profoundly patriotic, he desired India's political free-dom; at the same time he was repelled by many features of the nationalist movement. It seemed to him that Indian nationalism threatened India with the same evils that were destroying the West, and he refused to give his whole-hearted support to the Indian National Congress. This led him into conflict with some of the nationalist leaders, but *the greatest of them, including Gāndhi, recognized that his opposition arose from the splendor of his vision of India's role in the world, not from any attachment to British rule. He did not stress, as had Vivekānanda, the materialism of the West over against the spirituality of India, but he saw India's destiny as the creator of a new order of civilization and culture. A narrow and parochial nationalism, he believed, would make this impossible; therefore, India should strive to keep open the channels of spiritual communication with all the world. Although his vision fades with the passing years, he remains as one of the most attractive exponents of a vital element of the Hindu tradition.*

The career of Aurobindo Ghose (1872-1950) was very different from that of Tagore, although they came from somewhat similar backgrounds. His father wanted him to receive a thoroughly Western education to fit him for public service under the British government, so he was sent as a small boy to England to be educated, and a deliberate attempt was made to cut him off from all Indian contacts. After his return to India in 1893, however, he threw himself whole-heartedly into the nationalist movement, and became the great exponent of a nationalism that would be wholly Indian in its origin. The result was a fusing of the demand for political freedom with a mystical interpretation of India's past that made an irresistible appeal to many Hindu students at the end of the century. Accused by the Government of advocating terrorism and violence, Aurobindo withdrew from all political activity and dramatically retired to Pondicherry, the small French territory in South India, to devote himself to religious exercises and writing.

Aurobindo's intention in his years of retirement was to create a new synthesis of truth by drawing upon both Hindu and Western thought in such a way that an original theological and philosophical construct would emerge. In engaging in this task he was attempting to do for the modern world what Shankarāchārya had done for Hinduism in

the ninth century and St. Thomas Aquinas for Christian-
ity in the thirteenth, but it is impossible to say how suc-
cessful he has been. His writings are frequently obscured
by a use of the familiar language of Western philosophy to
apply to states and conditions of existence that are related
to his private religious experience; furthermore, he gives
terms meanings peculiar to his own system. Yet at all
times his writings are marked by brilliant insights that illu-
mine Hindu thought.

The heart of Aurobindo's system is a complex doctrine
of spiritual evolution, of the movement of the human soul
from lower to higher forms of spiritual consciousness. This
evolution can be aided by man's own efforts. This view is
elaborated at great length in works of a half poetical, half
philosophical nature, and while it has not won wide ac-
ceptance in India, it is conceivable that it may play an im-
portant part in Hindu religious thought. In any case, his
life as an ardent nationalist and then as a yogi has won
him the place assigned in the tradition to those who
through rigorous discipline attain enlightenment.

The third figure, Mohandas K. Gāndhi (1869-1948),
was very different from the others. This is partly because
of his unique political role, but also because of his intense
desire to express the values of the tradition in ethical terms
that would be immediately understandable by the Indian
masses. His achievements are so well-known that they
neither need nor permit summarization, and the selections
chosen for inclusion emphasize his attempt to find sanc-
tions for a revolutionary social ethic within the Hindu tra-
dition. Building on the work of previous reformers, but
chiefly relying on his own genius for creative improvisa-
tion, he gave the Indian independence movement a qual-
ity unique in human history. Non-violence, ahimsa, was
more than a technique to be used by the weak against the
strong: it was primarily a way of life, of which political
freedom was but one manifestation. Equally important
was the creation of self-respect, which was impossible, he
believed, under the conditions imposed by foreign rule.

*While he drew freely upon Western ideas and ideals—
from the New Testament, Ruskin, and Tolstoy—his ethical positions can be seen as derived from the ancient
Indian insistence on an order that undergirds both the
cosmos and the life of man. He called his autobiography*
Experiments with Truth, *and in this he was faithful to the
Hindu understanding of truth as an experience to be realized and made manifest in one's own personal life.*

*Sarvepalli Rādhakrishnan (b. 1888) crowned a career of
great academic distinction that included the posts of Vice
Chancellorship of Banaras Hindu University and the
Spalding Professorship of Eastern Religions at Oxford
with his election to the Vice Presidency of India in 1952
and to the Presidency in 1962. His many publications on
religion and philosophy have made him the best-known
interpreter of Indian thought. To his commitment to the
Hindu religious and philosophical tradition he adds a deep
and sympathetic knowledge of the Western tradition. Out
of this has come a persuasive statement of Hindu thought
expressed in a felicitous literary style. For him, Hinduism
is above all a union of reason and mystical intuition that
refuses to define its creed, and that is continually being
enriched by its hospitable attitude to new ideas and experiences. His interpretation has been widely accepted by
educated Hindus as the statement of their faith that
permits an attachment to the past but which is not cir-
cumscribed by it. From Rādhakrishnan, as from Tagore,
Aurobindo and Gandhi, comes the assurance that as India
enters a period of great social change her central values will
find eloquent spokesmen. In a world utterly remote in
time and spirit from the one that gave them birth, these
values remain to provide form and color to the new age.*

RABĪNDRANĀTH TAGORE:
A VISION OF INDIA

Tagore did not throw himself whole-heartedly into the nationalist movement because he questioned the direction it
seemed to be taking. The leaders of the Indian movement
had, he believed, accepted a Western conception of the meaning of the nation that was alien to India. His own vision
was of India as the center of a new and revitalized humanity,
and it seemed to him that nationalism was the enemy of this
dream. In the first selection, which is taken from a speech
made to a Bengali nationalist meeting in 1910, he presented
his view that the English had performed a notable work in
India. They had broken down the walls of separation between
East and West, and because of this the spirit of India was
free to spread throughout the world. Nothing should be done
to hinder this possibility. In the poem the same ideas are
expressed in a different form. When the West has spent itself
in the madness of nationalist wars, it will turn to "the patient
dark" of India for a message of healing peace.

In the evolving History of India, the principle at work is
not the ultimate glorification of the Hindu, or any other
race. In India, the history of humanity is seeking to elaborate a specific ideal, to give to general perfection a special
form which shall be for the gain of all humanity;—nothing
less than this is its end and aim. . . .
    . . . So, for ourselves, we must bear in mind that In-
dia is not engaged in recording solely our story, but that it
is we who are called upon to take our place in the great
Drama, which has India for its stage. If we do not fit ourselves to play our part, it is we who shall have to go. If we
stand aloof from the rest, in the pride of past achievement,
content with heaping up obstacles around ourselves, God
will punish us, either by afflicting us with sorrow unceasing
till He has brought us to a level with the rest, or by casting

us aside as mere impediments. If we insist on segregating ourselves in our pride of exclusiveness, fondly clinging to the belief that Providence is specially concerned in our own particular development; if we persist in regarding our *dharma* as ours alone, our institutions as specially fit only for ourselves, our places of worship as requiring to be carefully guarded against all incomers, our wisdom as dependent for its safety on being locked up in our strong rooms; then we shall simply await, in the prison of our own contriving, for the execution of the death sentence which in that case the world of humanity will surely pronounce against us.

Of late the British have come in and occupied an important place in India's history. This was not an uncalled for, accidental intrusion. If India had been deprived of touch with the West, she would have lacked an element essential for her attainment of perfection. Europe now has her lamp ablaze. We must light our torches at its wick and make a fresh start on the highway of time. That our forefathers, three thousand years ago, had finished extracting all that was of value from the universe, is not a worthy thought. We are not so unfortunate, nor the universe, so poor. Had it been true that all that is to be done has been done in the past, once for all, then our continued existence could only be a burden to the earth, and so would not be possible.

With what present duty, in what future hope, can they live who imagine that they have attained completeness in their great grandfathers,—whose sole idea is to shield themselves against the influence of the Modern behind the barriers of antiquated belief and custom?

The Englishman has come through the breach in our crumbling walls, as the messenger of the Lord of the world-festival, to tell us that the world has need of us; not where we are petty, but where we can help with the force of our Life, to rouse the World in wisdom, love and work, in the expansion of insight, knowledge and mutuality. . . .

The India to which the Englishman has come with his

message, is the India which is shooting up towards the future from within the bursting seed of the past. This new India belongs to humanity. What right have *we* to say who shall and who shall not find a place therein. Who is this "We"? Bengali, Marathi or Panjabi, Hindu or Mussalman? Only the larger "We" in whom all these,—Hindu Moslem and Englishman, and whosoever else there be— may eventually unite shall have the right to dictate who is to remain and who is to leave.

On us to-day is thrown the responsibility of building up this greater India, and for that purpose our immediate duty is to justify our meeting with the Englishman. It shall not be permitted to us to say that we would rather remain aloof, inactive, irresponsive, unwilling to give and to take, and thus to make poorer the India that is to be.

(R. Tagore, *Greater India,* pp. 82-87)

Nationalism

1

The last sun of the century sets amidst the blood-red clouds of the West and the whirlwind of hatred.
The naked passion of self-love of Nations, in its drunken delirium of greed, is dancing to the clash of steel and the howling verses of vengeance.

2

The hungry self of the Nation shall burst in a violence of fury from its own shameless feeding.
For it has made the world its food.
And licking it, crunching it, and swallowing it in big morsels,
It swells and swells,
Till in the midst of its unholy feast descends the sudden shaft of heaven piercing its heart of grossness.

3

The crimson glow of light on the horizon is not the light
of thy dawn of peace, my Motherland.

It is the glimmer of the funeral pyre burning to ashes the
vast flesh—the self-love of the Nation—dead under its
own excess.

Thy morning waits behind the patient dark of the East,

Meek and silent.

4

Keep watch, India.

Bring your offerings of worship for that sacred sunrise.

Let the first hymn of its welcome sound in your voice and
sing

"Come, Peace, thou daughter of God's own great suffering.

Come with thy treasure of contentment, the sword of for-
titude,

And meekness crowning thy forehead."

5

Be not ashamed, my brothers, to stand before the proud
and the powerful

With your white robe of simpleness.

Let your crown be of humility, your freedom the freedom
of the soul.

Build God's throne daily upon the ample bareness of your
poverty

And know that what is huge is not great and pride is not
everlasting.

(R. Tagore, *Nationalism*, pp. 157-59)

SRI AUROBINDO:
A VISION OF SPIRITUAL EVOLUTION

In *The Life Divine,* which was first published as a series of articles in the journal *Arya* from 1914 to 1916, Aurobindo stated his theory of spiritual evolution. Man must progress from the normal state of mental awareness to what he calls Supermind, "the truth-consciousness, the Real-Idea which knows itself and all that it becomes." The achievement of this state of Divine Life would lead to an enriched order of humanity. Aurobindo's concern with the social results of mystical intuition is in rather striking contrast with that of many other mystics. As man developed, he argued, he would become "acutely aware of the discord and ignorance that governs his relations with the world, acutely intolerant of it, more and more set upon finding a principle of harmony, peace, joy and unity."

The earliest preoccupation of man in his awakened thoughts and, as it seems, his inevitable and ultimate preoccupation,—for it survives the longest periods of scepticism and returns after every banishment,—is also the highest which his thought can envisage. It manifests itself in the divination of Godhead, the impulse towards perfection, the search after pure Truth and unmixed Bliss, the sense of a secret immortality. The ancient dawns of human knowledge have left us their witness to this constant aspiration; to-day we see a humanity satiated but not satisfied by victorious analysis of the externalities of Nature preparing to return to its primeval longings. The earliest formula of Wisdom promises to be its last,—God, Light, Freedom, Immortality.

These persistent ideals of the race are at once the contradiction of its normal experience and the affirmation of higher and deeper experiences which are abnormal to humanity and only to be attained, in their organised entirety, by a revolutionary individual effort or an evolutionary general progression. To know, possess and be the divine being in an animal and egoistic consciousness, to convert our twi-lit or obscure physical mentality into the plenary supramental illumination, to build peace and a self-existent bliss where there is only a stress of transitory satisfactions besieged by physical pain and emotional suffering, to establish an infinite freedom in a world which presents itself as a group of mechanical necessities, to discover and realise the immortal life in a body subjected to death and constant mutation,—this is offered to us as the manifestation of God in Matter and the goal of Nature in her terrestrial evolution. To the ordinary material intellect which takes its present organisation of consciousness for the limit of its possibilities, the direct contradiction of the unrealised ideals with the realised fact is a final argument against their validity. But if we take a more deliberate view of the world's workings, that direct opposition appears rather as part of Nature's profoundest method and the seal of her completest sanction.

For all problems of existence are essentially problems of harmony. They arise from the perception of an unsolved discord and the instinct of an undiscovered agreement or unity. To rest content with an unsolved discord is possible for the practical and more animal part of man, but impossible for his fully awakened mind, and usually even his practical parts only escape from the general necessity either by shutting out the problem or by accepting a rough, utilitarian and unillumined compromise. For essentially, all Nature seeks a harmony, life and matter in their own sphere as much as mind in the arrangement of its perceptions. The greater the apparent disorder of the materials offered or the apparent disparateness, even to irreconcilable opposition, of the elements that have to be utilised, the stronger is the spur, and it drives towards a more subtle and puissant order than can normally be the result of a less difficult endeavour. The accordance of active

Life with a material of form in which the condition of activity itself seems to be inertia, is one problem of opposites that Nature has solved and seeks always to solve better with greater complexities; for its perfect solution would be the material immorality of a fully organised mind-supporting animal body. The accordance of conscious mind and conscious will with a form and a life in themselves not overtly self-conscious and capable at best of a mechanical or subconscious will is another problem of opposites in which she has produced astonishing results and aims always at higher marvels; for there her ultimate miracle would be an animal consciousness no longer seeking but possessed of Truth and Light, with the practical omnipotence which would result from the possession of a direct and perfected knowledge. Not only, then, is the upward impulse of man towards the accordance of yet higher opposites rational in itself, but it is the only logical completion of a rule and an effort that seem to be a fundamental method of Nature and the very sense of her universal strivings.

We speak of the evolution of Life in Matter, the evolution of Mind in Matter; but evolution is a word which merely states the phenomenon without explaining it. For there seems to be no reason why Life should evolve out of material elements or Mind out of living form, unless we accept the Vedantic solution that Life is already involved in Matter and Mind in Life because in essence Matter is a form of veiled Life, Life a form of veiled Consciousness. And then there seems to be little objection to a farther step in the series and the admission that mental consciousness may itself be only a form and a veil of higher states which are beyond Mind. In that case, the unconquerable impulse of man towards God, Light, Bliss, Freedom, Immortality presents itself in its right place in the chain as simply the imperative impulse by which Nature is seeking to evolve beyond Mind, and appears to be as natural, true and just as the impulse towards Life which she has planted in certain forms of Matter or the impulse towards Mind which she has planted in certain forms of Life. As there, so here, the impulse exists more or less obscurely in her different vessels with an ever-ascending series in the power of its will-to-be; as there, so here it is gradually evolving and bound fully to evolve the necessary organs and faculties. As the impulse towards Mind ranges from the more sensitive reactions of Life in the metal and the plant up to its full organisation in man, so in man himself there is the same ascending series, the preparation, if nothing more, of a higher and divine life. The animal is a living laboratory in which Nature has, it is said, worked out man. Man himself may well be a thinking and living laboratory in whom and with whose conscious co-operation she wills to work out the superman, the god. Or shall we not say, rather, to manifest God? For if evolution is the progressive manifestation by Nature of that which slept or worked in her, involved, it is also the overt realisation of that which she secretly is. We cannot, then, bid her pause at a given stage of her evolution, nor have we the right to condemn with the religionist as perverse and presumptuous or with the Rationalist as a disease or hallucination any intention she may evince or effort she may make to go beyond. If it be true that Spirit is involved in Matter and apparent Nature is secret God, then the manifestation of the divine in himself and the realisation of God within and without are the highest and most legitimate aim possible to man upon earth.

Thus the eternal paradox and eternal truth of a divine life in an animal body, an immortal aspiration or reality inhabiting a mortal tenement, a single and universal consciousness representing itself in limited minds and divided egos, a transcendent, indefinable, timeless and spaceless Being who alone renders time and space and cosmos possible, and in all these the higher truth realisable by the lower term, justify themselves to the deliberate reason as well as to the persistent instinct or intuition of mankind. Attempts are sometimes made to have done finally with questionings which have so often been declared insoluble by logical thought and to persuade men to limit their mental activities to the practical and immediate problems of their material existence in the universe; but such evasions are never permanent in their effect. Mankind returns from them with a more vehement impulse of inquiry or a more violent hunger for an immediate solution. By that hunger mysticism profits and new religions arise to replace the old that have been destroyed or stripped of significance by a scepticism which itself could not satisfy because, although its business was inquiry, it was unwilling sufficiently to inquire. The attempt to deny or stifle a truth because it is yet obscure in its outward workings and too often represented by obscurantist superstition or a crude faith, is itself a kind of obscurantism. The will to escape from a cosmic necessity because it is arduous, difficult to justify by immediate tangible results, slow in regulating its operations, must turn out eventually to have been no acceptance of the truth of Nature but a revolt against the secret, mightier will of the great Mother. It is better and more rational to accept what she will not allow us as a race to reject and lift it from the sphere of blind instinct, obscure intuition and random aspiration into the light of reason and an instructed and consciously self-guiding will. And if there is any higher light of illumined intuition or self-revealing truth which is now in man either obstructed and inoperative or works with intermittent glancings as if from behind a veil or with occasional displays as of the northern lights in our material skies, then there also we need not fear to aspire. For it is likely that such is the next higher state of consciousness of which Mind is only a form and veil, and through the splendours of that light may lie the path of our progressive self-enlargement into whatever highest state is humanity's ultimate resting-place.

(Aurobindo Ghose, *The Life Divine*, pp. 1-7)

MAHĀTMA GĀNDHI:
A VISION OF THE GOOD LIFE

Gāndhi was aware that there were very great differences between his teachings and those of Hinduism in general. Other reformers, including such notable ones as Rāmmohan Roy and Dayānanda Saraswatī, had argued that the original religion had been corrupted, and that the true teachings of Hinduism could be recovered by a return to the great scriptures. But Gāndhi, with the frankness that was part of the secret of his power, admitted that his teachings were reinterpretations of the past. "I have endeavoured," he once wrote, "in the light of prayerful study of the other faiths of the world, and what is more, in the light of my own experiences in trying to live the teachings of Hinduism, . . . to give an extended but by no means strained meaning to Hinduism, not as buried in its ample scriptures, but as a living faith speaking like a mother to her aching children." In his interpretation of the *Bhagavad Gītā*, one of the two religious books of the Hindus that he claimed to know (the other was the Rāmāyana of Tulasīdās), he expounded his central idea of non-violence, although admitting that the *Gītā* apparently approves of war. His explanation was that the great stories of Hinduism are allegories, not historical accounts, and that each age must read them in the light of their spiritual knowledge. For him, therefore, the *Gītā* becomes above all a book of ethics, emphasizing selfless devotion in the cause of human brotherhood.

Krishna of the *Gita* is perfection and right knowledge personified; but the picture is imaginary. That does not mean that Krishna, the adored of his people, never lived. But perfection is imagined. The idea of a perfect incarnation is an aftergrowth.

In Hinduism, incarnation is ascribed to one who has performed some extraordinary service of mankind. All embodied life is in reality an incarnation of God, but it is not usual to consider every living being an incarnation. Future generations pay this homage to one who, in his own generation, has been extraordinarily religious in his conduct. I can see nothing wrong in this procedure; it takes nothing from God's greatness, and there is no violence done to Truth. There is an Urdu saying which means, "Adam is not God but he is a spark of the Divine." And therefore he who is the most religiously behaved has most of the divine spark in him. It is in accordance with this train of thought, that Krishna enjoys, in Hinduism, the status of the most perfect incarnation.

This belief in incarnation is a testimony of man's lofty spiritual ambition. Man is not at peace with himself till he has become like unto God. The endeavour to reach this state is the supreme, the only ambition worth having. And this is self-realization. This self-realization is the subject of the *Gita*, as it is of all scriptures. But its author surely did not write it to establish that doctrine. The object of the *Gita* appears to me to be that of showing the most excellent way to attain self-realization. That which is to be found, more or less clearly, spread out here and there in Hindu religious books, has been brought out in the clearest possible language in the *Gita* even at the risk of repetition.

That matchless remedy is renunciation of fruits of action.

This is the centre round which the *Gita* is woven. This renunciation is the central sun, round which devotion, knowledge and the rest revolve like planets. The body has been likened to a prison. There must be action where there is body. Not one embodied being is exempted from labour. And yet all religions proclaim that it is possible for man, by treating the body as the temple of God, to attain freedom. Every action is tainted, be it ever so trivial. How can the body be made the temple of God? In other words how can one be free from action, i.e. from the taint of sin? The *Gita* has answered the question in decisive language: "By desireless action; by renouncing fruits of action; by dedicating all activities to God, i.e., by surrendering one-self to Him body and soul."

But desirelessness or renunciation does not come for the mere talking about it. It is not attained by an intellectual feat. It is attainable only by a constant heart-churn. Right knowledge is necessary for attaining renunciation. Learned men possess a knowledge of a kind. They may recite the *Vedas* from memory, yet they may be steeped in self-indulgence. In order that knowledge may not run riot, the author of the *Gita* has insisted on devotion accompanying it and has given it the first place. Knowledge without de-votion will be like a misfire. Therefore, says the *Gita*, "Have devotion, and knowledge will follow." This devo-tion is not mere lip worship, it is a wrestling with death. Hence the *Gita's* assessment of the devotee's qualities is similar to that of the sage's.

Thus the devotion required by the *Gita* is no soft-hearted effusiveness. It certainly is not blind faith. The devotion of the *Gita* has the least to do with externals. A devotee may use, if he likes, rosaries, forehead marks, make offerings, but these things are no test of his devotion. He is the devotee who is jealous of none, who is a fount of mercy, who is without egotism, who is selfless, who treats alike cold and heat, happiness and misery, who is ever for-giving, who is always contented, whose resolutions are firm, who has dedicated mind and soul to God, who causes no dread, who is not afraid of others, who is free from exultation, sorrow and fear, who is pure, who is versed in action and yet remains unaffected by it, who renounces all fruit, good or bad, who treats friend and foe alike, who is untouched by respect or disrespect, who is not puffed up by praise, who does not go under when people speak ill of him, who loves silence and solitude, who has a disciplined reason. Such devotion is inconsistent with the existence at the same time of strong attachments. . . .

While on the one hand it is beyond dispute that all ac-tion binds, on the other hand it is equally true that all living beings have to do some work, whether they will or no. Here all activity, whether mental or physical, is to be included in the term of action. Then how is one to be free from the bondage of action, even though he may be acting? The manner in which the *Gita* has solved the problem is to my knowledge unique. The *Gita* says: 'Do your allotted work but renounce its fruit—be detached and work—have no desire for reward and work.'

This is the unmistakable teaching of the *Gita*. He who gives up action falls. He who gives up only the reward rises. But renunciation of fruit in no way means indifference to the result. In regard to every action one must know the result that is expected to follow, the means thereto, and the capacity for it. He, who, being thus equipped is, without desire for the result and is yet wholly engrossed in the due fulfillment of the task before him is said to have renounced the fruits of his action.

Again let no one consider renunciation to mean want of fruit for the renouncer. The *Gita* reading does not warrant such a meaning. Renunciation means absence of hankering after fruit. As a matter of fact, he who renounces reaps a thousandfold. The renunciation of the *Gita* is the acid test of faith. He who is ever brooding over result often loses nerve in the performance of his duty. He becomes impatient and then gives vent to anger and begins to do unworthy things; he jumps from action to action never remaining faithful to any. He who broods over results is like a man given to objects of senses; he is ever distracted, he says goodbye to all scruples, everything is right in his estimation and he therefore resorts to means fair and foul to attain his end.

From the bitter experiences of desire for fruit the author of the *Gita* discovered the path of renunciation of fruit and put it before the world in a most convincing manner. The common belief is that religion is always opposed to material good. "One cannot act religiously in mercantile and such other matters. There is no place for religion in such pursuits; religion is only for attainment of salvation," we hear many worldly-wise people say. In my opinion the author of the *Gita* has dispelled this delusion. He has drawn no line of demarcation between salvation and worldly pursuits. On the contrary he has shown that religion must rule even our worldly pursuits. I have felt that the *Gita* teaches us that what cannot be followed out in day-to-day practice cannot be called religion. Thus, according to the *Gita*, all acts that are incapable of being performed without attachment are taboo. This golden rule saves mankind from many a pitfall. According to this interpretation murder, lying, dissoluteness and the like must be regarded as sinful and therefore taboo. Man's life then becomes simple, and from that simpleness springs peace.

Thinking along these lines, I have felt that in trying to enforce in one's life the central teaching of the *Gita*, one is bound to follow Truth and *ahimsa*. When there is no desire for fruit, there is no temptation for untruth or *himsa*. Take any instance of untruth or violence, and it will be found that at its back was the desire to attain the cherished end.

(M. Gāndhi, in Desai, *The Gita According to Gāndhi*, pp. 128-32)

SARVEPALLI RĀDHAKRISHNAN:
A VISION OF HINDUISM

In a series of lectures delivered in England and the United States in 1926 Rādhakrishnan developed the interpretation of Hinduism that has since become associated with his name. Many of the ideas had been expressed by previous Indian thinkers, but the combination of systematic presentation, great erudition, and deep religious feeling, gave his views a wide audience. Especially significant has been his argument that Hinduism finds a place within itself for all the varieties of religious experience, thus creating a religion of tolerance, while Christianity and Islam, the inheritors of Judaism, display "the intolerance of narrow monotheism." The selection given here summarizes his understanding of the nature of Hinduism.

We are now at the end of our course. We see that the Hindu recognises one supreme spirit, though different names are given to it. In his social economy he has many castes, but one society. In the population there are many races and tribes, but all are bound together by one common spirit. Though many forms of marriage are permitted, there is only one ideal aimed at. There is a unity of purpose underlying the multitudinous ramifications. It may perhaps be useful to conclude this course with a brief résumé of the central spirit of Hinduism and its application to the problems of religion and society.

The world which is a perpetual flow is not all. Its subjection to law and tendency to perfection indicate that it is based on a spiritual reality which is not exhausted in any particular object or group of objects. God is *in* the world, though not *as* the world. His creative activity is not confined to the significant stages in the evolutionary process. He does not merely intervene to create life or consciousness, but is working continuously. There is no dualism of the natural and the supernatural. The spiritual is an emergent of the natural in which it is rooted. The Hindu spirit is that attitude towards life which regards the endless variety of the visible and the temporal world as sustained and supported by the invisible and eternal spirit.

Evil, error and ugliness are not ultimate. Evil has reference to the distance which good has to traverse. Ugliness is half-way to beauty. Error is a stage on the road to truth. They have all to be outgrown. No view is so utterly erroneous, no man is so absolutely evil as to deserve complete castigation. If one human soul fails to reach its divine destiny, to that extent the universe is a failure. As every soul is unlike all others in the world, the destruction of even the most wicked soul will create a void in God's scheme. There is no Hell, for that means there is a place where

God is not, and there are sins which exceed his love. If the infinite love of God is not a myth, universal salvation is a certainty. But until it is achieved, we shall have error and imperfection. In a continuously evolving universe evil and error are inevitable, though they are gradually diminishing.

In religion, Hinduism takes its stand on a life of spirit, and affirms that the theological expressions of religious experience are bound to be varied. One metaphor succeeds another in the history of theology until God is felt as the central reality in the life of man and the world. Hinduism repudiates the belief resulting from a dualistic attitude that the plants in my garden are of God, while those in my neighbour's are weeds planted by the Devil which we should destroy at any cost. On the principle that the best is not the enemy of the good, Hinduism accepts all forms of belief and lifts them to a higher level. The cure for error is not the stake or the cudgel, not force or persecution, but the quiet diffusion of light.

In practical religion, Hinduism recognises that there are those who wish to see God face to face, others who delight in the endeavour to know the truth of it all. Some find peace in action, others in non-action. A comprehensive religion guides each along his path to the common goal, as all woo the same goddess though with different gifts. We must not give supreme and sole importance to our specialty. Perfection can be attained as a celibate, or a householder, or an anchorite. A rigid uniform outlook is wrong. The saintliness of the holy man does not render the steadfastness of the devoted wife or the simple innocence of the child superfluous. The perfection of every type is divine. "Whatsoever is glorious, good, beautiful and mighty, understand that it goes forth from out of a fragment of my splendour." [1]

The law of Karma tells us that the individual life is not a term, but a series. Fresh opportunities will be open to us until we reach the end of the journey. The historical forms we assume will depend on our work in the past. Heaven

[1] *Bhagavadgītā*, x. 41.

and Hell are higher and lower stages in one continuous movement. They are not external to the experiencing individuals. Purification is by means of purgation. The wages of sin is suffering. We need not regard sin as original and virtue as vicarious. We should do our duty in that state of life to which we happen to be called. Most of us have not a free hand in selecting our vocation. Freedom consists in making the best of what we have, our perentage, our physical nature and mental gifts. Every kind of capacity, every form of vocation, if rightly used, will lead us to the centre.

While the ideal of monogamy is held up as the best means for a complete mental and spiritual as well as physical understanding between husband and wife, other forms were permitted in view of the conditions of people with different ideals and interests, habits and desires. A happy marriage requires to be made by slow steps and with much patient effort. If incompatibility of temper is enough to justify divorce, many of us will be divorced. While women's functions are distinguished from those of men, there is no suggestion of their inferiority.

While caste has resulted in much evil, there are some sound principles underlying it. Our attitude to those whom we are pleased to call primitive must be one of sympathy. The task of the civilised is to respect and foster the live impulses of backward communities and not destroy them. Society is an organism of different grades, and human activities differ in kind and significance. But each of them is of value so long as it serves the common end. Every type has its own nature which should be followed. No one can be at the same time a perfect saint, a perfect artist, and a perfect philosopher. Every definite type is limited by boundaries which deprive it of other possibilities. The worker should realise his potentialities through his work, and should perform it in a spirit of service to the common weal. Work is craftsmanship and service. Our class conflicts are due to the fact that a warm living sense of unity does not bind together the different groups.

These are some of the central principles of the Hindu

faith. If Hinduism lives to-day, it is due to them, but it lives so little. Listlessness reigns now where life was once like a bubbling spring. We are to-day drifting, not advancing, waiting for the future to turn up. There is a lack of vitality, a spiritual flagging. Owing to our political vicissitudes, we ignored the law of growth. In the great days of Hindu civilisation it was quick with life, crossing the seas, planting colonies, teaching the world as well as learning from it. In sciences and arts, in trade and commerce it was not behind the most advanced nations of the world till the middle of this millennium. To-day we seem to be afraid of ourselves, and are therefore clinging to the shell of our religion for self-preservation. The envelope by which we try to protect life checks its expansion. The bark which protects the interior of a tree must be as living as that which it contains. It must not stifle the tree's growth, but must expand in response to the inner compulsion. An institution appropriate and wholesome for one stage of human development becomes inadequate and even dangerous when another stage has been reached. The cry of conservatism "it has always been thus" ignores the fundamentals of the theory of relativity in philosophy and practice, in taste and morals, in politics and society, of which the ancient Hindus had a clear grasp. The notion that in India time has stood still for uncounted centuries, and nought has been changed since the primeval sea dried up, is altogether wrong. While there has been continuity with the past, there has also been progress. The Upaniṣads are products of a perfectly spiritual movement which implicitly superseded the cruder ceremonial religion of the Vedas. When the movement of the Upaniṣads became lost in dogmatic controversies, when the fever of disputes and dialectics lulled the free spirit of religion, Buddhism called upon the people to adhere to the simplicity of truth and the majesty of the moral law. About the same period, when canonical culture and useless learning made religion inhuman scholasticism, and filled those learned in this difficult trifling with ridiculous pride, the *Bhagavadgītā* opened the gates of heaven to all those who are pure in heart. When the ritualists succeeded in imprisoning the living faith in rigid creeds, the true prophets of the spirit, the Śaiva and the Vaiṣnava saints, and the theologians like Śamkara and Rāmānuja, summoned the people to the worship of the living God. The influence of Madhva and Caitanya, Basava and Rāmānanda, Kabīr and Nānak is not inconsiderable. There has been no such thing as a uniform stationary un-alterable Hinduism whether in point of belief or practice. Hinduism is a movement, not a position; a process, not a result; a growing tradition, not a fixed revelation. Its past history encourages us to believe that it will be found equal to any emergency that the future may throw up, whether on the field of thought or of history.

After a long winter of some centuries, we are to-day in one of the creative periods of Hinduism. We are begin-ning to look upon our ancient faith with fresh eyes. We feel that our society is in a condition of unstable equilib-rium. There is much wood that is dead and diseased that has to be cleared away. Leaders of Hindu thought and practice are convinced that the times require, not a sur-render of the basic principles of Hinduism, but a restate-ment of them with special reference to the needs of a more complex and mobile social order. Such an attempt will only be the repetition of a process which has occurred a number of times in the history of Hinduism. The work of readjustment is in process. Growth is slow when roots are deep. But those who light a little candle in the dark-ness will help to make the whole sky aflame.

(S. Rādhakrishnan, *The Hindu View of Life*, pp. 124-30)

SOURCES OF ENGLISH
TRANSLATIONS
AND SELECTIONS

〰〰〰〰

Apastamba Dharma Sūtra. Translated by George Buhler, in *Sacred Books of the East,* Vol. II, Part I, American Edition. New York: Christian Literature Company, 1898.

Atharva Veda. Translated by R. T. H. Griffith in *The Hymns of the Atharva Veda.* Benares: E. J. Lazarus and Co., 1896.

Bāna. *The Harsacarita of Bāna.* Translated by E. B. Cowell and F. W. Thomas. London: Royal Asiatic Society, 1897.

de Bary, W. T., Stephen Hay, Royal Weiler and Andrew Yarrow, *The Sources of Indian Tradition.* New York: Columbia University Press, 1958.

Besant, Annie. *Avatāras.* London: Theosophical Society, 1900.

Bhagavad Gītā. Translated by Sir Edwin Arnold in *The Song Celestial.* Boston: Roberts, 1885. Translated by K. T. Telang in *Sacred Books of the East,* Vol. VIII. Oxford: Clarendon Press, 1882.

Bhartrihari. *The Satakas or Wise Sayings.* Translated by J. M. Kennedy. London: Laurie, 1910.

Bhavabhūti. *Mālati and Mādhava.* Translated by H. H. Wilson in *The Theatre of the Hindus.* London: Trubner, 1871.

Dayānanda, Saraswatī. *Satyārtha Prākāsh.* Translated by C. Bharadwaja. Lahore, 1906.

Desai, M. K., *The Gita According to Gandhi.* Ahmedabad: Navjivan Trust, 1956.

Ghose, Aurobindo. *The Life Divine.* Calcutta: Arya Publishing House, 1939.

Gotama. *Nyāya Sūtras.* Translated by S. C. Vidyābhusana in *Sacred Books of the Hindus,* Vol. VIII. Allahabad: Panini Office, 1913.

Griffith, R. T. H. See *Rig Veda.*

Hitopadeśa. Translated by Sir Edwin Arnold. London: Smith, Elder, 1861.

Hume, R. E., *The Thirteen Principal Upanishads*. Bombay: Oxford University Press, 1954.

Jayadeva. *Gītā Govinda*. Translated by George Keyt. Bombay: Kutub, 1947.

Kabīr. Translated by Rabīndranāth Tagore in *Songs of Kabīr*. New York: Macmillan, 1915; also translated by G. H. Westcott in *Kabīr and the Kabīr Panth*. Cawnpore: Christ Church Mission Press, 1907.

Kaegi, Adolf. *The Rig Veda: the Oldest Literature of the Indians*. Translated by R. Arrowsmith. Boston: Ginn and Co., 1886.

Kālidās. *Shakuntalā*. Translated by Monier Williams. New York: Dodd, Mead, 1885.

Kanāda. *The Vaiśeṣika Sūtras of Kanāda* in *Sacred Books of the Hindus*, Vol. VI. Allahabad: Panini Office, 1911.

Kautilya. *Arthaśāstra*. Translated by R. Shamasastry. Mysore: Sri Raghuveer Press, 1956.

Kennedy, M. T. *The Chaitanya Movement*. Calcutta: Association Press, 1925.

Kingsbury, F., and G. E. Phillips. *Hymns of the Tamil Śaivite Saints*. Calcutta: Association Press, 1921.

Kumārila. *Ślokavārtika*. Translated by G. N. Jha. Calcutta: The Asiatic Society, 1902-1908.

Macauliffe, M. A., *The Sikh Religion*. Vol. I. Oxford: Clarendon Press, 1909.

Macdonnell, A. A. See *Rig Veda* below.

Mahābhārata. Translated by P. C. Roy. 14 vols. Calcutta: Bharata Press, 1883-1890; selections from this translation edited by S. C. Nott in *The Mahabharata*. New York: Philosophical Library, 1956.

Majumdar, R. C., editor. *The Classical Age*. Vol. III, *The History and Culture of the Indian People*. Bombay: Bharatiya Vidya Bhavan, 1954.

Mānikkavāchakar. *Tiruvācagam*. Translated by G. U. Pope. Oxford: Clarendon Press, 1900.

Manu. *Manu Smriti*. Translated by George Buhler in *Sacred Books of the East*, Vol. XXV. Oxford: Clarendon Press, 1886.

Muir, John. *Original Sanskrit Texts*. 5 vols. London: Trubner, 1884-1890.

Orr, W. G., *A Sixteenth Century Indian Mystic*. London: Lutterworth Press, 1949.

Patanjali. *Yogasūtra*. Translated by Rama Prasad in *Sacred Books of the Hindus*, Vol. IV. Allahabad: Panini Office, 1924.

Rādhakrishnan, S., *The Hindu View of Life*. London: Allen & Unwin, 1927.

Rāmakrishna. *The Gospel of Rāmakrishna*. Translated by "M." New York: Vedanta Society, 1947.

Rāmānuja. *The Vedānta Sūtra with Commentary of Rāmānuja.* Translated by George Thibaut in *Sacred Books of the East*, Vol. XLVIII. Oxford: Clarendon Press, 1906.

Rammohan Roy. *Translation of the Isa Upanishad.* Calcutta, 1816; and *The English Works of Raja Rammohan Roy.* Allahabad: Panini Office, 1906.

Rānade, M. G., *Religious and Social Reform.* Bombay: Gopal Narayan, 1902.

Rig Veda. Translated by R. T. H. Griffith, in *The Hymns from the Rig Veda.* 2 vols. Benares: E. J. Lazarus, 1920; also, A. A. Macdonnell, *Hymns from the Rigveda.* Calcutta: Association Press, 1923.

Śatapatha Brāhmana. Translated by Julius Eggeling in *Sacred Books of the East*, Vol. XII. Oxford: Clarendon Press, 1882.

Sen, K. C. *Lectures in India.* Calcutta: Brahmo Tract Society, 1899.

Sources of Indian Tradition. See de Bary, W. T., *et al.*, above.

Tagore, Debendranāth. *The Autobiography of Maharishi Devendranath Tagore.* Translated by S. Tagore and I. Devi. London: Macmillan, 1914.

Tagore, Rabīndranāth. *Greater India.* Madras: Ganesan, 1921.

Tagore, Rabīndranāth. *Nationalism.* New York: Macmillan, 1917.

Tilak, B. G. *Writings and Speeches.* Madras: Ganesan, n.d.

Tukārām. *The Poems of Tukārām.* Translated by J. N. Fraser and K. B. Marathe. Madras: Christian Literature Society, 1909.

Tulasīdās. *Rāmacaritamānasa.* Translated by F. S. Growse in *The Rāmāyana of Tulsīdās.* Allahabad: NWP and Oudh Government Press, 1887.

Valmiki. *Rāmāyana.* Translated by H. P. Shastri. Vol. I. London: Shanti Sadan, 1952.

Vishnu Purāna. Translated by H. H. Wilson. London: John Murray, 1840.

Vivekānanda, Swami. *Complete Works*, Vol. I. Almora: Prabuddha Bharata, 1919.

INDEX

Absolute, the, 234, 246
Ādityas, 235
Aesthetics, 157
Afghanistan, 71, 230
Agni, 10, 20-21, 25, 39, 44, 45
Ahimsa (non-killing), 71
Akbar, 230
Almsgiving, duty of, 34
Ālvārs, 246-247
Amrita, 210-211
Anarchy, danger of, 106-09
Animals, killing of, 113, 114-15, 134-35
Apastamba Dharma Sūtra, 84-86, 88
Appar, 233, 237-38
Apsarases, 211
Aquinas, St. Thomas, 198, 328
Āranyakas (Forest Books), 6; see also Brihad Āranyaka
Arjuna, 120, 126-29, 137, 301
Arthashāstra (Treatise on Material Gain), 102-03, 110; selection from, 110-12
Aryaman, 14
Aryans, 3, 4, 7, 17, 18, 35, 86, 118, 300
Ārya Samāj, 300

Asceticism, 86, 80, 138, 164
Ashoka, 71-72, 103, 112-13, 304; vision of true conquest, 112-16
Ashwins, 235
Astronomy, 155
Āśvalāyana Grihya Sūtra, 86-88
Atharva Veda, 5, 12, 23, 33, 36; selections from, 15, 24, 37-39, 40-41, 42-43, 44-45, 46-47
Ātman, 49, 55-58, 59-62, 64, 198, 199
Atomic nature of reality, 184-86
Aurangzīb, 71, 230, 274
Aurobindo, Sri, see Ghose, Aurobindo
Avatāras, 322-24
Ayodhya, 137

Bāna, 98-100, 170-74
Bāni, 268-70
de Bary, William Theodore, ix
Bāuls, 326
Benares, 7, 248
Benares Hindu University, 329
Bengal, 230, 233, 278, 279, 280, 281, 301, 326
Besant, Annie, 303, 322-24

Bhagavad Gītā, 73, 80, 118, 120, 126, 129, 168, 189; selections from, 83-84, 120-22, 123-24, 125-26, 126-29, 129-30, 246, 250, 301, 310-12, 339

Bhakti (attitude of devotion or adoration), 117

Bhakti movements and literature, 229, 243, 244, 248, 251, 261, 262, 268, 275, 280, 301

Bharata, 146

Bhāratavarsha, vii, 218, 219

Bhartrihari, 164-67

Bhavabhūti, 162-64

Bhīma, 137

Bhīsma, 80

Bible, the, 4, 6, 249, 279

Bihar, 70, 153

Bimbisāra, 70

Bombay, 281

Brahmā, 11 n., 46, 214, 215, 220

Brahman, 11 n., 41, 49, 50, 52-54, 63, 64, 92, 97, 98, 104, 198-207, 235, 236; identity of, with *ātman*, 59-62

Brāhmanas, 5-6, 28; selection from, 28-29

Brahmanaspati, 45

Brahmanism, 7

Brāhmans (priestly class), 11, 25, 28, 41-43, 59, 75, 77, 79, 80-81, 84, 93, 94, 102, 209, 250, 275; place of, 41-43

Brahmasūtra Bhāsya, 197-205

Brāhmo Samāj, 279-80, 281, 292, 302, 326

Brihad Āranyaka, 51-54, 55, 62-63

Brihaspati, 45

British in India, 230, 274-75, 281, 295, 301, 330

Buddha, *see* Gautama Buddha

Buddhism, 51, 70, 71, 72, 78, 119, 133-34, 180, 181, 198, 220, 232, 237

Burden of the past, 252

Cārvāka, 181

Caste system, 76, 83, 102, 209, 228, 247, 262, 279, 280

Caution and Commonsense, 176-179

Ceylon, 72

Ceylon, demon king of; *see* Rāvan

Chaitanya, 247, 255-56

Chāndogya, 55-58, 59-62, 63

Chandragupta Maurya, 71, 102

Change, possibility of, 95-96

Charity, duty of, 33-34

Charms, 36-39

Child marriage, 280

Chosen One, the, 44-45

Christianity, 275, 276, 279, 299, 300, 303, 305, 310, 343; against, 307-08; India and, 292-95

Classical Age, 153-56

Class structure, 42, 70, 74, 75-76, 78-84, 101, 102, 228, 231, 262; mutual dependence of the classes, 80-84

Concentration, 49

Consecration to Shiva, 237-38

Cosmic law, order; *see* Rita

Cosmology, Vedic, 10

Cow, the, in praise of, 40-41; place in Hindu tradition, 39-40

Creation Hymn, 24

Creation of the universe, 10, 23-27

Cults and sects, 117, 118, 119, 156, 233, 246, 248, 262, 268, 275, 326

Dādū, 262, 268-70

Daityas, 210, 211

Dānavas, 210, 211

Dandaniti (science of chastisement), 106

Dānu, 19

Dasratha, 146

Datta, Narendra Nāth, *see* Vivekānanda

Dayānanda Saraswatī, 276, 277, 300, 303, 304-09, 322, 339

Death, 12, 29-31

Decimal system, 155

Deism, 279

Deities, *see* Gods, Vedic

Delhi, 137, 230

Demons, 36, 55, 56, 210, 212

Demon king of Ceylon; *see* Rāvan

Devotion, price of, 212-14; way of salvation, 126-29

Dhanwantari, 211

Dharma, 70, 74-75, 76, 77, 78, 80, 90, 95, 104, 122, 180, 181, 228; defence of, 146-50

Dharmashāstra texts, 72-73

Dhritarāshtra, 137, 138

Discipline, 194-97; *see also* Yoga

Divorce, 86

Dravidian languages, 4, 228

Dualism, of matter and spirit, 189-94

Durgā (Kālī), 233, 244, 302

Duryodhana, 137

Dushyanta, 158

Dutch in India, 274

Duty, way of salvation, 122-24

Dvāparā Yuga, 221-22

Earth as motherland, 45-47

East India Company, 278

Education, system of, 84-86

Ends of life (man), four, 77-78, 228

Enduring Ruler, the, 45

English, *see* British in India

Epics, universe of the great, 136-150

Ethical theory and practice, 75

Ethics, Hindu, 147

European expansion into India, 273-77

Evil spirits, 36; *see also* Demons

Experiments with Truth, 329

Family life, second stage of life, 86-90

Fertility cults, 233

First Principle, 24

Forbidden acts, 233

Four ages (*yugas*), 220-23

Gama, Vasco da, 274

Gandhāra, 61

Gāndhi, Mahātma, 71, 276, 326, 327, 328-29, 339-43

Ganesh, 209

Ganges River (Gangā), vii, 70, 71, 218, 219

Gangetic Plain, 7

Gārgī, 52-54

Gautama Buddha, 70-71, 133, 248, 302; first sermon of, 133-134; *see also* Buddhism

Gautama Dharma Sūtra, 97-98

Geography, sacred, 45, 218-20

Ghori, Muhammad, 230

Ghose, Aurobindo, 69, 276, 326, 327-28, 329, 333-38

Gītā Govinda, 169-70

Goa, 274

Gods, Vedic, 9-10, 12-23, 55, 73, 168, 209, 210-12, 214-18, 232-45, 246-60; origin of, 10

Gokhale, 276

Golden age (*Krita Yuga*), 220-23

Good life, the, 101; charms and spells for, 36-39; vision of, 339-43

Gopāl, 253, 254

Gospel of Rāmakrishna, 313-17

Gospel of Selfless Action, 339-43

Grace, 117, 118; prayer for, 250-251

Greater India, 330-32

Growth, Age of, 117; possibility of, 95-96
Guptas, 72, 153-54

Hanumān, 137
Harappa, 3
Harsacarita, 98-100, 171-74
Harsha, 98, 170, 171
Heresies, 132-35, 181; *see also* Buddhism; Jainism
Hermit, third stage of life, 77, 90-91
Himālayas, 218
Hinduism, viii, 4, 7, 40, 45, 51, 72, 117, 119, 156, 205, 208, 227, 229, 231, 232, 233, 237, 238, 249, 261, 262, 263, 268, 275, 276, 277, 278, 279, 280, 281, 299, 300, 303, 304, 329, 343, 344; defence of, 284-88; original, 282-84; theosophy's interpretation of, 322-24; vision of, 343-48
Hindu Renaissance, 299, 309
Hindu View of Life, 343-48
Hiranyakashipu, 212
History, nature of, 220-23; sacred, 208-23
Hitopadesha, 177-79
Holi, 171
Homeless wanderer, fourth stage of life, 77, 91-93
Horoscopes, 155
Horse Sacrifice, 51-52
Householder, second stage of life, 77, 86-90
Huns, 221
Hymn of Man (*Purusha Sukta*), 23, 27, 32
Hymns, 228, 229, 239
Hymn to Earth (*Prithivī*), 45, 46-47

Ideal, statement of the, 78-80
Idol worship, 119, 156, 240, 279, 300

Ila, 214
Images in worship, *see* Idol worship
Immolation, 98-100
Immortality, 21, 50, 64
Incantations, 36-39
Incarnation, 129-30, 262
India, British in, 230, 274-75, 281, 295, 301, 330; Dutch in, 274; European expansion into, 273-77; Portuguese in, 274; vision of, 330-32; *see also* North India; South India
Indian National Congress, 301, 322, 326
Indian Ocean, 274
Indo-Aryan languages, 228
Indra, 10, 17-20, 21, 23, 25, 27, 35, 38, 44, 45, 55-58, 212, 236
Indus River, vii
Indus Valley civilization, 3-4, 18, 118, 130, 232
Initiation, 75, 77, 84
Invasions, 153, 156, 221, 229-31, 273-77
Isha Upanishad, 282-84
Ishvarakrishna, 189-94
Islam, 229, 230, 261, 262, 266, 268, 300, 305, 343; against, 308-09

Jahān, Shāh, 230
Jahāngīr, 230
Jaimini, 186
Jainism, 51, 70, 71, 72, 78, 119, 133, 180, 181, 220, 232, 237; vision of life, 134-35
Jaipur State, 268
Jambudvīpa, vii
Japjī, 266-67
Jatāvu (Vulture King), 256-60
Jaundice, spell against, 37
Jayadeva, 169-70
Jnānadeva, 248, 250-51

Jnānasambandha (Sambandar), 233, 239
Judaism, 343

Kabīr, 248, 261, 262, 263-65
Kaikeyī, 146
Kāla (Time), 23, 24
Kālī (Durgā), 233, 244, 302
Kali Yuga, 221-23
Kālidās, 158-61, 164, 167-68
Kalinga, 113, 114
Kalki, 221
Kāma (physical pleasure), 78
Kāmasūtra, or *Aphorisms on Love*, 174-76
Karma, 50, 51, 62-63, 70, 117, 119, 154, 180, 181, 228, 266; emancipation from, 64-65
Karma yoga, 122
Karnataka, 249
Kashmir, 244, 245
Katha, 64-65, 187-188
Kautilya, 102, 110
Kingdoms, Hindu, 7, 70, 230
King of Kings, 44
Kings and kingship, anarchy, danger of, 106-09; Ashoka's vision of true conquest, 112-16; crowning of, 44-45; divinity of, 102; duties and functions of, 102-16; lineage of, 138-46, 214-18; place in Hindu tradition, 43-44; remedy for an evil society, 103-06; war and peace, 110-12
Knowledge, way of salvation, 124-126
Koran, the, 6, 308-309
Krishna, 73, 118, 120, 122, 124, 126-30, 168-69, 210, 246-48, 252-53, 254, 301, 322; bride of, 253
Krita Yuga (golden age), 220-23
Kshatriyas (warriors), 42, 63, 75, 79, 81-82, 93, 94, 102, 268

Kumārila, 186-89
Kurus, 137

Lakshman, 137, 256
Lakshmī, 210, 211
Lallā, 244-45
Languages of India, 4, 228, 248, 279, 304
Legends, *see* Mythology
Life, duties of, exposition of, 74-100; four ends of, 77-78, 228; Jain vision of, 134-35; limitations of, recognition of, 93-95; as a sacrament, 97-98; four stages (*āshrams*) of, 76-77, 78, 84-93, 228; *summum bonum* of, 180-81; *see also* Family life; Good life, the
Life Divine, The, 334-38
Lineage of kings, 138-46, 214-18
Literature, 157-79
Logical thinking, basis of, 181-184
Lokāyata, 181
Love, divine and human, 168-70; pain of, 162-64; perils of, 164-167; physical, 86; pleasures of, 158-61; woman's, charm to compel, 38

Magadha, 70, 71, 153
Maghavan, 58
Magic, sympathetic, 37
Mahābhārata, 80, 103, 118, 136-137, 138, 234; selections from, 80-83, 104-06, 107-09, 138-46, 234-37
Mahāvira, 70-71
Mālati and Mādhava, 162-64
Man, four ends of, 77-78, 228; four stages of life of, 76-77, 78, 84-93, 228; origin of, 10; true nature of, 119-22
Mānikkavāchakar, 233, 240-41
Manu, 96, 106

Manu Smriti, 73, 78, 96, 103; selections from, 79-80, 86-87, 90-91, 91-93, 93-95, 95-96
Marāthas, 274
Marāthi, 247-48, 250, 281
Marriage, 86, 88, 97, 98; child, 280
Material gain (*artha*), 77-78; treatise on, 102-03, 110-12
Mathematics, 155
Mathura, 247
Matter and spirit, dualism of, 189-94
Mauryan Empire, 71, 102, 106, 153, 215
Medicine, 155
Meditation, 49, 77
Megasthenes, 110
Mewār, 252
Mīmāmsā, 181, 186-89, 202
Mīrābāī, 247, 252-53
Missionaries, Christian, 279, 300
Mitra, 14
Mohenjodaro, 3
Monogamy, 86
Monotheism, 263, 266, 268, 300, 344
Moral order, 9, 70
Morning prayer, 266-67
Mughals, 230, 251, 274
Munis, 212
Muslims, 156, 229-31, 247, 248, 263, 266, 273, 274, 279; see also Islam
Mutiny of 1857, 274, 276
Mysore, 249
Mysticism, reform and, 288-92
Mythology, Vedic, 9, 10, 45, 137, 168, 209

Nāgas, 211
Nakula, 137
Nānak, 262, 265-67, 268
Nationalism, 301, 327, 332-33
Nationalism, 332-33
Nāyanārs, 232, 246

Non-Dualism, 197-205; Qualified, 205-07
Non-existence, 29
Non-violence, 328, 339
North India, 70, 71, 98, 153, 228, 229, 232, 247, 248, 249, 262, 268
Nyāya, 181-84
Nyāyā Sūtras of Gotama, 182-84

Origin of gods and men, 10, 210-212
Orissa, 255
Outcasts, 76, 86
Oxford University, 329

Painting, Hindu, 154
Panchatantra, 176
Pāndu, 137, 138
Pāndya Kingdom, 240
Pānini, 204
Panjab, 7, 300
Pantheism, 50
Parliament of Religions (Chicago), 302, 317
Pārvati, 209
Pātaliputra, 71
Patanjali, 194-97
Peace, war and, 110-12
Peasants; see Vaishyas
Phallic symbols, 119, 234
Philosophy, Hindu, 156, 180-207
Pleasure, physical (*kāma*), 78; science of, 174-76
Poet-saints, 228, 229, 231, 232-233, 234, 248, 251, 261, 262
Polytheism, 279, 300
Pondicherry, 327
Popular Hinduism, 227
Portuguese in India, 274
Prahlāda, 212-14
Prajāpati (Lord of Offspring), 23, 24, 55-58
Prākrits, 228
Prārthana Samāj, 281
Price of devotion, 212-14

Priests, *see* Brāhmans

Prince's birth, celebration of, 170-74

Prithivī (Hymn to Earth), 45, 46-47

Prithvi Rāj, 230

Purānas, 156, 208-09, 212, 214, 220, 246, 300

Purandaradāsa, 249-50

Purūravas, 215

Purusha, 25-26, 56

Purusha Sukta (Hymn of Man), 23, 27

Qualified Non-Dualism, 205-07

Quran; *see* Koran

Rādhā, 168, 247, 302

Rādhakrishnan, Sarvepalli, 329, 343-48

Rājanya, 25

Rajasthan, 253

Rāma, 118, 137-38, 146-47, 246, 248, 249, 256-60, 263

Ramācharitamanas, 249, 257-60

Rāmakrishna, Srī, 276, 301-03, 313-17

Rāmakrishna Mission, 303

Rāmānanda, 248, 261, 263

Rāmānuja, 205-07, 246

Rāmaprasād, 243-44

Ramāyana, 136, 137-38, 146, 339; selection from, 147-50

Rāmmohan Roy, 276, 277, 278-280, 282-88, 299, 339

Rānade, Mahadev Govind, 276, 281, 295-98

Rāvan, 137, 256-60

Reality, 49, 50; atomic nature of, 184-86

Rebirths, cycle of, 62-63, 64, 70, 119, 180, 266; *see also* Transmigration

Reform in India, 278-98, 301; mysticism and, 288-92; social, need for, 295-98

Righteousness, Rule of, 112-16

Rig Veda, 5, 9, 12, 23, 24, 33, 42; selections from, 13-14, 16-17, 18-20, 20-21, 21-23, 25-26, 26-27, 30-31, 34, 35-36, 79, 204, 300

Rishis, 25

Rita, 9, 10, 11, 12, 28, 29

Rohinī (the Red One), 37

Royal line, founding of the, 138-146

Rudra, 130, 235

Sacrament, 97; life as a, 97-98

Sacred geography, 45, 218-20

Sacred history, 208-23

Sacred texts, proof of, 186-89

Sacrifice, 11, 25-26, 27-29, 32, 44, 49, 50-52, 83

Sādhyas, 25, 79

Sahadeva, 137

Salvation (*moksha*), 78, 233-34, 261; way of, 117-35

Sāman, 79

Sāma Veda, 5

Sambandar, 233, 239

Samhitā, 5, 6

Samyutta Nikāya, 133-34

Sānkhya, 181, 189-94, 195

Sanskrit, 154, 157, 228, 229, 304

Satapatha Brāhmana, 28-29

Satī, 98-100, 279

Satyārtha Prākāsh, 304-09

Savitar, 16

Science, 155

Science of pleasure, 174-76

Sculpture, Hindu, 154

Sects, *see* Cults and sects

Self, the, 50, 55-58, 59, 64, 180-81, 198-207; *see also* Ātman and *Brahman*

Semi-divine beings, 10

Sen, Keshub Chunder, 276, 280, 292-95, 302

Serfs; *see* Shūdras

Serpents, charm against, 37-38

Shakti, 233

Shakuntalā, 158-61, 167-68

Shankara, 198-205, 227, 234, 245, 246, 327

Shaivism, 118, 119, 244

Shiva, 4, 73, 118-19, 130, 209, 229, 232-33, 237, 238, 240, 242, 243, 244, 262; *Consecration to*, 237-38; consort of, Kālī, 244; description of, 234-237; dwelling places of, 242-243; everythingness of, 239; glory of, 239; indwelling lord, 245; in praise of, 232-45; song to awaken, 240-41; triumph through, 238

Shruti, 6, 96

Shūdras (serfs), 25, 42, 75-76, 79, 80, 82-83, 95

Shvetaketu, 59-62

Sikhism, 262, 265-66

Sītā, 137-38, 249, 256, 256-60

Sivaji, 304

Ślokavārtika, 186-89

Smriti (sacred law), 6, 88, 95, 96

Social life, 74, 86, 102; maintenance of, 101-16

Social order, 32-47, 75, 101, 102

Social reform, need for, 295-98, 301

Soma (drink), 11, 21-23, 41, 94, 97

Soma (god), 10, 21-23, 45

Sorcerers, 36

Soul, the, 71, 93, 97; transmigration of, *see* Transmigration

Sources of Indian Tradition (de Bary *et al.*), ix, x

South India, 70, 118, 228, 229, 232, 233, 246, 275, 327

Spells, 36-39

Spirit and matter, dualism of, 189-94

Spiritual evolution, vision of, 334-38

Sringāra Sataka, 164-67

Stages (*āshrams*) of life, four, 76-77, 78, 84-93, 228; hermit, 77, 90-91; homeless wanderer, 77, 91-93; householder and family life, 77, 86-90; student, 77, 84-86

Statecraft, 43; *see also* Kings and kingship

Stomach Austerity, 249-50

Student, first stage of life, 77, 84-86

Sūfīs, 261-62

Sundaramūrthi, 233, 242-43

Surabhi, 211

Sūrdās, 247, 254

Surya, 10

Sūtras, 182, 184; see also *Apastamba Dharma Sūtra; Brahmasūtra Bhāsya; Nyāyā Sūtras of Gotama; Vaiśesika Sūtras of Kanāda; Vedānta Sūtra; Yogasūtra*

Śvetāśvatara, 50, 63, 130; selection from, 130-32

Tagore, Debendranāth, 280, 288-292, 326

Tagore, Rabīndranāth, 263-65, 326-27, 329, 330-33

Tamil, 4, 228, 229

Tantras, 233

Tanūnapat, 28

Telugu, 4, 228

Temples, 156, 240

Temporal power, 101-16

Theater, Hindu, 154

Theism, 73, 130, 186, 229

Theosophical Society, 303, 322-324

Tilak, Bāl Gangādhar, 276, 301, 303, 309-13

Time (Kāla), 23, 24; as creator, 24

Tirunāvukkarashu, *see* Appar

Trading, charm for success in, 38-39
Transmigration, 12, 50-51, 62-63, 117, 181
Tretā Yuga, 221-22
Tribal system, 7
Triumph of Prahlāda, 212-14
Triumph Through Shiva, 238
Tukārām, 248, 251-52
Tulasīdās, 248, 249, 256-60, 261, 339
Turks, 221, 230
Tvashtar, 18

Umā, 236
Universe, the, control of, 33; creation of, 10, 23-27; of the great epics, 136-50; ground of, search for, 52-54; ordering of, 9-31
Upamanyu, 234
Upanishads, 6, 48-65, 90, 117, 120, 130, 197, 205, 279, 280, 288, 289; *see also Āranyaka*; *Chāndogya*; *Isha*; *Katha*; *Śvetāśvatara*
Urvashī, 215
Usha, goddess of dawn, 10, 15-17
Uttarādhyayana, 134-35

Vaiśesika Sūtras of Kanāda, 184-186
Vaisheshika, 181, 184-86
Vaishnavism, 118, 119
Vaishyas (peasants), 25, 42, 63, 75, 79, 80, 82, 93, 94, 95, 228
Vallabāchārya, 247, 254
Valmīki, 137, 248
Varuna, 10, 12-15, 17, 21, 23, 43, 45
Vātsyāyana, 174-76
Vedānta, 181, 197-207, 227
Vedānta Mīmāmsā, 202

Vedānta of Rāmānuja, 205-07
Vedānta of Shankara, 197-205
Vedānta Sūtra, 197, 199; *Commentary on the*, 205-07
Vedas, 3, 4-8, 33, 59, 72, 80, 81, 83, 84, 92, 104, 155, 186, 208, 250, 291, 300, 304, 305-307; *see also Atharva Veda*; *Rig Veda*; *Sāma Veda*; *Yajur Veda*
Vedic Age, 3-4, 7, 8, 48, 70, 72
Vijayanagar, 230
Virochana, 55-57
Vishnu (or Hari), 41, 73, 118, 129, 209-12, 221, 229, 235, 236, 246, 248, 262; in praise of, 246-60
Vishnu Purāna, 208, 214; selections from, 210-12, 212-14, 215-18, 218-20, 221-23
Vishwedevas, 235
Vitobhā, 248
Vivekānanda (Narendra Nāth Datta), 276, 302-03, 317-22, 327
Vritra, 18, 19
Vulture King, 256-60

War, 34-36; peace and, 110-12
Warrior class, *see* Kshatriyas
Widow's act of devotion, 98, 100
Wife's devotion, 167-68
Women, status of, 86-87

Yājnavalkya, 52-54
Yājnavalkya Smriti, 88-90
Yajur Veda, 5
Yajus, 79
Yoga, 93, 125, 181, 194-97, 235; *see also Karma yoga*
Yogasūtra, 194, 195-97
Yudhishthira, 137
yuga, 220-21

MODERN LIBRARY GIANTS

A series of sturdily bound and handsomely printed, full-sized library editions of books formerly available only in expensive sets. These volumes contain from 600 to 1,400 pages each.

THE MODERN LIBRARY GIANTS REPRESENT A SELECTION OF THE WORLD'S GREATEST BOOKS

G76 ANDERSEN & GRIMM: *Tales*
G74 AUGUSTINE, ST.: *The City of God*
G58 AUSTEN, JANE: *Complete Novels*
G70 BLAKE, WILLIAM & DONNE, JOHN: *Complete Poetry*
G2 BOSWELL, JAMES: *Life of Samuel Johnson*
G17 BROWNING, ROBERT: *Poems and Plays*
G14 BULFINCH: *Mythology* (ILLUSTRATED)
G35 BURY, J. B.: *A History of Greece*
G13 CARLYLE, THOMAS: *The French Revolution*
G28 CARROLL, LEWIS: *Complete Works*
G15 CERVANTES: *Don Quixote*
G33 COLLINS, WILKIE: *The Moonstone* and *The Woman in White*
G27 DARWIN, CHARLES: *Origin of Species* and *The Descent of Man*
G43 DEWEY, JOHN: *Intelligence in the Modern World: John Dewey's Philosophy*
G70 DONNE, JOHN & BLAKE, WILLIAM: *Complete Poetry*
G36 DOSTOYEVSKY, FYODOR: *The Brothers Karamazov*
G60 DOSTOYEVSKY, FYODOR: *The Idiot*
G51 ELIOT, GEORGE: *Best-Known Novels*
G41 FARRELL, JAMES T.: *Studs Lonigan*
G82 FAULKNER, WILLIAM: *The Faulkner Reader*
G39 FREUD, SIGMUND: *The Basic Writings*
G6
G7 } GIBBON, EDWARD: *The Decline and Fall of the Roman Empire* (COMPLETE IN THREE VOLUMES)
G8
G25 GILBERT & SULLIVAN: *Complete Plays*
G76 GRIMM & ANDERSEN: *Tales*
G37 HAWTHORNE, NATHANIEL: *Compl. Novels & Selected Tales*
G78 HOLMES, OLIVER WENDELL: *The Mind and Faith of Justice Holmes*
G19 HOMER: *Complete Works*
G3 HUGO, VICTOR: *Les Miserables*
G18 IBSEN, HENRIK: *Eleven Plays*
G11 JAMES, HENRY: *Short Stories*
G52 JOYCE, JAMES: *Ulysses*
G4 KEATS & SHELLEY: *Complete Poems*
G24 LAMB, CHARLES: *The Complete Works and Letters*
G20 LINCOLN, ABRAHAM: *The Life and Writings of Abraham Lincoln*
G84 MANN, THOMAS: *Stories of Three Decades*
G26 MARX, KARL: *Capital*
G57 MELVILLE, HERMAN: *Selected Writings*
G38 MURASAKA, LADY: *The Tale of Genji*
G30 MYERS, GUSTAVUS: *History of the Great American Fortunes*
G34 NIETZSCHE, FRIEDRICH: *The Philosophy of Nietzsche*
G88 O'HARA, JOHN: *49 Stories*

G55   O'NEILL, EUGENE: *Nine Plays*
G68   PAINE, TOM: *Selected Work*
G86   PASTERNAK, BORIS: *Doctor Zhivago*
G5   PLUTARCH: *Lives* (The Dryden Translation)
G40   POE, EDGAR ALLAN: *Complete Tales and Poems*
G29   PRESCOTT, WILLIAM H.: *The Conquest of Mexico* and *The Conquest of Peru*
G62   PUSHKIN: *Poems, Prose and Plays*
G65   RABELAIS: *Complete Works*
G12   SCOTT, SIR WALTER: *The Most Popular Novels* (Quentin Durward, Ivanhoe & Kenilworth)
G4   SHELLEY & KEATS: *Complete Poems*
G32   SMITH, ADAM: *The Wealth of Nations*
G61   SPAETH, SIGMUND: *A Guide to Great Orchestral Music*
G92   SPENGLER, OSWALD: *The Decline of the West* (one volume)
G91   SPENSER, EDMUND: *Selected Poetry*
G75   STEVENSON, ROBERT LOUIS: *Selected Writings*
G53   SUE, EUGENE: *The Wandering Jew*
G42   TENNYSON: *The Poems and Plays*
G23   TOLSTOY, LEO: *Anna Karenina*—tr. revised
G1   TOLSTOY, LEO: *War and Peace*
G49   TWAIN, MARK: *Tom Sawyer* and *Huckleberry Finn*
G50   WHITMAN, WALT: *Leaves of Grass*
G83   WILSON, EDMUND: *The Shock of Recognition*

MISCELLANEOUS

G77   *An Anthology of Famous American Stories*
G54   *An Anthology of Famous British Stories*
G67   *Anthology of Famous English and American Poetry*
G81   *An Encyclopedia of Modern American Humor*
G47   *The English Philosophers from Bacon to Mill*
G16   *The European Philosophers from Descartes to Nietzsche*
G31   *Famous Science-Fiction Stories*
G85   *Great Ages and Ideas of the Jewish People*
G89   *Great Classical Myths*
G72   *Great Tales of Terror and the Supernatural*
G9   *Great Voices of the Reformation*
G87   *Medieval Epics*
G48   *The Metropolitan Opera Guide*
G46   *A New Anthology of Modern Poetry*
G69   *One Hundred and One Years' Entertainment*
G93   *Parodies: An Anthology from Chaucer to Beerbohm and After*
G90   *Philosophies of Art and Beauty: Readings in Aesthetics from Plato to Heidegger*
G21   *Sixteen Famous American Plays*
G63   *Sixteen Famous British Plays*
G71   *Sixteen Famous European Plays*
G45   *Stoic and Epicurean Philosophers*
G22   *Thirty Famous One-Act Plays*
G66   *Three Famous Murder Novels, Before the Fact*, FRANCIS ILES, *Trent's Last Case*, E. C. BENTLEY, *The House of the Arrow*, A. E. W. MASON
G10   *Twelve Famous Plays of the Restoration and Eighteenth Century* (1660–1820): Dryden, Congreve, Wycherley, Gay, etc.
G56   *The Wisdom of Catholicism*
G59   *The Wisdom of China and India*
G79   *The Wisdom of Israel*